DATE DUE

DEMCO 38-296

Cost Reduction Systems

Cost Reduction Systems

Target Costing and
Kaizen Costing

Yasuhiro Monden

Translation by Bruce Talbot
Publisher's Message by Norman Bodek

Productivity Press
Portland, Oregon

ryoku o Tsukeru Genka-kikaku to
Shimposha, Tokyo, Japan, © 1994.

English edition © 1995 by Productivity Press, Inc. All rights reserved.

Productivity Press
P.O. Box 13390
Portland OR 97213-0390
United States of America
Telephone: 503-235-0600
Telefax: 503-235-0909

Cover design by Cabazon Design
Graphics by Productivity Press (I) Private Ltd. (Madras, India)
Composition by Caroline Berg Kutil
Printed and bound by Maple-Vail Book Manufacturing Group in the
    United States of America

Library of Congress Cataloging-in-Publication Data

Monden, Yasuhiro, 1940-
    [Kakaku kyōsōryoku o tsukeru genka kikaku to genka kaisen no gihō.
English]
    Cost reduction systems: target costing and kaizen costing / Yasuhiro
Monden; translation by Bruce Talbot.
        p. cm.
    Includes bibliographical references and index.
    ISBN 1-56327-068-4
    1. Cost control. 2. Value analysis (Cost control) 3. Automobile industry
and trade—Japan—Cost control. I. Title.
HD47.3.M66 1995
658.15'52—dc20   95-7751
                                                                               CIP

00 99 98 97 96 95 10 9 8 7 6 5 4 3 2 1

Contents

Publisher's Message

Productivity Press is pleased to bring you *Cost Reduction Systems*, the first book available in English to systematically document the target costing and kaizen costing systems that support the profitability of Japanese manufacturing giants such as Toyota, Nissan, and NEC. Target costing is a cost management approach that applies in the development phase of the product life cycle, whereas kaizen costing supports continued cost reduction of existing components and products during the remainder of the life cycle.

First developed in the automotive industry, target costing is an approach for helping companies achieve the basic goal of "making good products at low cost"—a prerequisite for success in today's global market. The twin objectives of target costing are 1) to lower costs of new products to ensure the required profit in meeting the quality, delivery, and price required by the market, and 2) to motivate employees to achieve the target profit through a companywide profit management activity. A complex organization such as a vehicle manufacturer needs a systematic approach to new product development that coordinates the cost-related planning activities of numerous divisions, departments, and suppliers. Target costing provides the framework for team-based cross-functional planning and development, clarifying the role of each party in the process.

Kaizen costing is cost reduction to maximize profit on products that are in production or already on the market. It is applied to ensure profitability of products in the declining period of product life, when customers are turning to other options and price must be reduced to maintain a profit. Kaizen costing involves improvement activities at the workplace and value analysis to determine cost-effective ways to fulfill necessary functions.

Author Yasuhiro Monden, an international expert on production and managerial accounting, describes the internal structure and process of target and kaizen costing as only an insider can. His presentation begins with basic definitions and an overview of the organizational structure in which target costing is deployed in Japanese companies. Part I of the book is devoted to the 14 basic steps involved in target costing, with a full chapter for each step.

Part II presents more details of target costing, with chapters on how it works in division-based companies, how companies do target costing semi-concurrently with their parts manufacturers, how to implement target costing as a companywide approach, and how to use value engineering (VE) in target costing

Part III gives the reader the nuts and bolts of the cost estimation system, with specific information not available elsewhere on the target costing approach to estimating direct materials costs and processing cost rates, estimating labor-hours using time tables, and combining the main cost elements of cost estimation for new products.

In Part IV, Monden thoroughly covers the kaizen costing approach, describing the rationale as well as the method used. The final chapter of the book compares kaizen costing with activity-based costing (ABC) practiced in some western companies.

Included in *Cost Reduction Systems* is a comprehensive bibliography of important works in English and Japanese related to management accounting, target costing, and kaizen costing; the reference list is arranged by specific companies and by author.

Monden draws his discussion from the automotive industry because it has the longest implementation history and hence the most case material from which to learn; the book includes examples from Toyota and Nissan, and one from General Motors. However, these approaches can be applied in other industries as well, and the author points out that in fact they have been implemented in a wide array of peripheral industries related to the automakers. Any industry that produces complex products can benefit from learning about these systems.

We express our appreciation to Yasuhiro Monden for permitting us to publish the English edition of his book. Dr. Monden is a prolific author and a top writer in the field of profit management and production systems. We are honored to be his English-language publisher for three previous books: *Japanese Management Accounting* (Michiharu Sakurai, coauthor), *Cost Accounting for the New Manufacturing Age,* and *Toyota Management System.*

We would like to thank the many people involved in producing this book: Bruce Talbot, translator; Miho Matsubara, text clarification; Cheryl Berling Rosen, series editor; Ron Bridenthal and Karen Jones, manuscript editors; Lisa Hoberg, word processing; Aurelia Navarro, proofreading; William Stanton, type design; Productivity Press (India) Private Ltd., Caroline Berg Kutil, and Frank Loose Design, graphics; Caroline Berg Kutil, composition; Catchword, Inc., index; Cabazon Design, cover design and composition.

Norman Bodek, Publisher

Diane Asay, Editor in Chief

Preface

This book describes cost-cutting methods that increase profits.

Today, competition among companies in many industries is turning global. The companies competing on this global market are now racing neck-and-neck in terms of quality levels, and to get ahead each company must come up with technological innovations. Because technological innovation has become a key part of this competition, competing companies are also faced with severe "cost competition" as they seek to provide customers with desired quality at an affordable cost.

Thus, for companies to survive, they must now set prices that are competitive in today's market while also setting costs that allow a profit margin. As prices are increasingly determined by market competition, costs must be cut to create profits.

The idea of lowering prices is generally a nightmare for manufacturers and a dream for consumers. However, lower prices mean a higher standard of living for society as a whole. Hence companies are having to return to the basic philosophy of "making good products at low cost."

"Making good products at low cost" is something that begins at the product development stage. Planners must identify and plan the quality features desired by customers and then accomplish cost levels that both ensure a profit and enable market-competitive product prices. This type of cost-cutting system is called "target costing."

As a teamwork effort, cost-cutting effectively encourages individual creativity and brainstorming to develop the best methods.

This book seeks to present, in a standardized and organized manner, the approaches and systems (methods) involved in target costing and kaizen costing. As yet, there have been no systematic studies or books published on these two systems. By a "systematic study," we mean more than an interest-based survey of the various topics related to target costing and the like. For example, it is impossible to systematically explain a target costing system if the explanation does not cover essential elements such as cost table systems for cost estimations or methods for determining target sales prices. In fact, it is impossible to implement target costing without understanding elements such as these. Neither is it enough to explain only the approach behind these systems. The explanation must at least afford a systematic presentation of the minimum conditions readers must understand before actually introducing and deploying target costing and kaizen costing at their own companies.

Each chapter in this book includes several figures and charts. Readers who take the time to study these illustrations in the order presented can gain a general grasp of the book's content.

The automotive industry was specifically selected as the context of this book because it is the industry in which the target costing system can be most easily understood and put into practice by many people. This is also an industry that can be described in its entirety. Another reason for selecting the automotive industry is that it is the industry that gave rise to both of these systems (target costing and kaizen costing) and naturally it is also the industry where they have been most widely implemented. In addition, having our scope include several types of industries would have made it very difficult to provide a complete description in a clear, well-timed sequence.

However, this is not to say that the systems described here cannot be readily applied to other industries. The way in which they have already been extended into a wide array of automotive-related peripheral industries is proof of this point.

Research Methods

This book brings information resulting from numerous case studies of individual companies together into a general, standardized system. As the author, I have adopted a KJ approach in developing this system. These corporate case studies have been decomposed into a subsystem organized into the sequence of cost control, to which I have added my own new information and descriptive scheme. This new information was not garnered all at once but rather was gradually collected over the course of my research. While the traditional KJ method has relied on index cards as an organizational tool, in this case I have given this role to a powerful personal computer.

When the case studies show different companies using different implementation methods, I have sought to present what appears to be the most effective method, and sometimes two methods are described in parallel.

Another consideration is that, for example, long-term profit planning and target costing must be closely tied, yet in the business world there are very few companies that coordinate these two elements in any logical, systematic manner. As a researcher, however, I have felt obliged to present these two interrelated elements logically. In addition, I will confidently present some methods I have developed myself, such as a method for determining target sales prices or for decomposing product target costs into function-based categories.

The research that went into this book differs greatly from research that analyzes and evaluates current responsibilities and methods. If we were to divide research that takes society as its object of study into descriptive research and normative research, this book would be on the side of the latter. The reason is that this book not only describes current conditions but also seeks to devise better methodology, including some of my own inventions.

Looking at two other categories—theoretical and empirical—we should say that this book is again almost entirely on the side of the latter. The reason in this case is that the book is deeply rooted in a large number of case studies. However, the book does include some theoretical parts, such as where I present a logically sound method that has only rarely been used by any company.

Thus, we may sum up this book's approach by saying that it is basically both an empirical book that includes a wealth of case study material and a normative book that seeks promising new methods which have been logically developed. This combination has already been referred to as a "constructive approach" (by Kasanen, Lukka, and Siitonen in 1993), and indeed research methods used for the book do fit well with this term's definition.

The book's main intention has been to provide a systematic description of the most important elements in the "drive trains" that power the target costing and kaizen costing systems. This book is intended to provide readers with what they need to at least introduce target costing and kaizen costing and begin deploying them. Readers should be aware that there are many topics peripherally related to target costing and kaizen costing that could not be included in the scope of this book. I hope to conduct further studies in these peripheral fields at a later date. Although there may be times when critics disagree with parts of this book, I am confidant that the true value of the systems described herein will be determined over the long run.

Because this book's focus is limited to target costing and kaizen costing, discussions of new product development steps will be limited to aspects directly related to target costing and kaizen costing. For an introduction to the new product development system, see Chapter 2 of my *Toyota Management System* (Productivity Press, 1993). In addition, the subject of quality assurance (or quality control) systems as part of new product development is a separate subject that will not be discussed much in this book.

Finally, nothing would please me more than for the modest results of my research to receive feedback from those in the business world who are struggling day and night to cut costs, so that an even better system of target costing and kaizen costing can be developed in the future.

Acknowledgments

"Target costing" is a system that was developed in Japan from the foundation provided by U.S.-born value engineering (VE). The Japanese automobile industry was the first to use target costing. "Kaizen costing" was developed completely in Japan.

On both sides of the Pacific, there have been numerous essays and books resulting from research into target costing's precursor, VE. In Japan, Masayasu Tanaka and his colleagues were among the first researchers to produce valuable results from VE-related studies. Indeed, I owe much to the results of the recent target costing-related research results published by these same researchers.

As for this book's focus on how the Japanese automotive industry has developed target costing and kaizen costing for profit planning, I am particularly indebted to Mr. Yoshiteru Noboru of Daihatsu Motors for the joint research he and I conducted (see essay published in 1983), which was the springboard for this endeavor.

Since the time of this joint research, the staff of Daihatsu's target costing office have very graciously lent me their cooperation and support. The results of case studies conducted with Daihatsu were published in my "Target Costing and Kaizen Costing in the Japanese Automobile Industry" (*Journal of Management Accounting Research*, 1991). However, this was the first book to be published in Japan with the term *Target Costing* (*Genka Kikaku*) in its title. Again, I would like to thank my many supporters in Daihatsu for their assistance.

I was fortunate enough to chair the Cost Management Research Council's symposium on the Japanese automotive industry's creation of a new target costing and kaizen costing system, an event sponsored jointly by the Chubu Industrial Alliance (*Chubu sangyo renmei*) and the Chubu Value Engineering Association (*Chubu VE kyokai*) in 1993. At this symposium, we conducted joint research using many case studies provided by Toyota and other major automobile manufacturers. This book includes excerpts from those joint studies that have been generalized and standardized. Accordingly, I would like to offer my heartfelt thanks to Mr. Kenji Kimura of the Chubu Industrial Alliance and to the other speakers at this symposium.

Recently, the academic world, along with researchers in the accounting field, have shown renewed interest in conducting target costing-related research. In particular, some very sharp observations have been made concerning the significance and characteristics of business management-related target costing activities, and I am indebted to the splendid research results produced by the many scholars and researchers listed at the end of this book.

Thus, this book would not have been possible without input and information from a wide variety of sources.

Finally, I offer my profound gratitude to my publisher Mr. Takeo Utsumi of Toyo Keizai, Inc. In addition, I would like to thank Yoshimasa Minegishi of Tsukuba University's Graduate Program of Management Science and Public Policy Studies for his contributions to Part III (Cost Estimation System). My thanks also to Rumi Ohata, for assisting in the general organization of the materials presented.

Cost Reduction Systems

Introduction

The Need for Price Competitiveness and Cost Reduction

Today, competition among companies has transcended national boundaries as companies from all countries compete on international markets. In brief, all of this competition is toward a common goal: to provide products with customer-pleasing quality and affordable prices. This kind of competition is becoming increasingly tough in the global marketing arena.

This trend is particularly conspicuous in product fields such as microcomputers and electronics goods and in the automotive market. Companies in these industries have been hard pressed to lower prices while devising a cost system that will still ensure profitability. Accordingly, such companies have had to systematically and rationally construct management systems that realize price-competitive cost levels. This type of system has become known as the "target costing" system, developed in Japan over the course of many years following the introduction of value engineering (VE).

1

Taking the perspective of companies' needs for increased price competitiveness, this introduction explains the need for cost reduction and the significance of a cost reduction system.

The Need for Price Competitiveness and Cost Reduction among Automobile Manufacturers

For an example, consider the Chrysler Neon, a compact model that debuted in January 1994. This four-door sedan with a four-cylinder engine (SOHC 16-valve, 132 hp max output, 17.8 kg/m max torque) measures 4.362 meters in length, 1.712 meters in width, 1.392 meters in height, and 2.642 meters in wheelbase, making it slightly larger than Japanese compacts such as the Corolla and Civic. Its engine size (2,000cc displacement) is comparable to the largest engine available in the Corolla.

The most inexpensive basic model Neon sells for about $9,000. Although this model is progressive in that it features a standard-equipped air bag, automatic transmission is not available, and its other standard-equipped features include only power steering and a radio. However, the Chrysler Neon is phenomenal as a two-liter vehicle that sells for less than $10,000.

By contrast, the Honda Civic and Toyota Corolla each sell for about $12,000. American buyers are not as attracted by extra accessories and functions as they once were, which makes the Neon a very price-competitive product in America's compact car market.

Since the Plaza Agreement of 1985, the share of Japanese vehicles in the U.S. automobile market has grown from 20.3 percent (in 1985) to 30.3 percent (in 1991) despite the increase in yen's value during this period from ¥225/$1 to ¥140/$1. How did the share of Japanese vehicles manage to increase even as the yen's value was rising so rapidly?

One reason is that, in 1985, U.S. automobile manufacturers were lagging behind their Japanese competitors technologically. They were behind, for instance, in engine development technology and other hardware-related technologies. Buyers recognized this technology gap and saw greater quality and value in Japanese vehicles, so they kept buying Japanese products even as prices rose due to yen appreciation. For their part, U.S. automakers were playing catch-up in terms of quality, but as they were also following the Japanese automakers in raising prices, they forfeited the advantage of price-competitiveness.

Since about 1992, analysts have been remarking that U.S. vehicles are now approaching the level of Japanese vehicles in terms of technology and quality. Moreover, American vehicle prices have not been rising on a level with the yen during that period. As a result, there is no longer a conspicuous quality gap between Japanese and American vehicles, but a sizable price gap has emerged.

This closing of the quality gap has led more buyers to focus solely upon price when choosing a vehicle.

Faced with this recent situation, Japanese automakers have launched a new strategy of avoiding price increases by working instead to lower manufacturing costs. They recognize that lowering costs is the only way they can hope to increase their price competitiveness.

The only other means of improving all-around competitiveness would be to again incorporate innovative technologies that would establish a new quality edge over American vehicles. When considering such a strategy, however, Japanese automakers would be wise to study what has occurred recently among Japanese consumer electronics manufacturers who have found that simply adding more functions or improving existing functions as a justification for higher prices does not always work—consumers today tend to reject products they perceive as having "too many functions."

Price Competitiveness and "Experience Curves" among Business Machine and Consumer Electronics Manufacturers

Selling prices among manufacturers of personal computers and other business machines and among consumer electronics manufacturers have been following a downward curve recently.

We might call this curve an "experience curve." For example, if we consider a popular brand of VCR and assign a value of 100 to its market price as of 1985, a model with the same functions sold in 1989 would be worth only about half of that value (see Figure I-1). The VCR's devaluation during those four years comes to about 12.5 percent per year on the average. (See Takubo 1991, p. 15.)

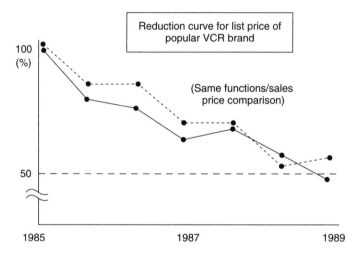

Figure I-1. Cost Reduction Curve

This experience curve theory also postulates that, as the years go by, total production output accumulates to ever higher levels and technological improvements help lower costs. In the case of business machines, one main factor behind cost reduction is the technological progress that has been raising the integration factor of LSIs. Figure I-2 shows how we can relate long-term trends in prices, costs, and profits based on the experience curve shown in Figure I-1.

A widely accepted theory concerning how these issues affect the electronics industry can be outlined as follows (see Abe 1993).

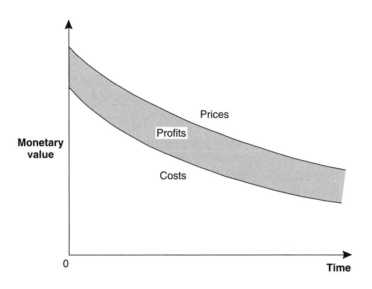

Figure I-2. Price, Profit, and Cost Trends

1. First, there have been four main factors affecting the market's competitive environment.
   a) More companies are entering the market.
   b) Price competition and other types of competition (such as in quality) have become increasingly severe.
   c) Product life cycles are becoming shorter.
   d) Wide-variety, small-lot production is increasing in response to diversification of customer needs.

2. Faced with these changes in the market environment, companies are working toward the following types of technological innovations in product development and manufacturing.

   Product development:
   a) Progress in microelectronics technologies (especially LSI integration)
   b) Development of new materials and new fabrication methods

Manufacturing:
a) Factory automation
b) Broadening the scope of production lines (broadly defined flexible manufacturing systems)
c) Computer-based control of production processes (computer-integrated manufacturing)

3. Companies have also been responding to market environment trends by globalizing their business activities in many areas, including product sales regions, parts procurement sources, manufacturing sites, and product development centers.

Given these market conditions, companies are adopting a new strategy with regard to competitiveness in price and quality. They recognize that technological progress enables development of qualitatively superior products as well as significant reduction in costs. Therefore, companies are closely watching technological developments and are looking for ways to implement promising new technologies into their new product development systems.

However, for companies to develop new products that incorporate new technologies while globalizing operations to take advantage of less expensive sources of materials, parts, labor, and other manufacturing costs, they must plan for all of these things early in the planning and development process.

Cost Management and Total Systems

The cost management systems established by Japanese manufacturing companies are essentially management systems oriented toward profit management. Their three main pillars are target costing, kaizen costing, and cost maintenance. Toyota was the first to develop this kind of system, and today it is used widely not only in the automotive industry but in many other manufacturing fields as well.

If we divide the model life of a product into (1) the planning and development stages and (2) the manufacturing stage, then we can say that target costing signifies the cost-cutting activities carried out for profit management during the product's planning and development stages. Kaizen costing refers to cost-cutting activities carried out for profit management during the product's manufacturing stage. Cost maintenance means taking the cost level achieved in the previous term as the standard for the current term and working to ensure that actual costs do not exceed the new standard.

Of these three main pillars, target costing is currently receiving the greatest emphasis. The reason is simple: companies that are competing amidst an environment characterized by rapid technological advances and, consequently, shorter product life cycles must find a way to bring effective cost-cutting into the product planning and development stages.

Effects of Target Costing and Kaizen Costing for Cost Curves and Sales Prices

Let us now consider how target costing and kaizen costing affect cost curves (see Figure I-3). First, once product development is completed and manufacturing begins, target costing significantly reduces costs in comparison to the previous product model; kaizen costing then continually devises small cost-cutting improvements during the manufacturing stage. However, after a certain amount of time, costs for a particular product model may reach their practical minimum, after which they can only rise. This minimum-cost point marks the final part of the model's product life cycle.

Nevertheless, other companies in the market are always working to cut their own costs, so that each company is obliged to begin again with new product development that aims in part to further reduce costs.

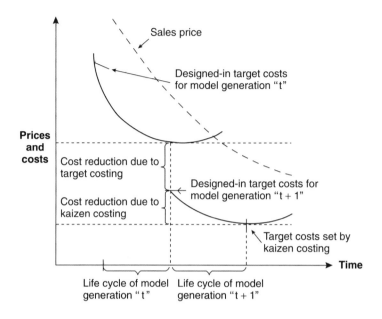

Figure I-3. Effects of Target Costing and Kaizen Costing on Cost Curve and Sales Price Trends

Part I

Target Costing System

Regarding Corporate "Missions" (Objectives) and Cost Reduction Efforts

Our company's mission is to develop not only housing but also various goods, services, information, and other intangible products that help raise people's quality of life, and to market these products at fair prices and in stable supply.

As we carry out that mission, our company's compensation from society will be an appropriate profit.

People will pay a certain price for a product if they recognize that the product is worth more than its price. Someone would likely buy an item priced at $1.00 if they saw at least $1.10 or $1.20 worth of value in it. Looking at this from the supply side, our company strives to manufacture products worth $1.20 at a unit cost of $.90 and then sell them for $1.00. Having made a considerable effort to achieve this service to society, the company receives a reward of $.10 per product.

(From "Practical Economic Philosophy" by Kōnosuke Matsushita, 1978.)

1
What Is Target Costing?

Definitions

Target costing incorporates companywide profit management during the product development stage. Specifically, such company-wide efforts include (1) planning products that have customer-pleasing quality, (2) determining target costs (including target investment costs) for the new product to produce the target profit required over the medium to long term given the current market conditions, and (3) devising ways to make the product design achieve target costs while also satisfying customer needs for quality and prompt delivery.

The target costing system is a companywide management system that supports the target costing process just described.

The target costing process is integrated with the company's profit management process and starts with general profit planning for the medium to long term. The main elements within this general plan are the new product development plan, sales plan, plant investment plan, personnel plan, and so on. These plans are used to set target profits for each product model. The *target profit* is the one target that all target costing activities seek to achieve.

Target costing itself also includes the process in which a customer-pleasing product is planned in detail and the target costs are determined based upon the product's target profit, and the process in which the product's target costs are achieved through a VE approach by the design department and are confirmed by checking the actual cost estimates.

Objectives

Broadly speaking, a target costing system has two objectives:

1. To lower the costs of new products so that the required profit level can be ensured while the new products meet the levels of quality, delivery timing, and price required by the market.
2. To motivate all company employees to achieve the target profit during new product development by making target costing a companywide profit management activity.

   • Any system that supports decision making in an organization must direct and motivate staff from many departments to use their creativity and reach set goals. The ideas of company employees must be brought together for the sake of achieving common goals and must not be left scattered and disorganized. In other words, the company needs to have a unified and rational system for consensus building and decision making.
   • A target costing system is one kind of system that helps rationalize group decision making in an organization. As such, its objectives include the following:

      (a) Establish target costs for new products that enable the company to achieve its target profit, and also make this target more achievable by setting a goal of reducing costs to below the design stage's cost estimates (the goal may be to reduce costs to eliminate any gap by which estimated costs exceed target costs; this is called setting goals and motivating staff).

(b) Create a set of steps that follow a schedule for a certain period, such as two years or four years (this is called successive decision-making scheduling).

(c) Use the creativity of people from various departments to devise alternative plans that enable further cost reductions (this is called brainstorming for alternative plans).

(d) Using the method that appeals to the most people, critically study the proposed alternative plans and select the best one (this is called evaluation and selection of alternative plans).

The key point is that a target costing system operates at the new product development stage as a highly efficient mechanism for reducing costs by enlisting the cooperation of many people throughout the organization. The essential ingredients for such a system are (1) the ability to enlist the cooperation of many employees and (2) the ability to raise efficiency by devising bigger cost savings with shorter lead times.

Steps

The steps in target costing may differ in timing and other respects according to the industry concerned, but the basic steps are similar. Below we will examine the basic, general steps that are used in the automotive industry's target costing process.

There are 14 steps in all, as can be seen in the flowchart in Figure 1-1. Chapters 3 to 16 of Part I address each of these steps in order, and thus all of the steps are summarized in Part I. It should be stressed, however, that these steps are not necessarily sequential—some can be carried out in parallel, such as by taking the concurrent engineering approach.

Target costing can be divided broadly into five phases:

1. Corporate planning
2. Developing the specific new product project
3. Determining the basic plan for a specific new product
4. Product design
5. Production transfer plan

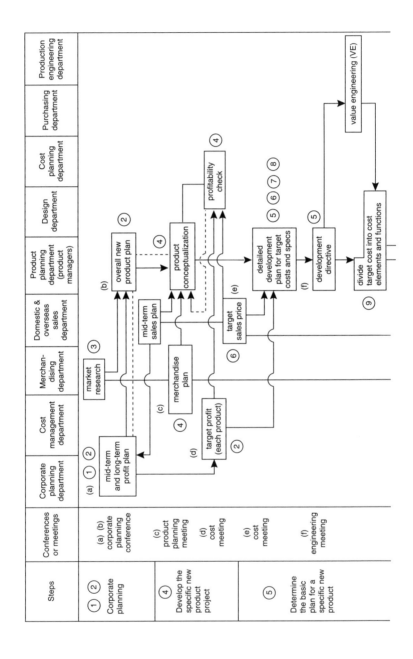

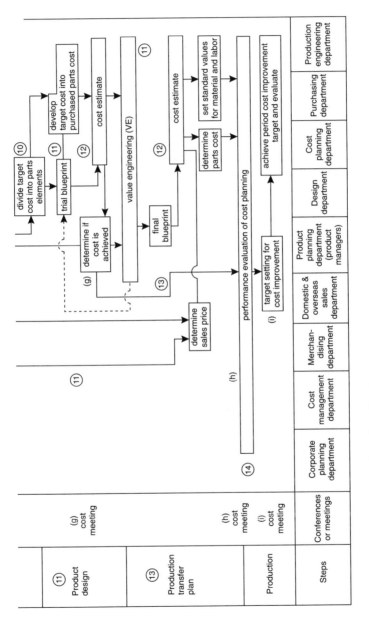

Figure 1-1. The Target Costing System

Corporate planning is the phase when medium- and long-term plans are established. As such, it includes the first two steps enumerated below.

Developing the specific new product project is the phase when the company forms specific new product development plans for various models. This phase includes Steps 3 and 4 below.

Determining the basic plan for a specific new product is the phase when the new product's detailed function-specific structures (formats), plant investment schedule, target sales price, and target cost are determined. Determining the target costs and their allotment is a key element in target costing. This major phase includes Steps 5 to 10 below.

Product design is the phase when designers draft a trial blueprint incorporating the target costs. Next, cost estimates are made based on the trial blueprints and product prototypes, and VE activities are undertaken to close any gap between estimated costs and target costs. This phase includes Steps 11 and 12 below.

The production transfer plan phase includes checking the production setup status, such as the installation of new equipment and the procurement of parts, to help ensure the achievement of target costs. This phase principally includes only Step 13, but Step 14 has also been included here for convenience.

Step 1. Life Cycle Planning for a Specific New Product

At this step, the product planning section creates a life cycle plan, which includes plans for the first year of development, the first year of full-scale production, and the next model-change year. Life cycle planning also includes estimating various related costs, such as personnel costs for design, prototype development, and production setup, as well as the corresponding equipment and materials costs. After completing this process, planners can formulate a provisional profit plan based on the product's model life (starting from the launch of full-scale production and ending when the next model-change period begins).

Step 2. Medium- and Long-Term Profit Planning and Overall New Product Plan

At this step, planners create three-year (medium-term) and/or five-year (long-term) profit plans and funds plans for the entire company. As part of the process for formulating the profit plans, planners determine model-life-based profit targets for each product line and, taking the perspectives of profit planning and fund planning, they also coordinate and adjust various specific structural plans in order to determine the basic structure of the corporate plan. Model-specific new product development plans, sales plans, plant investment plans, personnel plans, and fund procurement plans are all examples of specific structural plans.

The overall new product plan is a life cycle plan for a specific new product (product model or line) that has been generally worked into the long-term profit plan. In other words, the model life of each vehicle model is spread out over several years in a general plan that takes into account the model changes and minor changes planned for each model.

Step 3. Merchandising

The merchandising office conducts market surveys and evaluates the survey results with a threefold focus on (1) understanding user needs, (2) analyzing trends among competitors in the market, and (3) identifying quality-related issues based on market feedback (to look for causes of defects and other abnormalities). This information helps planners determine the goals and specific contents of the next model change or minor change.

The product planning department (product managers) receives the final version of the merchandising plan. The merchandising plan is also useful as an information source for the specific product life cycle plan described in Step 1 above.

Step 4. Product Conceptualization and Development Proposal

Product conceptualization refers to a process by which the product managers determine the basic concepts for new vehicle models. Part of this process is gauging user needs, competitive trends, and quality issues: product managers request the final merchandise plan based on the merchandise planning office's survey results and also refer to the results of any market surveys their own department has conducted. (See Chapter 5 for a further description of merchandise planning.) In addition, they keep track of advances in automotive technology. The product conceptualization that results from this process includes the vehicle's purposes, market potential (appeal), life-style image, body type, major functions (engine, etc.), and size.

As for the development proposal, the product manager works in collaboration with managers in the design department, prototype department, technology management department, and other relevant departments in finalizing the product conceptualization based on their input concerning new concepts.

In contrast to product planning at Step 1, where estimates are made based on a sales plan, cost estimates, and estimated fund requirements, planning at Step 4 is a much more specific type of product planning.

Step 5. Detailed Development Plan and Development Directive

The detailed development plan includes a detailed breakdown of the development proposal that is in turn based on the basic development concepts. As such, it specifies the vehicle's style design plan and structural elements, such as the engine, drivetrain, and wheelbase (chassis). It also proposes a per-vehicle target cost for the proposed new product.

The development directive is part of the output from the process that formulates the detailed development plan. It is submitted to top management's technology meeting for approval. However, the per-vehicle target cost for the proposed new product is submitted to top management for approval at the cost meeting held just before the technology meeting, about 30 months before the new product reaches the full-scale production and sales stages.

Step 6. Determination of Target Sales Price

Determining the target sales price is part of the detailed development planning process carried out at Step 5. Planners study the actual sales prices of numerous competing products on the market as well as their functions (function and performance grades) before setting a target sales price for their own new product.

Step 7. Establishment of Target Cost for Product

The vehicle's target cost, also determined as part of the detailed development planning process carried out at Step 5, is the per-vehicle cost that the new product must achieve to reach the target profit set for the product life period.

This target cost can be established using either of the following two formulas:

$$\text{Target cost} = \text{target sales price} - \text{target sales profit}$$

OR

$$\text{Target cost} = \text{target sales price} \times (1 - \text{target sales profit ratio})$$

During the target costing process, costs are divided into costs subject to cost reduction activities and costs not subject to cost reduction activities. In other words:

$$\text{Target cost} = \begin{array}{c} \text{Costs subject to} \\ \text{cost reduction} \\ \text{activities} \end{array} + \begin{array}{c} \text{Costs not subject} \\ \text{to cost reduction} \\ \text{activities} \end{array}$$

Step 8. Plant Investment Proposal

Plant investment proposals are made at various steps, including the long-term profit planning step, the product conceptualization step, the detailed development planning step, and the production transfer step (or production setup step). The most important parts of these proposals, however, are (1) the determination of the plant investment scope in the product conceptualization and (2) the determination of cost and function elements and parts-related investment costs in the detailed development plan.

Step 9. Divide Target Costs into Cost and Functional Elements

The engineering planning department's product manager plays the leading role in breaking down the target cost established per vehicle into cost and functional elements.

The term *function-based deployment* refers to the division of the target cost into functional elements that roughly correspond to the various design department sections. The following is a sample list of sections and corresponding functions:

Departmental Section	Function
Engine design section	Engine functions
Drivetrain design section	Drivetrain functions
Chassis design section	Chassis functions
Body design section	Body functions
Interior design section	Interior functions
Electronic engineering section	Electronics functions

Step 10. Divide Target Costs into Parts Elements

The design department takes the function-specific target cost elements provided by the engineering planning department and further separates them into part-specific target cost elements. The various sections within the design department do their own cost breakdown, starting with the most costly parts. The following is a sample list of functional elements and corresponding parts:

- Chassis functions   Front axle, front brakes, rear brakes, etc.

- Body functions   White body metal, bumpers, window glass, trim, etc.

- Interior functions   Seats, air conditioner, interior panels, audio system, etc.

The units used for part-specific target costs are the units of purchase (procurement units) in the case of purchased goods and the smallest part units in the case of parts manufactured at one of the company's own plants.

Step 11. Product Design and Cost-Building Activities

Product design refers to the designers' work in designing product part blueprints that meet two goals: required quality grade and part-specific target cost.

From the perspective of target costing, the goal of product design is to work part-specific target costs into the design blueprints—in other words, to "design to cost." On a companywide basis, everyone should work toward these two goals of achieving both required functions (quality and target costs).

Step 12. Cost Estimates at Design Stage

At this stage, cost estimates can be made according to a cost table that is based on the product-specific, function-specific, and part-specific cost targets as well as the blueprints that incorporate these targets. The following example shows a detailed cost estimate comprising three categories of costs: direct materials costs, processing costs, direct operating costs, and plant management costs.

$$\text{Manufacturing costs} = \text{direct materials costs} + \text{processing costs} + \text{direct operating costs (including development costs)}$$

Step 13. Production Transfer Plan

The production transfer plan paves the way for reconciling target profits with target costs at the production stage. It sets up processes to check whether preparations are on schedule for installing production equipment at company and supplier plants and whether materials and parts purchases are proceeding according to the cost plan and schedule. In effect, this plan is the final determinant of standard values for the new product's sales price, parts prices, materials consumption rate, labor-hours, and other cost-related factors.

Step 14. Performance Evaluation of Cost Planning

This performance evaluation of the target costing results and process is done after the new vehicle has finally reached the production transfer stage and manufacturing and purchasing activities have begun.

2

The Target Costing
Organization

Definition

Target costing is a companywide profit management activity centered on the new product development phase. As such, it is a companywide challenge to achieve a dream, and the seekers of the target costing dream are from virtually all job categories. Accordingly, let us begin this chapter with a "cast list" much like that found at the beginning of plays or novels, but divided instead into organizational divisions and departments.

Corporate planning division
The corporate planning department establishes the business strategy and the long-term general profit plan (five-year plan).

Accounting division
1. Target costing department
   • This department carries out a profitability check of the *product conceptualization* drafted by product managers.

- They also calculate the estimated costs based on the product managers' *basic product plan.*
- As part of their cost estimation work, they draft and revise a *process cost table* for individual manufacturing processes.

In some companies, the target costing department is under the supervision of the product planning division instead of the accounting division.

2. Cost management department
- This department is responsible for general promotion of the kaizen costing system and target costing activities at workplaces.
- The budget managers are responsible for general supervision of short-term profit planning and budgeting.

3. Cost accounting department
- This department carries out cost accounting related to financial accounts (standard cost accounting and actual cost accounting).

Finance division
- This division is responsible for capital procurement and operations. They also help draft the plant investment portion of the long-term general profit plan.

Merchandise planning division
- This division presents a *merchandise plan* to the product managers.

Product planning division
The product managers (chief engineer, model supervisors, etc.) have the following responsibilities:

- Draft the product conceptualization
- Draft the basic product plan
- Establish the vehicle target cost
- Separate the vehicle target cost into costs for specific functions and subsystems

- Achieve vehicle target cost
- Be responsible for profitability of developed vehicles (overall responsibility for sales, costs, and profits)

The relations between product managers and design department staff are established in a matrix system such as the one shown in Figure 2-1. In this cross-functional management system, product managers assigned to specific vehicle models work with designers assigned to specific functions.

This matrix system requires very specialized, up-to-date, and advanced design engineering from each of the various design departments assigned to one of the vehicle's functional elements, and this requirement raises the possibility that individual design departments could gain too much authority. This scenario would make it difficult for product managers to implement their own product conceptualizations and would oblige them to simply accept the designers' views. The end result is that such a designer-centered system would make it very difficult to develop a vehicle model that has a distinct and consistent style. It would also be difficult to have a solid sense of the development process for a specific vehicle if this process were no longer principally led by a product manager.

For example, in the era of bubble economics a designer who has developed a new type of engine would probably want to see that engine used in an upcoming vehicle model, regardless of whether it suits the vehicle's overall design balance. Designers also generally want to add as many functions and features to a vehicle as possible, which can easily result in a vehicle that is too "loaded" (hence, too costly) to be marketable.

In addition, it is difficult for designers to remain genuinely motivated when they are assigned to highly specialized design work that is very narrow in scope, such as designing only the cylinder block or the headlamps.

By contrast, if the company establishes a system of collaboration between the product development and design department based on a group of vehicle models (such as a product line of related models), the result is a team led by the product manager and

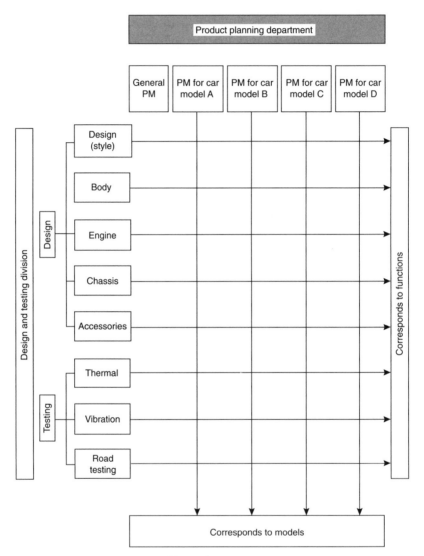

Figure 2-1. Relation between Product Managers and Vehicle Design Departments

composed of members who each maintain an overall perspective on the product development process. This plan makes it easier for designers to correctly understand their own role in this process, appreciate the results of their teamwork, and consequently feel a stronger sense of participation and motivation toward excellence. Under such a collaborative system, developers and designers can all feel they are part of a well-coordinated product development team in which each member can offer his or her own expertise.

Within such a system there may be subteams, such as a subteam assigned to the vehicle's front grille and another subteam for the instrument panel. These subteams can contribute their collective wisdom to the development process while maintaining a sense of overall design balance by virtue of their participation in the entire collaborative system. This system also facilitates information sharing among team members, which will help prevent errors in prototype development and will generally speed up the development process.

All of these advantages must be weighed against the consideration that building complicated model-specific organizations tends to incur higher equipment and personnel costs which in turn inflate vehicle development costs.

Case Study: Organization of Toyota's Product Development Division*

Development Center No. 1

Includes function-specific design groups** for development of rear-wheel drive (FR) vehicles. Such development is centered on the Crown model and other high-grade models.

---

* As of September 25, 1992.

** "Function-specific design groups" refers to departments assigned to planning, style design, body design, interior design, chassis design, engine design, and testing.

Development Center No. 2

Includes function-specific design groups for development of front-wheel drive (FF) vehicles. Such development is centered on the Corolla model and other midsize and compact cars.

Development Center No. 3

Includes function-specific design groups for development of wagons, vans, and commercial vehicles. Example: Town Ace.

Development Center No. 4

Carries out development of common elements (engine, drive-train parts, electronic devices, etc.).

Because the above vehicle categories (FR, FF, and wagon/van/commercial) use different functional parts, they work most closely with the function-specific design departments corresponding to their vehicle category. At the same time, within each development center priority is also placed on coordinating and unifying technology for common parts (such as drivetrain) to keep costs down. Such coordination among development centers is the responsibility of the technology management department. Compare the conventional type of organization shown in Figure 2-1 to Toyota's development center organization, shown in Figure 2-2 below. (In Figure 2-2, "CE" means chief engineer, which is another name for the product manager.)

Case Study: General Motors*

GM products are divided into six model lines: Cadillac, Buick, Pontiac, Oldsmobile, Chevrolet, and Saturn. Until recently, each of these lines had its own independent development and design departments and its own dealer network. Now GM has consolidated the development and design departments for all but the Saturn line into three sets: one each for luxury vehicles, midsize

---

*System in operation since October 23, 1992.

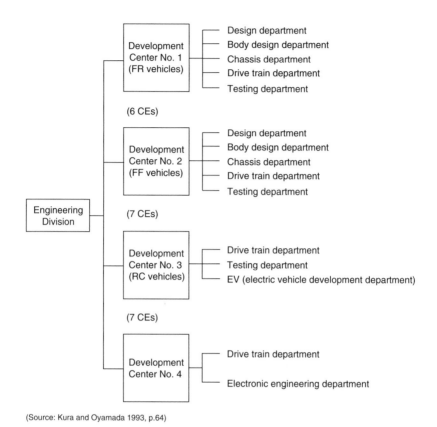

(Source: Kura and Oyamada 1993, p.64)

**Figure 2-2. New Organization for Toyota's
Product Development Division**

vehicles and compact vehicles. This consolidation effectively reduced requirements for white-collar design and development staff and helped achieve cost-cutting commonization of parts. (GM has not consolidated its six separate dealer networks, however.)

Style Design Department

Develops the style design of new products. Style design includes the exterior shape and interior design, the color design, clay model fabrication, and style CAD.

Design Division

Body design department
Responsible for body components, exterior trim, lamps, mirrors, exhaust pipes, windshield wipers, etc.

Interior design department
Responsible for instrument panels, interior ceiling, seats, seat belts, air conditioners, etc.

Engine department No. 1
Responsible for design and testing of commercial vehicle engines.

Engine department No. 2
Responsible for design and testing of passenger vehicle engines.
(Both engine departments develop the next generation of vehicle engines. This includes development of EFI systems, turbochargers, etc.)

Chassis design department
Responsible for the design of chassis parts such as suspension, steering, brakes, exhaust pipes, and fuel system.

Drivetrain department
Responsible for the design and testing of drivetrain parts, such as transmission, differential gears, and 4WD parts.

Electronic engineering department
Responsible for the design and testing of electronically controlled systems such as EFI systems, cruise control, batteries, TEMS, pneumatic suspension, ABS, navigation systems, displays, audio system, and wire harnesses.

Prototype Department

Responsible for fabricating prototypes, including prototype-related procurement and management of parts for testing, presses, sheet metal fabrication, and assembly.

Testing and Evaluation Division

Product testing department
Responsible for testing and evaluation of vehicles' overall performance.

Vehicle testing department No. 1
Responsible for testing and evaluation of thermal, vibration, noise, and operability items: air conditioner, vibration and noise, user-friendliness, field of view, visibility, etc.

Vehicle testing department No. 2
Responsible for testing and evaluation of strength, safety, running and performance items: body, chassis, drive strength, seats, windshield wipers, rubber parts, exhaust pipes, collision testing, endurance, etc.

Vehicle testing department No. 3
Responsible for testing and evaluation of operation and handling performance items: handling stability, drivability, and other general performance items.

Production Engineering Department

This department is positioned between the Design Division and the Manufacturing Division; its general function is to convert product design information into production-related information. Specifically, it is responsible for process planning. Process planning uses various input data, such as drawings, part configurations, and part shapes specified in drawings drafted by the Design Division, as well as engineering requirements (based on performance requirements). The Production Engineering Department's five main tasks include:

- determining the types and sequence of manufacturing methods
- determining the types and sequence of manufacturing processes
- determining the types and sequence of manufacturing equipment

- determining processing operations
- estimating operation labor-hours (i.e., standard times) and costs for each process.

Process planners use IE methods to integrate the "three Ms" (men/women [staffing], materials, and machines) to plan a highly efficient work system that minimizes waste. They plan processes based on the drawings they are given in order to reduce processing costs. In addition, they produce process-specific processing cost estimates, which are in turn submitted as a reference for the Design Division's VE activities.

Purchasing Department

- This department informs suppliers of the Design Division's concepts and detailed structural plans concerning main vehicle components and asks suppliers to submit VE proposals.
- They also give suppliers target costs for the final list of purchased parts.
- They make cost estimates based on the trial blueprints and present the estimates to the Target Costing Department.
- After the final blueprints are completed, they conduct a final cost estimate, which they use as a basis for negotiations on the price of purchased parts so that their prices can be determined before production begins.

Suppliers

Suppliers conduct their own target costing activities and keep track of GM's target costing activities.

3

Individual New Product Development Plan

Definitions

The individual new product development plan is a profit plan related to the model life of an individual vehicle model. The corporate planning department drafts a plan for the life cycle of each vehicle model (i.e., drafts a plan for the model's development start, production start, and model change year). In this plan, they estimate the labor requirements for the model's design, prototype development, and production setup as well as other costs related to the model's development and production plant investment needs. They are then able to project the model's profitability over its product life (from the start of full-scale production to the next model change).

For entirely new models, the individual new product development plan may extend as far as ten years into the future. For example, a new model whose development activities began on

April 1, 1994, would enter into full-scale production four years later and would then have a four-year sales period. This plan alone makes for an eight-year span. Thus, the first five years of this model's development plan must be taken into account in the company's long-term profit plan. However, since most new models are not entirely new but are either a major or minor model change, often their entire model life can be included in the company's long-term profit plan.

Objective

Each individual new product development plan should provide input for the corporate long-term profit plan (a five-year profit plan) and should also provide basic output data for coordinating the development plans for all vehicle models.

Input and Output

Input

Projections based on market trends (sales volume, sales price, etc.)

Output

1. Schedule for introducing new models, full model changes, and minor model changes
2. Anticipation of the following policy items regarding new models and model changes:

   • price range
   • sales volume
   • image
   • market segment
   • main sales regions (such as Japan, North America, and Europe)
   • target customers
   • introduction timing

- manufacturing plants
- life cycle plan for drivetrain (engine, transmission, etc.)
3. Profit planning for each product over each of the next five business years
4. Estimation of resources required for development

Steps

- The profit plan for each product (in other words, for each entire product series under development) in each year of its model life is drafted using either the direct costing (a.k.a. variable costing) or the contribution margin approach (see Figure 3-1). The elements in this contribution margin formula start with an overall profit total for the entire model life period, after which this sum is divided into the years in the period. The estimated gross sales figure is incorporated first so that other items can be compared in total sales using established ratios.

	1995	1996	1997	1998	1999
Total sales 　Variable costs 　　Direct materials cost 　　Direct labor cost 　　Variable indirect costs					
Marginal income 　Traceable fixed costs 　　Amortization cost of 　　　new equipment 　　Prototype development 　　　costs 　　Development costs					
Contribution margin 　Common fixed costs					
Manufacturing operating profit 　Direct sales costs 　Indirect sales costs					
Operating profit					

Figure 3-1. Profit Plan Based on Contribution Margin Approach

- As for the amortization of new equipment and deferred assets such as prototype development expenses and other development costs, these items are amortized according to the fixed installment method for estimated costs of products over either a four-year period (for full model changes) or a two-year period (for minor model changes). Engine units in new models are an exception; they are generally used for two model lives and are thus amortized over a period of eight to ten years.
- The common fixed costs and indirect sales costs are apportioned for each new product (i.e., model series) based on the current model's standard cost figures. Direct sales costs are apportioned for each new product based on the current model's results.
- The profit plan for the total model life of each model series is used to calculate the marginal income ratio (marginal income ÷ total sales), the contribution ratio (contribution margin ÷ total sales), the manufacturing operating profit ratio (manufacturing operating profit ÷ total sales), and the operating profit ratio (operating profit ÷ total sales). These profit-to-sales ratios for new models (under development) are all based on average figures for the current models.

Departments Responsible

1. The corporate planning department chief drafts the life cycle plan for each vehicle model.
2. The merchandising department gathers various information including market trends, market segments, price estimates, and sales volume estimates and presents the information to the corporate planning department.
3. The accounting division's target costing department collects past sales figures and various cost-related information concerning existing products and presents the information to the corporate planning department.

4

Long-Term Profit Plan and Corporate New Product Development Plan

Definitions

The long-term general profit plan describes the entire company's profit plans and fund plans for each business term over the next five years. As part of the process of creating this five-year plan, planners must determine (1) profit targets for each product line's model life and (2) the various strategic project plans that together comprise the company's basic management structure. Strategic project plans must be coordinated with the profit plans and the fund plans. Examples of strategic project plans include new product development plans for each vehicle model, plant investment plans, personnel plans, and capital procurement plans.

The corporate new product development plan coordinates the new product life cycle plans for each vehicle model (discussed in Chapter 3) with long-term profit plans as part of the long-term profit planning process.

Corporate new product development plans are set up for each year in the product's model life and cover all full model changes or minor model changes that are planned for all target models. Thus, all the production and sales plans for all of the company's vehicle models are coordinated under one plan that takes the perspective of the company's overall business strategy.

Objectives

1. To help achieve the profit target set by top management for a certain period by coordinating the various specific plans that together determine the basic management structure.
2. To help achieve term-specific target profits by determining target profits for the model life of each product (or product series).
3. To stagger the introduction of new products (new models) so that their timing is spread out evenly and so that several models do not get bunched together at the same time. Such staggered timing is important to make effective use of company resources such as personnel for design, prototype development, and production setup work, and development and plant investment capital.

Input and Output

Input

1. Life cycle plan for specific new products
2. Current position of company's vehicle models on product portfolio chart (cash flow chart)
3. Estimated values for the company's overall personnel capacity (for design, prototype development, and production setup work), manufacturing plant capacity, and new plant investment capacity (including capital procurement ability)

Output

1. Five-year general profit plan (including long-term profit plan and long-term fund plan)

2. Target profit for each product (product series)
3. Target return-on-sales ratio for each product (product series)
4. Plant investment plan for each product (product series)
5. Personnel plan
6. Overall new product plan

Steps

Step 1

The profit plans for each vehicle model in each business term over the next five years (i.e., individual model new product life cycle plans) are based on either a direct costing or contribution margin accounting method (see Figure 4-1).

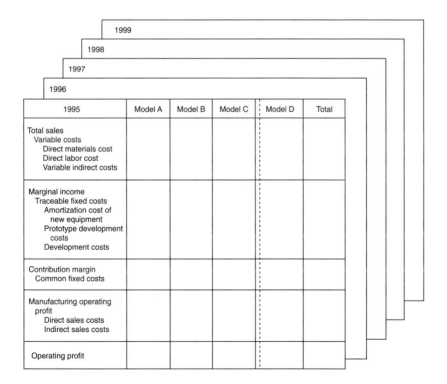

Figure 4-1. 5-Year Profit Plan

The companywide ratio of profit to target sales is established based on the company's business results from previous years and target values, as well as the business results among companies in similar industries in previous years. In other words:

$$
\begin{array}{ll}
\text{Company-wide ratio} & W_1 \times \text{company's past results } + \\
\text{of profit to} \quad = & W_2 \times \text{past results from same industry } + \\
\text{target sales} & W_3 \times \text{company's targets in five years}
\end{array}
$$

Here, $W_1 + W_2 + W_3 = 1$. In the beginning, the values of W_1 and W_2 are relatively large, but gradually the value of W_3 will increase so that in five years $W_3 = 1$ and $W_1 = W_2 = 0$.

The target values for gross sales in each term, inclusive of all of the company's vehicle models, are determined based on top management's strategic judgments, which take into account the estimated values on the regression curve set by past time-series data. Multiply the gross sales target value by the target value for the return-on-sales ratio to get the target value for the companywide operating profit. In other words:

$$
\begin{array}{l}
\text{Target} \\
\text{operating} \\
\text{profit per} \\
\text{term}
\end{array}
=
\begin{array}{l}
\text{target} \\
\text{gross sales} \\
\text{per term}
\end{array}
\times
\begin{array}{l}
\text{target} \\
\text{return-on-sales} \\
\text{ratio} \\
\text{per term}
\end{array}
$$

Note: Normally, the companywide target ratio of profit to total capital (i.e., the target return on investment or ROI) is determined in the same way as the target ratio of profit to gross sales. However, Japanese automobile companies have traditionally started by determining the target ratio of profit to gross sales, and they do not use an ROI target. For the future, they will need to use an ROI target to help improve productivity (i.e., the turnover of total capital).

Step 2

Product-specific profit proposals under the individual model new product life cycle plans are input into the formula described in Step 1, and the profits in each term over a five-year period are added up. The predicted profits per term are then compared with the target profits per term as established in Step 1. If there is a gap between these profit figures, the individual model development plans under the vehicle-model-specific new product life cycle plans must be revised to close the gap. In this case, costs, earnings, and profits within the development plans for specific products under new product life cycle plans must be revised. As described in Step 5 below, this threefold perspective (abbreviated as the C-E-P relationship) guides revisions in the product-specific gross sales plan (i.e., the sales plan), the product-specific traceable fixed cost plan (i.e., the product-specific plant investment plan), and the variable cost plan (i.e., the product-specific variable cost reduction plan). The end result is a set of product-specific operating profit target values that the company can use when striving to achieve term-specific operating profit target values.

Meanwhile, from the perspective of the company as a whole, there also need to be some lateral adjustments among product models as part of what is called *product portfolio management* (PPM), described next.

Step 3

One of the tasks in PPM is to determine how internal capital (capital obtained through sales activities) and external capital (capital obtained through financial activities) is distributed among the various vehicle models.

One strategy companies employ to help ensure their survival and ongoing development is to achieve a balance in the use of capital produced by mature business operations for investment in promising new business operations. This is part of PPM.

PPM managers study two facets of each business operation that they are considering for their PPM plan: market growth rate and market share.

Market growth rate is used to measure the capital demand (or required investment capital) for each business operation. If the market growth rate is high, capital demand is also high; conversely a slow-growth market has only modest demand for capital. Accordingly, large sums of investment capital are required for business operations in fast-growing markets to maintain and expand market share.

Although it is relatively easy to expand market share in a fast-growing market, once the market's growth rate declines, expanding or reversing a decline in market share becomes very difficult.

Market share studies measure the capital supply (i.e., capital flow) from each business operation. Products or business operations that have a large market share also have a high earnings rate and therefore provide a large capital supply (flow), while the opposite is true of products or business operations that have a small market share.

The *experience curve effect* verifies the earnings rate of each product or business operation as a function of market share. Experience curves include logarithmic tables describing functions for costs and total production volume. It verifies, for example, that when the total production volume is doubled, costs can be reduced from 20 to 30 percent. Because the market share of a business operation in a particular industrial field is related to the total production volume (i.e., the total "experience") in that business operation, business operations that enjoy a large market share have lower costs and higher cost-competitiveness plus higher profits (profit amounts and profit rates). Therefore, the return-on-sales ratio should be used as the horizontal axis.

Market growth rate and market share can be used as the vertical and horizontal axes of a matrix containing all of the company's business operations. Such a matrix is called a *portfolio chart*. Figure 4-2 shows the simplest possible matrix, which contains four quadrants.

In the figure, the horizontal axis, titled "relative market share," is not a percentage of the market but rather is the share relative to the competitor that has the largest share of the market. In other words:

$$\begin{array}{l} \text{Relative} \\ \text{market} \\ \text{share} \end{array} = \frac{\text{company's market share}}{\text{largest market share among company's competitors}}$$

Accordingly, only the company that has the largest market share (in the industrial field or market sector) rates a relative share of 1 or above.

The basic approach to managerial strategy using this portfolio chart is to combine the internal capital produced by current "money trees" with external capital gained via capital increases, loans, and the like, and then determine long-term investment schemes for these combined funds in areas such as (a) R&D for new hit products and (b) improvement of "problem child" products.

Thus, PPM is useful for long-term fund planning, which includes coordinating capital procurement and capital operations in

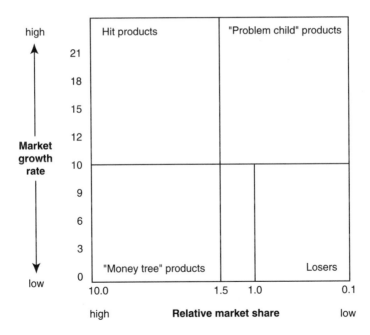

Figure 4-2. Portfolio Chart

step with the timing of model changes for each vehicle model and the debut of newly developed models.

Step 4

Long-term profit planning usually employs the fixed install-ment method for depreciating costs such as new plant investment costs and amortizing deferred assets such as prototype develop-ment and development costs over a period of four years (for full model changes) or two years (for minor model changes). A com-panywide fixed percentage on diminishing value plan is often pre-ferred for financial accounting of plant investment depreciation. In addition, some subassembly units (such as the engine units) in new products are generally used for two model cycles and are therefore depreciated over eight to ten years.

Some companies treat deferred assets as full-amount expenses at the time of payment, but this method makes it difficult to com-prehensively coordinate the profit proposals for all of the compa-ny's products within the long-term profit plan. It also breaks product managers' responsibilities after production startup into term-specific or product-specific contribution margins, which are difficult to evaluate.

Step 5

To achieve the target operating profit per term based on the contribution margin accounting method described in Step 1 above, the companywide profit/loss breakeven point must be lowered.

$$\text{Sales equal to profit/loss breakeven point} = \frac{\text{fixed costs}}{\text{marginal income ratio}}$$

In view of the above equation, new product development plans must be made suitable in relation to each product's traceable fixed costs (such as plant investment costs, prototype develop-ment costs, and other product development costs). In addition, raising the marginal income ratio requires planning to reduce each product's direct materials costs (costs for basic materials and purchased parts), as well as direct labor costs and variable indirect costs. The task of lowering direct labor costs falls under the category of personnel planning. To achieve this goal, revisions must be made in the individual new product development plan.

Step 6

The individual new product development plan is the profit plan proposal for each model series under development. The profit rate above shows average figures for each series of vehicles under development. Consequently, the target marginal income ratio as a series average, the target contribution margin rate, and the target operating profit rate are all determined based on the results of Step 5. At this point, the target profits for the various models within a series have not yet been determined.

Step 7

The coordination process includes spreading out the introduction of vehicle models to prevent any concentration of models within the same time period that might strain development personnel capacity, equipment capacity, or capital procurement capacity. The corporate new product development plan is supposed to determine how the introduction of vehicle models will be coordinated.

In this sense, the corporate new product development plan coordinates the life cycle plans for each model. This plan is presented in the format shown in Figure 4-3 after being authorized by the corporate planning council.

Step 8

Now comes the point when a capital procurement and operations plan can be made with respect to all of the strategic project plans that have been coordinated to facilitate achievement of term-specific target profits. In contrast to Step 5, in this case all of the disbursements for procured new plant investment capital,

Corporate New Product Development Plan					
◎ : New model development ○ : Full model change △ : Minor model change					
Model	**1993 Year**	**1994 Year**	**1995 Year**	**1996 Year**	**1997 Year**
A		○	△		○
B	○		△	○	
C		△		○	
D			◎		△

New model development entails creating a completely new model, designed to meet current customer needs for uses and new functions. With each new model development there are many important factors to consider, including the model's market position, its characteristics and new technologies, its production scale, sales network, and so on.

A full model change entails making comprehensive improvements in an existing model to better suit emerging customer needs, including not only the exterior design and vehicle body but also the engine and chassis. All major parts of the vehicle are upgraded to incorporate the latest technologies.

A minor model change is carried out to extend the model's life through partial improvements in the body, engine, and chassis. An attempt is made to incorporate as much new technology as possible without requiring a full model change.

(Model changes that are even more modest than "minor model changes" are called "facelifts.")

Figure 4-3 (Part 1). Corporate New Products Development Plan

prototype development costs, and development costs are paid in full at the scheduled time (see Figure 4-4).

Step 9

The long-term profit plan is then revised using the rollover method to add on each year over the next five years.

Step 10

Figure 4-5 serves as a reference for determining how the output from the long-term profit plan will relate to cost planning at later steps (such as the basic product planning step or the detailed development plan). The following section describes the roles of various departments in these activities.

Model name	Last model change before 1984	1985	1986	1987	1988	1989	1990	1991	1992
President	8/73						(10)		→
Infinity Q45 (*)						(10)			→
Cedric	6/83			(6)				(8)	→
Cima (*)					(1)			(10)	→
Gloria	6/83			(6)				(8)	→
Leopard	9/80		(2)						→
(240Z)	9/83					(7)			→
Cefiro (*)					(9)				→
Passat							(5)		→
Laurel	10/84					(1)			→
Skyline	8/81	(8)				(5)			→
Maxima	10/84			(5)	(10)				→
Bluebird	10/83			(10)				(9)	→
Silvia	8/83				(5)				→
180SX (*)					(4)				→
Primera (*)							(2)		→
Presea (*)									→
Stanza	6/81		(6)			→			
Auster	6/81	(10)				→			
Prairie	8/82				(9)				(1) →
Avenir (*)						(5)			→
Sunny	10/81	(9)				(1)			→
Laurel Spirit	1/81		(8)				→ Total production	10 million units	
Pulsar	4/81		(5)				(8)		→
Exxa		(10)				→			
NX coupe (*)							(1)		→
Langley	6/81		(10)			→			
Liberta Villa	6/82			(10)		→			
March	10/82								(1) →
Be⁻l (•*)				(1)	→				
PAO (•*)						(1)	→		
Figaro (•*)								(3) →	Limited to 2,000 units

1. ● Solid dots indicate models that are not currently being manufactured or sold (as of January 1992).
2. * Asterisks indicate models that have been introduced since 1985.
3. ○ Circled numbers indicate the month in which the model change was carried out.

(Source: Kado, 1993, p.159.)

Figure 4-3 (Part 2). List of Nissan Car Model Changes and New Models

Item	1994	1995	1996	1997	1998
I. Revenues and expenditures handled in business activities					
Revenues					
1. Sales revenues					
2. Other revenues					
(1) Income from interest, dividends, etc.					
(2) Other					
Subtotal (A)					
3. Income from sale of tangible fixed assets, etc.					
(1) Sale of tangible fixed assets					
(2) Sale of investment securities					
(3) Collection of loans outstanding (including short-term loans)					
(4) Other revenues					
Subtotal (B)					
Total revenues (C) = (A) + (B)					
Expenditures					
1. Sales expenditures					
(1) Purchase of basic materials and products					
(2) Personnel cost expenditures					
(3) Other sales expenditures					
2. Non-sales expenditures					
(1) Expenditures for interest expenses, discounts, etc.					
(2) Other non-sales expenditures					
Subtotal (D)					
3. Expenditures for acquisition of tangible fixed assets, etc.					
(1) Expenditures for acquisition of tangible fixed assets					
(2) Expenditures for acquisition of investment securities					
(3) Loans (including short-term loans)					
(4) Other expenditures					
Subtotal (E)					
4. Expenditures for account settlement, etc.					
(1) Dividend allotments					
(2) Corporate taxes, etc.					
(3) Other					
Subtotal (F)					
Total expenditures (G) = (D) + (E) + (F)					
Revenue/expenditure balance (H) = (C) − (G)					

Figure 4-4 (Part 1). Long-Term Fund Planning Chart (Business Activities)

Item	1994	1995	1996	1997	1998
II. Revenues and expenditures handled in capital procurement activities					
Revenues 1. Short-term loans (including promissory notes) 2. Discounted promissory notes 3. Long-term loans 4. Corporate bond issues 5. Capital increases 6. Other revenues					
Total revenues (I)					
Expenditures 1. Repayment of short-term debts 2. Repayment of long-term debts (including debts to be repaid within one year) 3. Debenture redemption 4. Other expenditures					
Total expenditures (J)					
Capital procurement revenue/expenditure balance (K) = (I) − (J)					
III. Current total capital revenue/expenditure balance (L) = (H) + (K)					
IV. Adjustment amount due to loss by valuation by lower of cost or market method (M)					
V. Capital balance at beginning of term (N)					
VI. Capital balance at end of term (O) = (L) − (M) + (N)					

Figure 4-4 (Part 2). Long-Term Fund Planning Chart (Financial Activities)

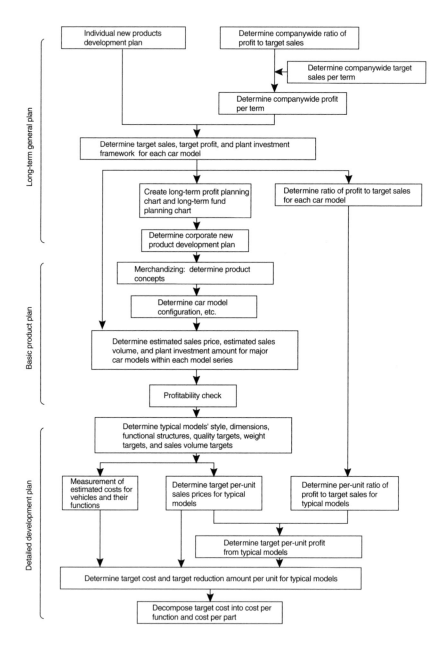

Figure 4-5. Profit Management Process within Target Costing System

Departments Responsible

- The long-term profit plan is proposed to the corporate planning department, which is responsible for providing information and advice to support top management's decision making; the final decision is made by the corporate planning council, which includes top managers. The individual new product development plan, after being incorporated into the long-term profit plan, is also first proposed to the corporate planning department. The corporate planning council also makes the final decision to approve the corporate new product development plan, which has been coordinated with the long-term profit plan.

- The engineering planning department as a whole participates in the general coordination of life cycle plans for all planned products to ensure efficient use of personnel capacities (for design, prototype development, and production setup) and existing plant capacity. They are also responsible for studying ways to further reduce costs, such as by reducing variety in vehicle models or by commonizing major vehicle parts.

- The accounting division's cost management department provides the corporate planning department with information on revenues, costs, and profits for each vehicle model and for the company in general.

- The financial division provides the corporate planning department with information concerning planning proposals for capital procurement, plant investment, and other companywide capital operations. This division also takes an active role in formulating these planning proposals.

5

Merchandising

Definitions

Merchandising starts with market studies and includes planning centered on which kinds of products should be introduced to which markets and how products can be accurately matched with their most receptive market segments.

Merchandising differs from product planning in that merchandising yields only general concepts of the types of products to be developed, whereas product planning works to develop actual products (automobiles, in this case).

The three main tasks in merchandising are understanding markets, defining market segmentation (or product positioning), and clarifying product concepts. The merchandising department studies products as "merchandise" for particular markets and carries out market surveys to gain an understanding of these markets. The merchandising department also receives input from the sales division concerning desired products, product ideas, and other topics in order to better understand changing user needs, trends among other companies competing in the same markets, and market quality issues (such as types of claims submitted by customers). This information enables the merchandising department to establish strategic positions for products to be developed (this is called *product positioning*) and to propose product objectives and characteristics (*product concepts*).

Objective

The objective of merchandising is to understand what kinds of products are in demand in view of the current market trends and market environment, and to provide product planning department managers with the information they need to establish a product planning concept for new products.

Steps

Step 1. Market Surveys

- Implement market surveys among users (and potential users). Study survey results to gain a grasp of why users buy products and which functions they use the most.
- Gather information from domestic and overseas offices concerning what users want to see in future models. In particular, study desired sales pricing and sales points that distinguish the company's models from competing models.
  A "competing model" is any other company's model that is similar to one's own model in terms of market position, product concept, and price range. Such similar products are in direct competition with each other. Because the sales strengths and weaknesses in a competing model are likely to be the same in one's own, it is important to thoroughly study competing models as part of merchandising. The results of such studies should be incorporated into the product plan.
- Study problems that have occurred on the market, particularly problems having to do with product quality, then make

recommendations to help prevent such problems from occurring (or reoccurring) in one's own products.

Figure 5-1 illustrates the tasks undertaken at Step 1.

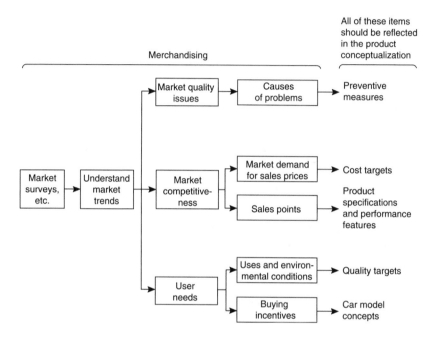

Figure 5-1. Merchandising Tasks

Step 2. Product Line Positioning

Product positioning is the matching of certain products with certain market segments. *Market segmentation* refers to managing how well the overall market (i.e., each market segment) is covered by the range of products being marketed. The former approach focuses on individual products whereas the latter approach focuses on the configuration of products for the entire market. Both approaches have the same basic functions.

Given today's merchandising trends toward individuality and diversity, it is no longer easy to manufacture and sell standard products in large lots. Instead, products must be diversified in correspondence with the various market segments, and targets must be set for each market segment. The merchandising department takes the market segmentation approach or the product positioning approach in matching their merchandising plans with targets in various market segments. Among automobile manufacturers, this is called a *full-line policy*.

At this step, the three main issues are

(a) how to divide the market into segments
(b) how to sell products in each target market segment, and
(c) which target market segments are most important.

The first two issues also relate to determining concepts for products to be introduced to various market segments. The third issue relates to product portfolio management as described in Chapter 4 in the discussion of long-term profit plans.

Even when a product's positioning does not change, the characteristics of target users are likely to change, and therefore product concepts must be reviewed before every model change.

Market segmentation strategies

Market segmentation (i.e., product segmentation) is the part of the full-line policy that determines when changes must be made in the positioning of vehicle models in the user perception chart. Some leading companies attempt to occupy all of the more popular positions in the user perception chart, so that there is little or no space left in the chart for newcomers to enter products without facing direct competition.

The first thing to consider when embarking upon a full-line policy is "localizing competition." Companies employ the market segmentation approach. When choosing brands, users think in terms of price and how close the current products' characteristics are to their own ideal product (as shown on the perception chart).

Figures 5-2 and 5-3 show examples of perception charts. Figure 5-2 includes only certain American and European vehicle

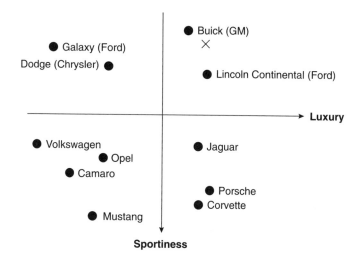

Figure 5-2. Perception Chart: Car Drivers

brands. In this figure, the horizontal axis is a continuum of luxury (with the most luxurious models at the right) and the vertical axis is a continuum of sportiness (with the sportiest models at the bottom). Researchers filled in this perception chart after conducting surveys among vehicle buyers and applying analytical methods such as factory analysis and discriminant analysis.

All other factors being equal, a vehicle buyer whose preferences put him or her at position X in Figure 5-2 would be psychologically closest to a Buick or Lincoln Continental and would be less likely to choose other brands. Using a market segmentation approach, we can see that few automobile manufacturers make much of an impression on this particular vehicle buyer and there are a only a few vehicle brands competing in this vehicle buyer's market segment. In fact, as shown in the figure, only two companies have products competing in that market segment. Thus, we can say that the competition is localized.

A slight change in a model's sales price or product characteristics can cause it to be repositioned within the preference chart, so that the vehicle enters a different segment, where it affects (and

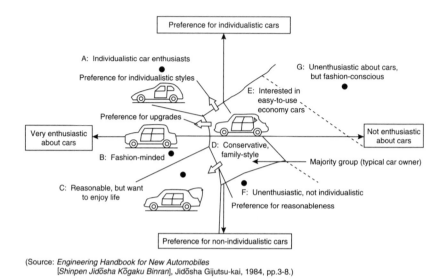

(Source: *Engineering Handbook for New Automobiles*
[*Shinpen Jidōsha Kōgaku Binran*], Jidōsha Gijutsu-kai, 1984, pp.3-8.)

Figure 5-3. Concepts Based on Knowledge and Values of Users

competes with) only a few other vehicle models. For this reason, companies are often more concerned with the marketing strategy of their products in particular market segments than with their total market share.

Vehicle brands must be repositioned to change their image among vehicle buyers. Such repositioning entails changing product characteristics and sales promotion strategies, which in turn incurs extra costs.

A newcomer who introduces a model that has exactly the same position on the perception chart as an existing model will face severe price competition that makes it difficult to maintain profitability. Therefore, newcomers try to introduce models that occupy unique positions with no direct competition. This is called the *market niche strategy*. However, when existing vehicle brands get well established in a position, it becomes difficult for other manufacturers to introduce a rival brand in a market niche anywhere close to that position.

Step 3. Clarification of Product Concepts

Product concepts define the products and what they mean to buyers. As such, a product's concept includes product characteristics, which depend upon the lifestyle, values, interests, tastes, behavior patterns, family configuration, and income of the product's target users. Product physical characteristics that should be built into a particular model include its dimensions, style, standard and performance features, design, colors, decor, intended use, and price. From a different perspective, we might also call these characteristics the model's sales points.

Product managers use the concepts clarified by the merchandising department as a guideline when planning the concrete development of vehicle models as products. Each model's target users are defined via the market positioning process described in Step 2 above, in which a specific type of user or market segment is set for the vehicle model. The people who define the model's product concept must first study the preferred characteristics among its target users.

For example, assume that there is a growing market for vehicles popular among young people and that our company wants to introduce a new product for young people as target users. Our merchandising department has concluded its market surveys and the results show that these target users are looking for the following characteristics:

- Style: A new look compared to existing models
- Size: Emphasis on functionality; larger than compacts but smaller than mass-market vehicles
- Performance: Superior to compact class
- Price: Best price for young buyers is between compacts and mass-market vehicles

In addition to the above characteristics specifically for young vehicle buyers, merchandising looks at:

- Target sales period: To be determined according to market growth trends and actions taken by competitors

- Target sales volume: To be determined according to market size prediction and target market share

All of the above factors go into formulating the merchandising proposal.

After the merchandising proposal comes the product planning proposal, which focuses on determining the actual configuration of the vehicle model to be developed, in line with the merchandising concept described in the merchandising proposal. Specifically, the following items must be determined:

- Vehicle size
- Vehicle weight
- Performance features
- Styling
- Major components (chassis, engine, etc.): includes deciding whether to modify and re-use existing designs or create new designs for major components
- Target price, target sales volume, and target costs
- Basic engineering configuration (vehicle's basic structure and design)
- Development master schedule

Step 4. Decision by Top Management

Although the product managers are responsible for responding to the requests presented by the merchandising department, the merchandising proposal is presented to the top managers who attend the merchandising meeting (see Figure 5-4).

Step 5. Final Decision on Product Concept by Product Managers

The merchandising proposal drafted by the merchandising department is used as a tentative plan by the relevant product manager in the engineering planning department, who must make the final decision concerning the product concept.

Merchandising Proposal	Creation date:
	Merchandising department
① Background	② Objectives
③ Contents	④ Vehicle Line
⑤ Sales price and estimated sales volume	⑥ Market entry period

Figure 5-4. Form for Merchandising Proposal

Departments Responsible

The merchandising department carries out market surveys and proposes the product's market positioning, product concept, and other characteristics in its merchandising proposal.

The domestic and overseas sales organizations provide market information (concerning user needs, trends among competitors, etc.) to the merchandising department.

The merchandising meeting (top management's decision-making body) reviews and decides to approve or reject the merchandising proposal.

The relevant product manager from the engineering planning department uses the merchandising proposal as a guide in drafting a final version of the product concept.

Supplement: Case Study of the Product Process: Nissan's Cima

According to Mr. Naoki Itai (see Itai 1991), product concepts necessarily involve meanings that are a subjective matter among the concept developers. Consequently, he thinks it best to have product concepts developed by large groups of people who can work cooperatively.

Inasmuch as product concepts set the direction to be followed by many product designers and developers, establishing a good product concept is a precondition for product development of any kind and is essential for successful product development. The following briefly describes the process by which Nissan created the product concept behind its Cima luxury model.

Step 1. Determine development targets for product positioning

The Nissan Cima started out as a concept for reaching target users who wanted a car even more luxurious than Nissan's Cedric and Gloria luxury models. This concept was developed after discerning latent user needs for higher luxury and after identifying problems with existing models.

Comparisons with competing vehicles

The development staff made extensive studies that took the user's perspective in comparing the Nissan Cedric and Gloria with competitors both domestic (e.g., Toyota Crown) and overseas (e.g., Mercedes-Benz, BMW, Jaguar).

Their studies showed that Japanese luxury vehicles tend to be perceived as formal vehicles for VIPs, which emphasize comfort and stability in the rear seats and lack the sporty, personal-car image of certain foreign luxury brands such as Germany's Mercedes-Benz and BMW.

Market surveys

Market research includes sampling surveys among users as well as interview surveys among owners of midsize vehicles. These surveys revealed the following types of dissatisfaction among users.

The Cima's design size is the same as compact vehicles. Like the Crown and the Cedric, the base vehicle is a 2000-cc (compact) vehicle while the midsize model has a 2800-cc engine mounted on the same base, which does not satisfy users who want a feeling of status.

The comparative studies and surveys described above showed that the design orientation should be toward a vehicle that affords users the status of a midsize vehicle while not sacrificing the performance features of a high-grade personal vehicle such as the German models. Hence the design objective of building a "new big car."

Step 2. Clarify the Product Concept

To clarify the idea of a "new big car" developed at Step 1, Nissan formulated a basic development policy and listed key words that would help clarify the product concept.

Basic Policy for Development of Cima:

1. We will not limit ourselves to the conventional "framework."
2. We will not simply copy European or American vehicles but will instead emphasize the vehicle as a "Japanese vehicle."
3. We will emphasize original, mature design in all aspects, to make a vehicle that will be well received all over the world.

Key Words for Development of Cima:

1. Expression of good taste
2. Expression of style and presence
3. Top-grade running performance
4. Meticulous, thoughtful design details
5. Top-quality comfort

We made the product concept more concrete by translating the above basic policy and key words into the following ideas concerning the vehicle's size, performance features, design, and price.

1. Size
   • Wider than previous domestic (Japanese) vehicles

- Midsize vehicle (not mid-size engine in a compact vehicle)

2. Performance features
   - A personal vehicle that emphasizes good running performance
   - Most powerful engine among domestic (Japanese) vehicles (at the risk of quality overkill, the vehicle will have a 255-hp 3-liter turbo-charged engine)

3. Design
   - Emphasis on beauty of form rather than beauty of function: use attractive lines that give a hint of the traditional Japanese aesthetic and the gentleness of a Buddha statue

4. Price
   - High price; about ¥5.1 million (US$50,000)
   - Emphasis on status

6

Product Conceptualization and Development Plan

Definitions

Product conceptualization is the process by which the responsible product manager in the engineering planning department determines the configuration of new product features, production scale, and other key product concepts after reviewing the merchandising requests (in the merchandising plan described in Chapter 5) based on market research undertaken by the merchandising department. The product manager also evaluates recent technological developments and applies the results of his or her own market research in considering user needs, market competitiveness, and market quality issues. Figure 6-1 illustrates this process.

The development plan presents a summary of the new vehicle's concept based on input provided by a group that includes the product manager, designers, engineers, prototype developers, and engineering managers. As such, it is the output from the product conceptualization process.

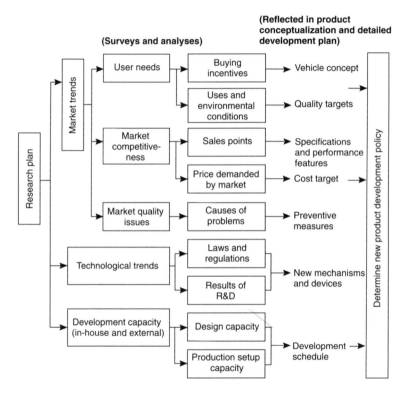

Figure 6-1. Planning Process for New Car Models

Objectives

1. To determine the new vehicle's model configuration (model number) and production scale to provide a starting point for the following design activities
2. To take the perspective of target costing in determine the vehicle model's cost outline based on the product conceptualization

Input and Output

Input

1. New product life cycle plan and corporate new product development plan
2. Market survey information and merchandising plan
3. Information on development of cutting-edge technologies

Output

The output is the development plan, which contains the following:

1. Development goals (including product concept): Define changes in (1) economic environment, (2) use environment and regulatory trends, (3) predictions for rival vehicle models, and (4) the company's vehicle model. The following points should be addressed with regard to (4).
   - How will the vehicle model's positioning and concept change, and exactly what kind of image is being sought?
   - What will the model's sales points be relative to rival vehicle models?
   - What is the design image?
   - What are the vehicle's dimensions?
   - Which performance features are most important to upgrade?
   - What are the "hard points" in the vehicle's design and structure?
   - What new mechanisms and equipment will the new model have?
   - Will parts be commonized?
   - How long is the model life?
   - What is the sales price?
   - What is the acceptable range of costs?

2. Model configuration (model number): The model configuration indicates the overall idea and scale of the development project.

(a) Destination: divided into various domestic and overseas sales regions; regulations, required quality and required performance features vary according to the destination.

(b) Body type: passenger vehicles include the following body types

> Sedan, hardtop, coupe, hatchback, van, wagon
> 1-box, 2-box, or 3-box
> Categories based on number of doors

(c) Grades: 5 to 10 grades is typical

(d) Engine: 4 to 6 types of engines, with various tradeoffs between power and fuel efficiency

> Categories based on type of fuel (e.g., gasoline, diesel, LPG)
> Categories based on number of cylinders
> Categories based on carburetor or EFI (Electronic Fuel Injection)

(e) Transmission

> Column shift or floor shift
> Manual (three-speed or four-speed) or automatic (three-speed, four-speed, overdrive, lockup)

Figure 6-2 describes a model configuration example based on the June 1992 model change implemented for the Toyota Camry.

3. Size: Determine full length, full width, wheelbase, and interior cabin size.

4. Estimated sales price and estimated sales volume: These estimates need to be more firmly established than they were in the new product life cycle plan for individual products (used in drafting the long-term profit plan).

5. Production scale and plant investment plan: Because there is an investment risk in setting up a plant investment plan based on estimated sales volume, the plant investment plan usually assumes a production scale somewhat lower than the estimated production scale.

Body/drive type	Engine	Grade		Trans-mission	Model No.	Unit price*
Sedan, 2WD	1,800-cc, 16 valves (4S FE)	XT		5F	E-SV 30-AEMDK	1,503
				4A/T	-AEPDK	1,578
		Lumiere		5F	-AEMMK	1,708
				4A/T	-AEPMK	1,783
		ZE		5F	-AEMEK	1,849
				4A/T	-AEPEK	1,924
	2,000-cc, diesel turbo (2C T)	Lumiere		5F	Y-CV 30-AEMMX	1,857
				4A/T	-AEPMX	1,932
		ZX		5F	Y-CV 30-AEMGX	2,024
				4A/T	-AEPGX	2,099
	2,000-cc, 16 valves (3S FE)	Lumiere	Normal	5F	E-SV 32-AEMMK	1,818
				ECT	-AEPMK	1,911
			4WS	5F	E-SV 33-AEMMK	1,898
				ECT	-AEPMK	1,991
		ZX	Normal	5F	E-SV 32-AEMGK	1,970
				ECT	-AEPGK	2,063
			4WS	5F	E-SV 32-AEMGK	2,030
				ECT	-AEPGK	2,123
		ZX touring P	Normal	5F	E-SV 32-AEMGK (R)	2,137
				ECT	-AEPGK (R)	2,230
			4WS	5F	E-SV 33-AEMGK (R)	2,197
				ECT	-AEPGK (R)	2,290
Sedan, 4WD	2,000-cc, 16 valves (3S FE)	Lumiere		5F	E-SV 35-AEMMK	1,996
				ECT	-AEPMK	2,095
		ZX		5F	-AEMGK	2,173
				ECT	-AEPGK	2,272
Hardtop, 2WD	2,500-cc, V6 (4VZ-FE)	Prominent X		ECT	E-VZV 32-ATPQK (X)	2,252
		Prominent	Normal	ECT	-ATPQK	2,423
			4WS	ECT	E-VZV 32-ATPQK	2,423
		Prominent G	Normal	ECT	E-VZV 32-ATPQK (G)	2,687
			4WS	ECT	E-VZV 33-ATPQK (G)	2,747

* In ¥1000

Figure 6-2. Example of Car Model Configuration (June 1992 Model Change for Toyota Camry)

6. Rough styling: At this stage, there are general images of the exterior and interior designs, but these designs have not been finalized. The images may be shown in idea sketches or one-fifth scale mock-ups.

7. Estimated development costs: This is an estimate of the prototype development costs and narrowly defined development costs.

The prototype development costs are proportionate to the number of prototypes. There are three stages in prototype development—the initial prototype, the formal prototype, and the production prototype. If we include all three generations of formal prototype development, the total number of prototype units manufactured rises to over 300. This pushes the manufacturing cost per prototype vehicle to tens of millions of yen (over US$100,000) excluding labor costs, and even more for luxury models. Accordingly, the company must invest around ¥10 billion (US$100 million) just to complete the prototype development stage.

8. Development schedule: This includes the production schedule and the sales startup schedule

Steps

Step 1. Determine Model Life

Typical model changes are implemented every four years, which means a four-year model life. The product development lead time (the time from the model's product conceptualization to its full production startup) is four years. Thus, the model life is the same length of time as the development period.

Conceptual work on the next-generation model begins immediately after the latest model has reached the stage of full-scale production and sales.

The product manager and staff spend about one year (from P minus 48 months to P minus 36 months where "P" indicates the start of full-scale production) completing the product conceptualization and obtaining approval for the development plan.

Step 2. Make a Schedule for Early Development Stages

- From product conceptualization to approved development plan: by P minus 36 months. (This stage is the theme of this chapter; the following stages are taken up in subsequent chapters.)
- Start of target costing: by P minus 36 months
- Establishment of target costs: by P minus 30 months
- Approval of styling design and establishment of basic structure of each major function: by P minus 30 months

Step 3. Determine the Styling (Exterior and Interior Design)

Style is the most important ingredient for making successful passenger vehicles. Style is the first thing people notice, whether they see the vehicle in a catalog, on television, or wherever. If the style is a turn-off for buyers, the vehicle will not sell well. Style is what attracts a potential customer to the showroom; only afterward does the customer begin to ask about the engine, suspension, and so on.

During model changes, the new product concept closely follows the style of the preceding model, so that many major structural elements and specifications are already determined to some extent. The style design may change somewhat later on, and the development plan shows only a rough styling as part of the image description.

The process for determining the body design includes the following steps:

(a) First, the product manager formulates a preliminary style image (about P minus 40 months).

(b) At that time (about P minus 40 months), the design department's preliminary design team begins its exterior design work (the line team has not yet begun).

(c) Once the design department's line team completes its preparations for the latest new model's next minor change, they begin design work for the next-generation model. This new work begins usually about ten months after the latest new model enters the market, or about two months after the preliminary design team begins working.

(d) Making idea sketches is the first step in creating the image for the style design concept. Next, the designers make one-fifth-scale mock-ups of their designs. This occurs at about P minus 36 months.

(e) Last, they make a full-scale clay model. This model is submitted for approval along with the design proposal. It takes only one year for the design team to reach this point, which is about P minus 30 months.

Meanwhile, the interior design work proceeds slightly behind the exterior design work and receives style approval at about the same time.

Step 4. Develop Initial Prototype

Prototype development includes three major steps: initial prototype development, formal prototype development, and production prototype development. Formal prototype development is carried out after style approval is received, but initial prototype development comes even before the vehicle's style has been finalized. Initial prototype development includes the design, prototype manufacturing, and testing of components. Why must prototype work begin at such an early stage? There are several reasons.

The constant emergence of unprecedented new functions and new materials from high-tech research means longer development lead times, since there is little or no information (market data, test and evaluation data, etc.) from previous models. Thus vehicle components that use such new functions or new materials must be developed and tested basically from scratch. The initial prototype development step affords developers the opportunity to experiment with such functions and materials early on, before the ordinary (formal) prototype development step.

When a current model is improved upon, there are usually many new design units to be created. The engine room lends support by creating a full-size mock-up to facilitate study of the layout and assembly methods used for such design units.

Step 5. Make Component Development Plan

Automobile manufacturers that produce a wide range of models have component design and development programs that are to some extent independent of new-model vehicle bodies. Instead, designers select from among a variety of components, choosing those which best suit the basic configuration of their new model designs. After that, they move onto the detailed design stage.

Step 6. Determine Estimated Sales Price and Volume

The rule of thumb for setting the estimated sales price is "having competing products in a very competitive market requires that product prices be determined by the level of the product's functions." This rule means that the prices and the various functional levels found in all of the competing products must be taken into account when determining (estimating) a new product's sales price. Consequently, even when the model under development does not have any functional changes from the previous model, it may still be necessary to price the new model lower than the previous model. For example, suppose that a rival company starts turning out many new models that are lower in price than your own company's models with the same level of functions. Once this fact becomes known, your company must establish a lower, more competitive price for its own similar models under development.

Thus, we must abandon the old propositions that prices do not change unless there is a change in functions (use value), and that prices can be raised whenever functions are added or improved.

- Added function examples: 4WS (four-wheel steering for added stability on curves) or active suspension (an electronic control system for hydraulic suspension that uses sensors to detect road conditions)
- Improved function examples: more horsepower from engine or higher fuel efficiency

Hence the formula

$$\begin{matrix} \text{price of new} \\ \text{model} \end{matrix} = \sum_j \beta_j \times \begin{matrix} \text{main design parameters that} \\ \text{indicate the level of functions } j \end{matrix}$$

In the above formula, β_j represents the coefficient or weight assigned to the various main design parameters. This price estimation method is further described in Chapter 8.

The sales division determines the estimated sales volume after considering factors such as (1) past sales results, (2) current market trends, and (3) competing product trends. The most important factor is the first one—sales results for the current model. The people who determine this figure cannot afford to be overly optimistic but must instead take a conservative approach that relies as much as possible on solid evidence to yield a prudent figure. The reasons for this cautious approach include the following.

Given that "profit per vehicle unit = profit during model life ÷ sales volume during model life," greater sales volume tends to mean less profit per vehicle unit. Moreover, given that "target cost = target price − profit per target unit," a lower profit per vehicle unit tends to mean unnecessarily high target costs.

Note: Even when we use the formula "profit per vehicle unit = target sales price × target return-on-sales ratio," it still holds true that "target return-on-sales ratio = target profit during product life cycle period ÷ target gross sales during product life cycle period." Thus the estimated sales volume still serves as a premise.

Step 7. Profitability Check

The accounting division's target costing section (or product planning section) carries out a general study to determine whether or not the development plan will be profitable. They listen to the product manager's presentation about the basic structure of the planned vehicle model and make an approximate estimate of the costs per vehicle unit. They use the following two formulas when making this cost estimate.

$$\begin{matrix} \text{Estimated} \\ \text{costs} \end{matrix} = \begin{matrix} \text{actual costs} \\ \text{of current} \\ \text{model} \end{matrix} + \begin{matrix} \text{cost variables resulting from new model's} \\ \text{revised functions and specifications} \end{matrix}$$

Estimated profit = estimated sales price − estimated costs

When their estimate shows that the new model's development plan does not afford sufficient profitability, the development plan must be revised.

Departments Responsible

A product manager (who has division chief ranking) in the engineering planning department works with a group of subordinates to refine the product conceptualization and draft a development plan. This group usually includes staff from not only the engineering planning department but also from sales, design, engineering, prototype development, and engineering management. The product manager functions as the project leader and works directly with a core group of 10 to 15 staff members, who all have specialized knowledge and skills and are ranked as section managers or subsection managers.

When the development plan is completed, the general manager in charge of product planning (who has executive director ranking) presents it to the product planning cross-function meeting to receive their approval.

The members of the product planning cross-function meeting include about a dozen high-ranking staff from the engineering development division (including the engineering planning department, engineering departments, and prototype development department), the production engineering department, the sales division, the purchasing department, and the accounting department. The vice president in charge of engineering development chairs these meetings. As such, the product planning cross-function meeting comprises a cross-functional group that promotes lateral coordination among the above departments, which are vertically organized (i.e., function-based) groups.

7

Detailed Development Plan and Development Directive

Definitions

The detailed development plan is a more detailed breakdown of the development plan that was formulated as the output of the product conceptualization process. It describes the planned vehicle model's style design as well as the structure and specifications of its function-based categories, such as its engine (power train), transmission (drivetrain), and chassis, and an estimated target cost per vehicle unit.

The development directive is formulated as the output of the detailed development plan process and must receive the approval of the engineering cross-function meeting (attended by top managers). The estimated target cost per vehicle unit must receive approval from the costing cross-function meeting (also attended by top managers) before the development directive can be drafted. This meeting occurs at about P minus 30 months (30 months prior to full-scale production and sales).

Objectives

1. The objective of the detailed development plan is to serve as a resource for the target costing approach when establishing a formal target cost per vehicle unit.

2. The objective of the development directive is to serve the product manager as a resource for the target costing approach both when explaining the detailed development plan to the various departments concerned with the development project (particularly the design and engineering departments) and when enlisting their cooperation in proceeding to the next step, which includes function-based and component-based breakdowns of target costs. The cooperating departments who receive the development directive implement a thorough VE (Value Engineering) study.

Input and Output

Input

1. The development plan (see the description in Chapter 6)

2. Analysis of the relative strengths of the company's products and competing products (in terms of specifications, quality, performance characteristics, and costs)

3. Profit/cost analyses: analyses of the target and actual figures for the costs, profits, prices, and sales volumes of the target vehicle model and other similar vehicle models

Output

The following items are determined in addition to the items included in the development plan.

1. Style design
   Exterior and interior design, color design, and clay model fabrication

2. Dimensions, etc.: the most basic hardware specifications, such as

- passenger capacity
- interior cabin space
- exterior dimensions
- "hard points" in exterior design (window positions, height of belt line, height of door opening, height of hood and luggage compartment, height of bumper, etc.)
- wheelbase and treads

3. Function-based structural components

   The detailed specifications for each structural component are to be determined by the various corresponding design and engineering departments. At the product conceptualization stage, the product manager formulates a function-based list of basic structural components and specifies any mechanisms or equipment that will be newly adopted or modified.

   (a) Engine functions: engine model number, cooling system, intake and exhaust system, mounting method, etc.

   (b) Drivetrain functions: model numbers and layout of transmission, differential gears, propeller shaft, axles, etc.

   (c) Brake functions: model numbers and layout of boosters, master front brakes, rear brakes, parking brake, etc.

   (d) Suspension functions: model numbers, layout, and alignment of front suspension, rear suspension, tires, wheels, etc.

   (e) Steering functions: model numbers and layout of manual or power steering, steering wheel, etc.

   (f) Body functions: basic structure, principal dimensions, design "hard points," etc.

   (g) Interior functions: seats, trim, etc.

   (h) Other equipment functions

   (In addition, the list may also have "chassis functions" as a general category that includes the suspension, steering, brakes, and intake/exhaust systems.)

4. Establishment of targets for performance characteristics and quality factors

These targets include power performance, fuel economy performance, regulations, braking performance, handling stability and travel performance, ride comfort and vibration/noise control, durability, air conditioning performance, operability, and serviceability.

5. Establishment of key targets
   When setting targets to increase fuel efficiency and improve performance, the following items must be considered carefully as items profoundly related to target costing.
   • Is there any waste in the vehicle's dimensions?
   • Is there any room for improvement in terms of quality and performance?
   • Can checking of components be safely reduced?
   • Can parts be made more compact (are they unnecessarily large)?
   • Can the structural system as a whole be changed for the better in some way?

6. Establishment of cost targets: final determination of target cost per vehicle unit
7. Establishment of target profits for typical model numbers
8. Estimated costs for functions and entire vehicles
9. Development directive: includes items in development plan plus the above items

Steps

Step 1. Determine the Function-Specific Basic Structures

The product manager uses the development plan as a guideline in working with the various engineering departments to determine the vehicle model's design and basic structures categorized by functions. The target costing approach identifies the following caution points at this step.

Cost impact of styling

The body design may have the following kinds of impact on costs:

(a) Stricter tolerances for certain parts
(b) Increased labor-hours for machining and/or assembly
(c) Greater variety in the part configuration list

Example: Recently, bumpers have been fit closely to the vehicle body to give a feeling of integration with the body. Consequently, whereas there used to be several millimeters of space between the bumper and the vehicle body, this gap is now less than one millimeter. This change requires stricter tolerances for the bumper and its various related components, which tends to increase costs.

If body style modifications result in higher costs, it must be determined how much costs will be allowed to rise. The product manager must find a balance between higher costs and the aesthetic improvement offered by styling changes.

Reduction of life cycle cost to aid profitability

The life cycle cost of a product includes all of the costs incurred during the product's entire life cycle, from product development through manufacturing, sale, use, and disposal.

Even after a vehicle has been sold, costs are incurred not only by its user but also by its manufacturer. The following are two factors that should be considered at the target costing stage to help decrease such costs.

(a) Reduction of costs for processing claims. Claims processing costs are part of the costs borne by the manufacturer after its products are sold yet are excluded from the list of costs dealt with under the target costing approach. Most of the causes for quality-related claims are due to mistakes made during the design and development stages, and therefore it is usually necessary to design-in quality improvements to prevent and eliminate these causes. This process may required adding or modifying functions, which tends to increase the variable costs and/or special fixed costs for target costing, but it will also work to reduce the number of claims, which may result in a lower life cycle cost (total cost) for the product in question. In fact, it may even work to boost sales of the product. Therefore, we can justify slightly

higher target costs at the design and development stages under these circumstances.

(b) Cost of discarded wiring. When a vehicle dealer or individual buyer decides to install optional equipment, such as an audio system, the existing wiring for the standard equipment is often discarded. However, costs were incurred at the design and development stages to include such standard-equipped wiring.

While excluding any standard-equipped wiring would help lower variable costs for target costing, including such wiring reduces the user's cost burden (and inconvenience burden) and therefore helps reduce the product's life cycle cost. Slightly higher costs for the manufacturer and lower costs for the consumer also contribute to higher sales and, in turn, higher profits. Therefore, this is another case in which slightly higher target costs can be justified during target costing.

Lessons from current model

Once the current model enters the full production stage, there are lessons to be learned, such as ideas for cutting costs and ways to resolve or prevent current problems, that can be applied toward the next-generation model. They can also be used to reevaluate and further refine VA (value analysis) and VE (value engineering) programs that are being or are about to be implemented.

Reverse engineering (tear-down) studies of competing vehicles

Tearing down competing vehicles can provide valuable technical information and suggest ways to improve VE plans for next-generation vehicles. Competing vehicles should be disassembled down to the level of individual parts and studied by various experts including designers, engineers, procurement staff, and cost managers.

Cost-saving effects of parts variety reduction

Although style makes a key difference among products, at the same time it is important to reduce the number of different parts required wherever possible. Such variety reduction should be worked out in the detailed development plan, before the development process enters the first-generation prototype development stage.

A major theme in VE activities is studying possible parts variety reduction in the main subassembly units produced in-house by automobile manufacturers, such as the engine, transmission, and chassis. For example, Toyota's Celica line includes three "sister models"—the Celica, Corona EXiV, and the Carina ED. Toyota's production schedule for 1990 shows that about 10,000 units of each model were manufactured each month. The exterior design of each of the three sister models is radically different from the other two. However, their chassis, engines, and transmissions all contain many common parts.

Making parts variety reduction a high priority when selecting the parts for each model offers the following cost advantages:

(a) Effect of reducing overall number of parts: lower depreciation expenses and unit costs
When the number of common parts rises, the total number of parts declines and both plant investment costs and depreciation expenses decline as well, albeit only slightly. The per-unit cost of parts also goes down thanks to economy of scale in producing greater quantities of the same parts.

(b) Effect of using mass-produced parts: lower unit costs
Costs are lower when using mass-produced parts than when using small-lot parts.

These two types of effects comprise an important factor for determining the estimated production volume and the estimated unit cost of parts when making a part-specific breakdown of target costs.

Step 2. Cost Estimates for Specific Functions and Vehicles (Approximate Estimates)

At the detailed development planning stage, a cost estimate is done after all of the above cost-reducing measures have been adopted. This estimate is called an *approximate estimate*. The purchasing department makes its own cost estimate of parts to be supplied by vendors and the production engineering department estimates the costs of parts to be manufactured in-house. As soon as the cost target for a new product has been established, the detailed development plan is revised accordingly and another round of cost estimates is carried out based on the revised plan.

After the final cost estimates have been completed and analyzed by the target costing department, the product manager presents a target cost proposal to the cost meeting.

Step 3. Establishment of Target Profits for Typical Models

In the long-term profit plan, three categories of profit targets are set for the model life of an entire series of vehicles in the model line under development: marginal income, contribution margin, and operating profit. At the same time, series-average profit ratios are planned for the entire series as the marginal income ratio, contribution margin ratio, and operating profit ratio.

At the product conceptualization stage, the target profits over the model life of the entire series and the series-average return-on-sales ratio are used as a basis for calculating target values for the marginal income, contribution margin, and operating profit of typical models in the series over their model life. These calculations use the following formulas:

$$\begin{matrix} \text{Target marginal income} \\ \text{of typical model} \end{matrix} = \begin{matrix} \text{target sales of typical model} \\ \times \text{ series-average marginal profit ratio} \end{matrix}$$

$$\begin{matrix} \text{Target contribution} \\ \text{margin of typical model} \end{matrix} = \begin{matrix} \text{target sales of typical model} \\ \times \text{ series-average contribution margin ratio} \end{matrix}$$

$$\begin{matrix} \text{Target operating profit} \\ \text{of typical model} \end{matrix} = \begin{matrix} \text{target sales of typical model} \\ \times \text{ series-average operating profit ratio} \end{matrix}$$

(**Note**, however, the series-average profit ratio is revised when return-on-sales profits vary widely among typical models due to model grade differences.)

The following formula is used to calculate the per-unit target operating profit for typical models:

$$\text{Target profit per unit among typical models} = \frac{\text{target operating profit for model}}{\text{sales volume during life cycle of model}}$$

Step 4. Determine Target Cost per Vehicle Unit

Chapter 9 describes the method for determining the target cost per vehicle unit.

Departments Responsible

The product manager and his or her staff from the engineering planning department and other departments determine the items listed above under "Output" (e.g., style, dimensions, function-based structure, quality, weight, cost targets).

Engineers and designers from various departments help the product manager determine the function-based structure and draft a highly reliable VE proposal.

The purchasing department and production engineering department make cost estimates for purchased parts and in-house parts, respectively. These estimates are then compiled by the target costing department.

8

Setting Target Sales Prices

Cost-Based and Market-Based: Two Methods for Setting Prices

A cost-based method or a market-based method can be applied to set sales prices.

The *cost-based method*, also known as the cost-plus method, adds on a set profit margin to either the full cost or the variable costs to get a sales price for a particular product. This method is most effective when it is a seller's market and when your company's product is clearly superior to and distinct from competitors' products, so that setting a sales price based on your company's costs will not run the risk of losing out in price competition with rival companies. For example, Japanese automakers found themselves in such a situation when selling on the U.S. market during the 1980s.

With the *market-based method*, your company looks at the prices of competing products on the market and sets similar prices for its own products. This method is most effective in a much different kind of market environment, characterized by the following:

(a) No major distinctions between your company's products and competing products in terms of quality and functions. For example, in the U.S. auto market of the early 1990s, improved quality among American vehicles has narrowed the quality gap with Japanese vehicles.

(b) Short product life cycles as technological advances rapidly bring new generations of competing products into the market at low prices. This characteristic is especially true in product fields where technological progress has been rapid, such as personal computers and fax machines.

(c) The market has matured to the point that it has become a buyer's market.

Consequently, the market-based method for setting target sales prices rests upon the following proposition:

> Generally, the price of products (i.e., competing products) in a highly competitive market depends upon the functional level reached by the product's various functions.

Even if there is no conspicuous difference in the quality and functions of competing products on the market, prices may be set according to slight differences in a product's functional level or the inclusion of extra functions (which give the product a slight edge in functional level). In this context, functions include not only practical functions but also aesthetic functions such as the product's styling. Also, when setting costs, one must consider all competing products in the same market segment—including one's own company's competing products.

When one of the major functions of a product under development can be thought of as a major design parameter, it may be helpful to draw a *price-performance curve* (see Shapiro and Jackson 1978, p. 122). In such a curve, the prices of all competing products (including one's own company's competing products) are plotted along the vertical axis and the major design parameter is plotted along the horizontal axis (see Figure 8-1).

In Figure 8-1, "horsepower" is considered as a engine's major performance parameter (i.e., major design parameter), and the price/performance relationship between this parameter and prices of competing products has been plotted. In the figure, the price per horsepower of model A is shown as 2.0 whereas that of model B is 1.0. Based on this scatter diagram, prices can be predicted for specified performance values (i.e., design parameter values).

There are several methods for setting target sales prices based on the above proposition. Two such methods are described in the following sections.

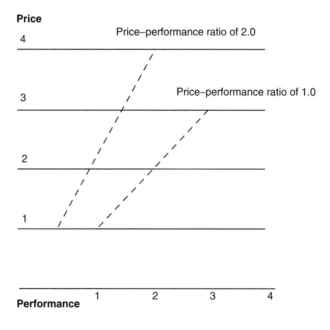

Figure 8-1. Price-Performance Curve

Weight Analysis Method

The following methods (also described by Masayasu Tanaka 1984, pp. 42-44, and Tanaka, Amagasa, and Ama 1988, pp. 211-217) have been proposed for cases where there are several variables among the major design parameters.

1. After finding a simple regression equation between each design parameter and price, a specialist evaluates the weights among the various design parameter values and adds this weight factor to the simple regression equation.
2. Apply main component analysis to make sales price estimates based on several main components (each component consisting of several design parameters).
3. Apply WADP (weight analysis by design parameters), a heuristic approach for price estimations in which a positive weight is added to each design parameter.

I recommend the relatively simple weighted regression analysis method (further described in Monden and Kanesawa 1994). This method includes the following steps.

Step 1

After the target competing product's major functions have been determined via the product conceptualization and detailed development planning stages, formulate a regression equation for the design parameter values representing the product's main functional level and the actual sales prices of currently sold versions of the competing products based on data from numerous competing products. Next, use this regression equation to postulate an equation for estimating sales prices. This equation uses weighted regression analysis.

$$P = \beta_1 X_1 + \beta_2 X_2 + ... + \beta_j X_j + ... + \beta_m X_m + \beta_{m+1}$$

Where

X_j = main design parameter values ($j = 1, ..., m$)

P = sales price
β_j = regression coefficient ($j = 1, ..., m + 1$)

However, the following caution points should be observed to help improve the reliability of the price estimation method (regression equation) used in weighted regression analysis.

The following method can be used to raise the determination coefficient to 0.85 or above.

(a) Effective selection of drivers (addition or deletion)
Although you should select drivers that have a strong correlation, you must restrict your selection of drivers that have a strong correlation between drivers. One way is to use the main component analysis method, but I recommend the co-ordinated scatter diagram method instead.

(b) Deletion of abnormal values
Create a graph to compare actual values with estimated values and delete data that have large gaps between the two (these are indicated as relative errors, not absolute error).

(c) Addition of data

(d) Restriction of application scope
In the use of linear regression analysis, the actual data for time values may change rapidly if the driver data values exceed a certain range. In such cases, divide the driver data into two or more areas and make a regression equation for each area.

Step 2

Find estimated sales price values (P^*) by incorporating into this estimation method the main design parameter values (X_j^*) for your company's new product (probably a model change or minor change) that were determined via the product conceptualization and detailed development plan stages.

If the product is still at the product conceptualization or detailed development plan stage, you can vary the design parameter values and do a simulation of the method for estimating sales prices.

Step 3

Using the estimated sales price as a base, measure the price image among consumers based on the product concepts derived from consumer surveys to get an idea of the price zone. Next, revise this value using the estimated sales volume or estimated costs to strategically determine the final target sales price.

Example: Let us suppose there are three major functions that influence the price of a vehicle: (1) development features, (2) functional distinctions, and (3) main equipment items.

As an example, Figure 8-2 shows data from December 1993 concerning major functions, equipment, and prices for Japanese midsize specialty vehicles that are competing in the sporty "specialty" market segment. Weighted regression analysis can be applied to these data to obtain a price estimation formula. Inasmuch as vehicles compete on a global market, data from similar European and American models should also be included to render a better estimation formula.

Coordinative Planning Method Using Secondary Planning

Described below is a price-setting method that I developed. I call it a coordinative planning method in that it uses a secondary planning method and a type of multitarget planning method. (This method can be used as an alternative to the method described in Steps 1 and 2 above.)

First, let us define the elements used in this method.

P_i = actual cost of current competing product i (i = 1, ..., n)

X_{ij} = main design parameter values (X_j) related to current competing product i (i = 1, ..., n, j = 1, ..., m)

$$\hat{P}_i = \frac{P_i - \bar{P}}{\sigma_p}$$

$\bar{P}$ = mean value of P_i

σ_p = standard deviation of P_i

Main Design Parameters for Silvia, Celica, and Prelude				
Grade	Silvia Q's Type S	Silvia K's Type S	Celica SS-II, SS suspension	Prelude Si VTEC
Price	SMT 208.7 4AT 218.4	5MT 249.7 4AT 259.4	5MT 222.5 4AT 226.8	5MT 246.8 4AT 256.3
Engine				
Category	In-line, 4-cylinder DOHC 16V	In-line, 4-cylinder DOHC 16V turbo	In-line, 4-cylinder DOHC 16V	In-line, 4-cylinder DOHC 16V VTEC
Displacement (cc)	1998	1998	1998	2156
Max. output (ps/rpm)	160/6400	220/6000	180/7000 (MT) 170/660 (AT)	200/6800
Max. torque (kgm/rpm)	19.2/48.00	128.0/4800	19.5/4800	22.3/4800
Fuel injection method	EGI	EGI	EFI	PGM-FI
Tank capacity (liters)	Premium	65/Premium	65/Premium	65/Premium
Dimensions and weight				
Total length (mm)	4500	4500	4435	4440
Total width (mm)	1730	1730	1750	1765
Total height (mm)	1295	1295	1305	1290
Wheelbase (mm)	2525	2525	2535	2550
Treads (F/R) (mm)	14801470	1480/1470	1510/1490	1525/1515
Vehicle weight (kg)	1160 (MT) 1180 (AT)	1220 (MT) 1240 (AT)	1210 (MT) 1230 (AT)	1250 (MT) 1270 (AT)
Performance	12.0 (MT) 10.0 (AT)	11.4 (MT) 9.2 (AT)	11.6 (MT) 10.6 (AT)	12.0 (MT) 10.6 (AT)
10 and 15 mode fuel consumption (km/l)				
Front suspension Rear suspension Tire size	Strut Multi-link 205/60R15	Strut Multi-link 205/55R16	Strut Strut 205/55R15	Double wishbone Double wishbone 205/55R15
Aluminum wheels	●	●		●
Air bag	▲ 13*	▲ 10*	▲ 6*	▲ 92.8* (set)
4WS	▲ 25.2* (HICAS package)	▲ 18* (HICAS package)	▲ 5* —	▲ 13*
ABS	▲ 13*	▲ 13*		▲ 23.7* (set)
Sun roof	▲ 11.5* (set)	▲ 11.5* (set)	▲ 12*	▲ 10.5* (set)
DSP audio system	▲ 22.5* (package)	▲ 22.5* (package)	▲ 9.5*	▲ 22.5* (set)

● Standard-equipped   ▲ Optional   *= 10,000 of yen

(Source: *Car and Driver,* Japan edition, December 10, 1993, p.43.)

Figure 8-2. Main Design Parameters for Leading Models of Japanese Midsize Specialty Cars

$$\hat{X_j} = \frac{X_{ij} - \bar{X_j}}{\sigma_{xj}}$$

$\bar{X_j}$ = mean value related to change of i for X_{ij}

σ_{xj} = average variation related to change of i for X_{ij}

At this point, we wish to find a value of β_j $(j = 1, ..., m)$ that satisfies the following equation:

min $(\hat{P_i} - \Sigma_j \beta_j \hat{X_{ij}})^2$

s.t. $\Sigma_j \beta_j = 1$

    $\beta_j \geqq 0,\ j = 1, ..., m$

We might also wish to satisfy the same equation for all competing products P_i $(i = 1, ..., n)$. To do this, we must find a value of β_j^* $(j = 1, ..., m)$ for which the following equation holds true:

min $\Sigma_i (\hat{P_1} - \Sigma \beta_j \hat{X_{ij}})^2$

s.t. $\Sigma_j \beta_j = 1$

    $\beta_j \geqq 0,\ j = 1, ..., m$

Using this value of β_j^*, we can make the following equation.

$P = (\Sigma_j \beta_j^* \hat{X_j})\ \sigma_p + \bar{P}$

Where

$\hat{X_j} = (X_{ij} - \bar{X_j}) \div \sigma_{xj}$

X_j = typical design parameter of new product to be priced

P = estimated sales price of new product to be priced

One advantage of this coordinative planning method over the weighted regression analysis method is that all the values for betaj are non-negative. This feature makes it easier to intuitively understand the positive effects of functional improvements or augmentations. (However, because β holds for non-negative conditions, for factors such as fuel consumption which have a correlation between price and negative values, the fuel consumption values should be inverted.)

In contrast to heuristic weighted methods, this method uses a secondary planning method as an optimization technique, which makes it a much faster method for obtaining the optimum result.

9

Setting Target Costs for Products

Definitions

Target costs for vehicles are set as per-unit cost targets for planned models, with a view toward achieving the model's target profit, which is set for the entire model life. Basically, there are two methods for determining such target costs.

Method Based on Sales Price

The target cost can be calculated as follows using the target return-on-sales ratio for the model series of vehicles, as was presented in the long-term profit plan (alternatively, you can use the target return-on-sales ratio for typical model numbers within the model series). Use either of the following formulas.

Target cost = target sales price × (1 − target return-on-sales ratio)

or

Target cost = target sales price − target operating profit

Method Based on Estimated Cost

The target cost can also be calculated by subtracting the per-unit profit improvement target value from the estimated cost. In other words:

Target cost = estimated cost − per-unit profit improvement target value

Target costs can be divided into (1) costs subject to target costing, i.e., costs that are the focus of cost-reduction activities within the target costing process, and (2) costs not subject to target costing. In other words:

$$\text{Target cost} = \begin{array}{c}\text{costs subject to}\\ \text{target costing}\end{array} + \begin{array}{c}\text{costs not subject}\\ \text{to target costing}\end{array}$$

1. Costs subject to target costing

Variable costs
- Materials costs (sheet metal, steel rods, die-cast products, etc.)
- Part transportation costs
- Coating, lubricant, and adhesive costs
- Purchased part costs
- Variable processing costs (labor-related): labor-hours × specified allocation rate
- Variable processing costs (based on allocations other than labor hours): management of cost drivers using allocation-based value × specified allocation rate

Direct fixed costs
- Depreciation of new equipment: management of equipment investments
- Prototype development costs
- Other development costs: management of development labor costs

2. Costs not subject to target costing
- Direct sales costs: set based on results from current model

- Indirect fixed manufacturing costs: reflects in-house and vendor manufacturing based on standard costs for current model (does not include depreciation of special-purpose equipment)
- Management-related indirect sales costs: set using specified allocation rate related to manufacturing costs

Target prime costs are also set as the improvement target for target costing activities; in other words, as cost reduction targets:

Cost reduction target = estimated cost of planned vehicle − target cost

Objective

The objective of having cost targets for vehicles is to help achieve the target profit set for the model life of the particular vehicle line by providing a basis for calculating target values to be used in cost-reduction activities at the design stage. The objective of target costing activities is to eliminate the difference (i.e., the cost-reduction target) between the estimated cost and the target cost.

In addition, it lays the foundation for the next step in target costing, namely breaking target costs down into categories based on functional elements and parts elements.

Input and Output

Input

1. Target sales price of typical model number: These prices are determined by the long-term profit plans for domestic and overseas sales. They incorporate new function evaluations contained in the product manager's development plan.
2. Target sales volume of typical model number: input from development plan.
3. Target profit for typical model number: To help achieve the target profit established for the vehicle line in the long-term

profit plan, these profits are set in three categories for each typical model number.
(a) by destination (country, etc.)
(b) by model
(c) by grade

4. Estimated cost data for planned model: calculated based on (a) to (e) below.
   (a) Current model's costs according to cost table: analysis of actual costs, contribution margin, and operating profit of current model and related models
   (b) Estimation of cost variables according to new functions described in detailed development plan
   (c) New plant investment (capital budget)
   (d) Development cost budget
   (e) Prototype development cost budget

5. Highly reliable VE plan

Output

1. Target cost formulated as overall cost per planned vehicle
2. Division between costs subject to target costing and costs not subject to target costing
3. Target cost reduction value for planned vehicle

Steps

There are two methods for setting target costs per vehicle: (1) the sales price-based method and (2) the estimated cost-based method. Either method can be used to determine the target cost needed to ensure the target profit over the planned vehicle's model life, and indeed both methods use the same kinds of data. The two methods differ chiefly in the sequence of their calculations. These methods are briefly described in sections (I) and (II) below.

Target costs are approved by top managers at the costing cross-function meeting. Before approving these cost figures, the managers check the feasibility of reaching the target contribution margin and operating profit for the entire model line being planned, based on the figures for the target marginal income, target sales volume, and target plant investment total. (This is called the second profitability check.)

Target costs do not include commodity price fluctuation predictions. Instead, target costs are predicated on commodity prices 30 months prior to the product's sales launch and normal production conditions typical of the third month of production. They are also held in comparison to the costs that the design engineers will aim toward in their design activities. Accordingly, fluctuations that occur prior to the production stage, such as changes in material costs or labor costs, are excluded from the target costing process from the production stage onward. These target costs are not intended to represent average costs for the life cycle of the planned vehicles.

I. Sales-Price-Based Method

Step 1. Determine the Target Profit per Vehicle

As was described in Step 3 in Chapter 7, figures such as the target profit over the model life of the planned model series or the series-average return-on-sales ratio are taken as a basis for calculating the target profit per vehicle for several typical model numbers. Although the long-term profit plan uses the model series' target profit rate as a basis for determining the target return-on-sales ratio, the actual return-on-sales ratio for the current model is also considered to help establish a more achievable target.

Method 1: First calculate the target profit rate for the model life period.

$$
\begin{array}{c}
\text{Model life target} \\
\text{profit for typical} \\
\text{model number}
\end{array}
=
\begin{array}{c}
\text{target sales for} \\
\text{same model} \\
\text{number}
\end{array}
\times
\begin{array}{c}
\text{series-average} \\
\text{target return-on-} \\
\text{sales ratio}
\end{array}
$$

$$
\begin{array}{c}
\text{Target profit per} \\
\text{unit of typical} \\
\text{model number}
\end{array}
=
\frac{\text{target profit for model life of same model number}}{\text{target sales volume of same model number}}
$$

Method 2: First calculate the target sales price.

$$
\begin{array}{c}
\text{Target sales price} \\
\text{per unit of typical} \\
\text{model number}
\end{array}
=
\begin{array}{c}
\text{target sales} \\
\text{price of same} \\
\text{model number}
\end{array}
\times
\begin{array}{c}
\text{series-average} \\
\text{target return-on-} \\
\text{sales ratio}
\end{array}
$$

Step 2. Calculate the Target Cost per Vehicle Unit

$$
\begin{array}{c}
\text{Target cost per} \\
\text{vehicle unit}
\end{array}
=
\begin{array}{c}
\text{target sales} \\
\text{price}
\end{array}
-
\begin{array}{c}
\text{target profit per} \\
\text{vehicle unit}
\end{array}
$$

In Step 1, factors such as the target operating profit ratio, the target marginal income ratio, and the target contribution margin ratio were applied toward calculating the target return-on-sales ratio.

- The target operating profit ratio is used to calculate the target value for all costs, including ordinary fixed costs, direct sales costs, and management-related indirect sales costs.
- The target marginal income ratio is used to calculate the target value for only the variable costs in developing the model (i.e., the direct materials costs, direct labor costs, and variable processing costs).
- The target contribution margin ratio is used to calculate target values related to all of the planned vehicle's direct costs (including depreciation of new equipment, prototype development costs, and other development costs). In other words, it is used to calculate the costs subject to target costing.

The target sales price is not the price at which the vehicle will be sold to ordinary buyers but is instead the manufacturer's invoice price (= sales company's sales price − sales company's profit). For further description of methods for determining the target sales price, see Step 6 in Chapter 6.

Step 3: Measure the Estimated Cost per Vehicle Unit

$$
\begin{array}{c}
\text{Estimated cost per} \\
\text{vehicle unit}
\end{array}
=
\begin{array}{c}
\text{actual cost of} \\
\text{current model}
\end{array}
+
\begin{array}{c}
\text{estimated cost variables} \\
\text{for specification revisions} \\
\text{(as noted in detailed} \\
\text{development plan)}
\end{array}
$$

Here, the cost variables are the cost adjustments required by design changes. These costs are estimated based on a highly reliable VE plan and cost tables. Estimates of the plant investment and cost depreciation expenses for typical models are needed to measure these cost variables (these will be described in Chapter 10, Chapter 14, and in Part III).

The "actual cost of current model" is not the current model's target cost at the time of full production start-up. Because of the effects of kaizen costing on production during the entire model life, such effects gradually lower the actual cost.

Step 4. Determine the Cost Reduction Target per Vehicle Unit

To determine this target, use the estimated cost per planned vehicle unit (calculated at Step 3) and the target cost per vehicle unit (calculated at Steps 2 and 3) as follows:

$$\text{Cost reduction target} = \text{estimated cost} - \text{target cost}$$

Figure 9-1 illustrates a formal application of this sales price-based method.

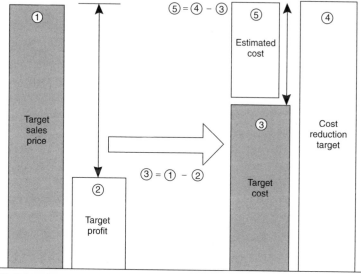

Circled numbers indicate calculation sequence

Figure 9-1. Determination of Target Cost Using Sales Price-Based Method

II. Estimated-Cost-Based Method

Use the following formula to calculate the target cost:

$$\begin{array}{c} \text{Target cost per} \\ \text{vehicle unit} \end{array} = \begin{array}{c} \text{estimated cost} \\ \text{per vehicle unit} \end{array} - \begin{array}{c} \text{profit improvement} \\ \text{target per vehicle unit} \end{array}$$

Here, the method used to measure the target cost per vehicle unit is the same as in Step 3 above. There are two methods for determining the profit improvement target per vehicle unit: (1) determination based on the profit improvement target for the model life period (called the target period profit method), and (2) determination based on the extent of improvements required in the return-on-sales ratio for the current model (the target improvement profit ratio method).

Method 1: Target Period Profit Method

$$\begin{array}{c} \text{Profit} \\ \text{improvement} \\ \text{target over} \\ \text{model life} \end{array} = \begin{array}{c} \text{target} \\ \text{profit over} \\ \text{model life} \end{array} - \begin{array}{c} \text{estimated} \\ \text{profit over} \\ \text{model life} \end{array} \qquad [equation\ 1]$$

The target profit can be determined as follows:

$$\begin{array}{c} \text{Target profit} \\ \text{over model life} \end{array} = \begin{array}{c} \text{target} \\ \text{sales over} \\ \text{model life} \end{array} \times \begin{array}{c} \text{target} \\ \text{return-on-sales} \\ \text{ratio} \end{array} \qquad [equation\ 2]$$

Although the amount is already known, the target profit can also be expressed using the following formula.

$$\begin{array}{c} \text{Target profit} \\ \text{over model life} \end{array} = \begin{array}{c} \text{(target sales price} \\ \text{- target cost} \\ \text{per vehicle unit)} \end{array} \times \begin{array}{c} \text{target sales} \\ \text{volume} \end{array} \qquad [equation\ 3]$$

Also:

$$\begin{array}{c} \text{Estimated profit} \\ \text{over model life} \end{array} = \begin{array}{c} \text{(target sales price} \\ \text{- estimated cost} \\ \text{per vehicle unit)} \end{array} \times \begin{array}{c} \text{target sales} \\ \text{volume} \end{array} \qquad [equation\ 4]$$

The estimated cost per vehicle unit has already been determined in Step 3 above and is thus a known value. The estimated profit, therefore, is also a known value. If we use the right side of equation 2 or 4 in place of the right side of equation 1, the left side of equation 1 (i.e., profit improvement target over model life) becomes a known value.

Also, if we use the right side of equations 3 or 4 in place of the right side of equation 1:

$$\begin{array}{c}\text{Profit} \\ \text{improvement} \\ \text{target over} \\ \text{model life}\end{array} = \begin{array}{c}\text{(target sales price} \\ \text{− target cost} \\ \text{per vehicle unit)}\end{array} \times \begin{array}{c}\text{target sales} \\ \text{volume}\end{array}$$

Here, the target cost per vehicle unit is an unknown value still to be determined, while all other variables are known values. Therefore, we should change the target cost per vehicle unit formula as follows:

$$\begin{array}{c}\text{Target cost per} \\ \text{vehicle unit}\end{array} = \begin{array}{c}\text{estimated cost per} \\ \text{vehicle unit}\end{array} - \frac{\begin{array}{c}\text{profit improvement target} \\ \text{over model life}\end{array}}{\text{target sales volume}}$$

$$= \begin{array}{c}\text{estimated cost per} \\ \text{vehicle unit}\end{array} - \begin{array}{c}\text{profit improvement target} \\ \text{per vehicle unit}\end{array}$$

Method 2: Target Improvement Profit Method

$$\begin{array}{c}\text{Profit} \\ \text{improvement} \\ \text{target per} \\ \text{vehicle unit}\end{array} = \begin{array}{c}\text{target} \\ \text{sales price}\end{array} \times \begin{array}{c}\text{(target return-on-sales ratio} \\ \text{− estimated return-on-sales ratio)}\end{array}$$

Here, the target return-on-sales ratio uses an estimated profit rate based on the actual return-on-sales ratio for the current model. Alternatively, the following formula can be used:

$$\begin{array}{c}\text{Profit} \\ \text{improvement} \\ \text{target per} \\ \text{vehicle unit}\end{array} = \text{estimated profit per vehicle unit}$$

$$= \begin{array}{c}\text{(target sales price} \\ \times \text{ target} \\ \text{return-on-sales ratio)}\end{array} - \begin{array}{c}\text{(target sales price} \\ \text{− estimated price per} \\ \text{vehicle unit)}\end{array}$$

Figure 9-2 illustrates this estimated-cost-based method.

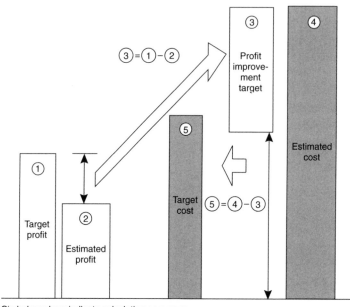

Circled numbers indicate calculation sequence

**Figure 9-2. Determination of Target Cost
Using Estimated-Cost-Based Method**

Finally, we can demonstrate the relation between the cost reduction target and the profit improvement target. The cost reduction target in the final equation using the sales-price-based method was calculated at Step 4 as follows:

$$\begin{array}{c}\text{Cost} \\ \text{reduction} \\ \text{target per} \\ \text{vehicle unit}\end{array} = \begin{array}{c}\text{estimated cost} \\ \text{per vehicle unit}\end{array} - \begin{array}{c}\text{target cost per} \\ \text{vehicle unit}\end{array} \qquad [equation\ 5]$$

If we change the final equation using the estimated-cost-based method, we can show the profit improvement target per vehicle unit as follows:

$$\begin{array}{l}\text{Profit improve-}\\ \text{ment target per}\\ \text{vehicle unit}\end{array} = \begin{array}{l}\text{estimated cost}\\ \text{per vehicle unit}\end{array} - \begin{array}{l}\text{target cost per}\\ \text{vehicle unit}\end{array} \qquad [equation\ 6]$$

Since the right sides of equations 5 and 6 are exactly the same:

$$\begin{array}{l}\text{Cost reduction target}\\ \text{per vehicle unit}\end{array} = \begin{array}{l}\text{profit improvement}\\ \text{target per vehicle unit}\end{array}$$

Departments Responsible

Target costs are set by the product planning departments mentioned in the detailed development plan along with the relevant product manager, and are authorized by the costing cross-function meeting attended by top managers. This meeting occurs about 30 months before the planned vehicle enters the market.

The costing cross-function meeting includes executive managers from the engineering development division, production division, sales division, purchasing division, and finance and accounting division, and is chaired by a vice-president (from the finance and accounting division).

After the target cost is authorized, the detailed development plan receives general authorization from the product planning meeting as a green light for development to begin. The authorization notice is sent as a development directive to all relevant divisions and departments.

Supplement: Target Cost Setting Method Used by a Large Automotive Parts Manufacturer

Parts manufacturers are not able to independently determine the sales prices of their parts (products). First, their parts are not original products that they developed themselves but are instead quite similar to other products on the market. Therefore, market prices must be a major consideration. Such prices also depend greatly upon the part designs required by the customer (vehicle manufacturer) and the customer's target cost plan. In fact, parts manufacturers at least provisionally take their customer's target cost for each part as their own target sales price.

First, they set their target profit ratio not in relation to their profit on total sales but rather in relation to their manufacturing costs, as follows:

$$\text{Target profit ratio} \;=\; \frac{\text{mark-up rate on manufacturing}}{\text{cost of part (product)}}$$

Thus, every year the same target profit ratio can be used. (However, in some cases an absolute value is set as the target profit, such as when product weight reductions, size reductions, or other cost-saving revisions have been made.)

When the target profit ratio and a given sales price are used to determine the target cost, the sales price ratio becomes an important yardstick.

$$\text{Sales price ratio} \;=\; \frac{\text{sales price}}{\text{estimated cost} + \text{target profit}}$$

If the actual sales price ratio is greater than 100, the actual profit exceeds the target profit. If the actual sales price ratio is 50, the actual profit is a negative value, meaning red ink.

Given that:

P^* = given sales price
A^* = given target profit ratio (i.e., mark-up rate over cost)
C = manufacturing cost

Then:
$$P^* = C \left(1 + \frac{A^*}{100}\right)$$

And:
$$\text{Sales price ratio} = P^* \left[C \left(1 + \frac{A^*}{100}\right)\right] = 1$$

Thus, the sales price ratio is 100 percent.

While the values of P^* and A^* have already been given, we can find the value of C (cost) as follows for a sales price ratio of 100 percent.

$$C = P^* \div \left(1 + \frac{A^*}{100}\right)$$

If the sales price ratio is over 100 percent, the actual profit exceeds the estimated profit. To make this happen, we must set a target cost (C^*) that is:

Target cost $C^* \leqq$ value of C in above equation

In other words, we must set a target cost that enables the sales price ratio to be 100 percent or higher.

10

Plant Investment
Planning Proposal

The Four Steps in the Plant Investment Planning Proposal

Similar to the target costing process, the plant investment planning process for new products also has four steps, which are described below.

Step 1

The long-term general profit plan includes annual breakdowns of budgeted capital expenditures. Within these annual budgets, the long-term general profit plan also includes a policy outlining plant investment expenditures for each vehicle series (as described in Chapter 4).

Step 2

At the product conceptualization step, the following three factors are major prerequisites for target costing of products under development:

111

(a) Sales price

(b) Number of vehicle units subject to target costing

(c) Amount of plant investment capital

To firmly establish these three prerequisites, a prerequisite meeting or coordination meeting for product conceptualization must be held before the development plan can be written. This same meeting should determine the plant investment requirements for a basic (typical) model number among the planned vehicle series.

Step 3

After the target cost per unit of the new model has been determined based on the detailed development plan, this cost is broken down into functional elements, and then broken down again into parts elements within those functional elements. As part of this process, planners work out a general outline of the plant investment plan. The finished plan will be a detailed, part-specific plant investment plan.

Step 4

At the product design step, production setup begins. The production setup phase extends from completion of the first-generation prototype (18 to 20 months prior to quality product startup) to completion of the production prototype.

At the production setup phase, the production engineering department uses drawings to develop detailed process designs and determine detailed equipment specifications. In addition, they write orders for purchased or in-house parts and inspect, install, test, and adjust the production equipment. (For further description of these activities, see Chapter 15.) Parts suppliers are also considered and selected at this point.

Plant Investment Planning at the Product Conceptualization Stage

The following methods can be used for plant investment planning at Step 2:

(a) Set the amount of plant investment funds so that it does not exceed the current model's depreciation cost per product unit.

(b) Set the amount of plant investment at a level where the estimated depreciation cost (part of the estimated costs for the planned model) can be lowered by the target cost reduction rate for per-unit costs.

(c) Use the ratio of plant investment costs to total manufacturing costs for the current model as a guideline in setting equivalent or lower plant investment costs for the planned model.

Plant Investment Planning at the Detailed Development Plan Stage

The following section describes plant investment planning at Step 3. First, however, the following plant investment planning-related issues must be considered before making cost-element and functional-element breakdowns of target costs per vehicle unit.

(a) Determine which parts are to be manufactured in-house and which are to be supplied by outside vendors. Purchase cost (i.e., purchase price) targets must be set for parts to be supplied by outside vendors. However, such "outside" parts usually do not require any new plant investment funds, and consequently there are no additional costs for depreciation or adjustment of new production equipment.

(b) Determine which companies (and plants) will be performing contracted assembly work. Major Japanese automobile manufacturers often contract out their assembly work to auto body manufacturers such as Toyota Auto Body, Daihatsu Motors, Kanto Auto Works, and Nissan Shatai.

In such cases, the automobile manufacturer provides the auto body company with major functional elements such as the engine and transmission but consigns all of the processes after pressing—such as welding, coating, and final assembly—to the auto body company. Accordingly, when an automobile manufacturer consigns the assembly of a particular model to an auto body company, it must of course pay for the cost of such consigned production, but it is free from paying for plant investment for new body press dies, welding equipment, assembly equipment, and the like.

Although the two issues described in (a) and (b) are part of what is broadly called process design, they should be addressed before the trial blueprint is made. However, process design also includes determining such things as in-house or consigned production of certain parts and the number and sequence of processes. Such factors can greatly affect plant investment requirements.

Stage 1

The design-related departments that receive the development directive from the product manager must carry out a thorough VE study. (Since the design work is still at a very basic stage, however, this VE study is done only to provide basic data for determining function-specific and part-specific target costs). The purchasing department requests similar VE studies from suppliers.

At this stage, the production engineering department becomes the hub of cooperative efforts among staff from the purchasing department and the various design departments to develop the process design based on the product manager's development directive and the above-mentioned VE studies.

The process design in turn becomes the basis for cost estimates carried out by various departments (the production engineering department estimates costs for in-house parts and the purchasing department estimates costs of parts from outside vendors). The sum of these estimates is divided by the number of planned vehicles to get the estimated cost per vehicle unit, which must be brought as close to the target cost as possible, such as by coming up with new VE plans and process designs. After this, the resulting estimated cost is broken down into lists based on cost elements, functional elements, and parts elements. At this point, the equipment investment plan can be at least outlined. To put it differently, if the process design work is centered in the production engineering department and if this work can be carried out within the restrictions set by the target cost per vehicle unit, the result of this work will help determine the framework of the plant investment plan. Naturally, this plant investment plan must also basically refer to the plan for dividing in-house and outside manufacturing.

Stage 2

The part-specific plant investment list is created, including the following items:

New and remodeled production equipment. When adding new kinds of parts and devices that are required for the planned model (for example, 4WD parts), the production line may have to be redesigned to accommodate new production equipment.

Model changes may also require changes in production methods (such as changes in die-casting and forging processes) which in turn necessitate production line redesigns and remodels.

New dies. Dies are used in press processes, plastic molding processes, and die-casting processes. Model changes typically require changes in many parts of the vehicle body and interior equipment, and this means that new dies must be made. The automobile manufacturer must pay not only for dies used for in-house manufacturing but also in some cases for dies used by contracted manufacturers.

Although the first-generation prototypes of the components are completed about 15 months before the first-generation vehicle body prototype, arrangements for manufacturing new dies for full-scale production of these components require that the second-generation prototype dies be started at about the same time as the first-generation vehicle body prototype is made.

Departments Responsible

The production engineering department creates the rough draft of the plant investment plan. The accounting division evaluates how the plan will affect costs and how well it will fit into the company's term-specific budget and model-specific plant investment policy, then makes its own revised version of the plan. This revised version of the plan receives formal authorization from the costing cross-function meeting, after which it becomes the plant investment budget.

Likewise, the production engineering department and the accounting division's target costing department work together in planning plant investment needs for product changeover. However, the production engineering department usually takes full control of the plant investment planning related to maintaining or expanding production capacity, in other words, items such as:

(a) Renovation of old production equipment (maintenance and rebuilding).

(b) Acquisition of new production equipment to boost production capacity. All such planning items must be authorized by top management.

11
Target Cost Breakdown into Cost Elements and Functional Elements

Definitions

The engineering planning department's product manager directs the breakdown of the target cost, expressed as the target cost per vehicle unit, into categories based on cost elements and functional elements.

The cost-element breakdown typically includes the following types of costs:

- Material costs
- Purchased parts costs
- Direct labor costs
- Variable indirect costs
- Depreciation costs for special-purpose equipment (such as press dies and welding jigs)
- Prototype development costs
- Other development costs

- Direct sales costs
- Management-related indirect sales costs
- Spare parts cost

The function-specific breakdown is based on the vehicle's structural components (which roughly correspond to the various design departments). These functional elements are assigned to their corresponding design departments as follows.

- Engine design department: Engine functions
- Drivetrain design department: Drivetrain functions
- Chassis design department: Chassis functions
- Body design department: Body functions
- Interior design department: Interior functions
- Electronic engineering
  department: Electronic functions

Objectives

The design division's first step toward achieving the target cost per planned vehicle unit is to break down this target cost into functional elements assigned to corresponding design departments. The next step is to establish a monetary framework that enables each design department to further break down its function-specific target costs into section-specific or part-specific target costs. After that, some departments may carry this cost breakdown further, such as by dividing part-specific costs into process-specific costs.

The function-specific cost breakdown gives a financial indication of which functions the product manager is emphasizing in comparison to the cost configuration for the current model.

Input and Output

Input

1. Target cost per vehicle unit (total estimated costs)
2. Cost-element and function-element breakdown of actual

costs of current model and cost share percentages of each cost element and functional element

3. Cost revisions (increases or decreases) in functional elements due to functional changes in planned model

4. Target cost reduction rate (percentage difference between target cost and estimated cost)

5. Priorities among functions (functions emphasized by product manager in product conceptualization)

6. VE plan from product conceptualization stage

7. VE results from previous models and technical difficulty estimates

Output

1. Target cost breakdowns into cost elements and functional elements (for each model number in the planned vehicle series)

The monetary values of function-specific costs are shown either as per-vehicle costs (in the case of new models or major model

Cost element / Functions	Material costs	Purchased parts costs	Direct labor costs	Variable indirect costs	Special-purpose equipment costs	Direct sales costs	Prototype development costs	Other development costs	Spare parts costs	Total
Engine										
Drivetrain										
Chassis										
Body										
Interior										
Electronic										
Total										

Figure 11-1. List of Cost-Specific and Function-Specific Target Costs

changes) or as differentials in comparison to the current model (in the case of minor model changes). (See Figure 11-1.)

2. VE plan

Steps

Step 1

The product manager holds a meeting to discuss the development directive and to enlist the cooperation of VE staff in relevant departments (such as the design departments and the plant management and purchasing departments) in carrying out thorough VE studies.

The VE plans resulting from these studies are first screened for technical accuracy and then are subjected to a cost estimation check and profitability check. Eventually, only the plans worth studying in more detail are kept. These remaining plans are then referred to when breaking down target costs into cost elements and functional elements.

Step 2

First, the overall estimated cost per vehicle unit is broken down into the cost elements listed under (1) in the "Definitions" section above. The current model's breakdown of cost elements and the provisional plans for dividing in-house and contracted manufacturing are both used as references for this cost-element breakdown. The objective of the cost-item breakdown is to exercise cost element-based control of efforts toward achieving target costs.

Step 3

Next, as part of the process of determining the target reduction amount for functional elements, the product manager meets several times with the design department staff in charge of the various functional elements to discuss and work out the target reduction amounts.

During this process, the design departments present their VE plans for the planned vehicle. In addition, the project team evaluates the relative importance of each functional element and votes on each element to establish priorities (using the Delphi method). They also consider past VE results and review the technical difficulty estimates.

Step 4

Figure 11-2 illustrates the steps by which the total target cost per vehicle unit (G) is broken down into functional allocations based on the input items described above. These steps are described below.

(a) Take the current model's actual function-specific costs A_i (where i is the function number) as the base.

(b) Next, estimate the function-specific cost fluctuation component $(\pm\, e_i)$ based on the functional configuration or specifications and design plan resulting from the product conceptualization stage.

For example, the above estimation would be needed if four-wheel steering (for more stability on curves) and active suspension (an electronically controlled suspension system that uses road condition sensors) were to be added in the planned vehicle. Some other possible changes are small, such as changing the specifications for the stainless steel used in the exhaust manifold.

(c) Using the results from steps (a) and (b) above, measure the function-specific target cost for the planned vehicle based on the following formula:

Function-specific estimated cost $(\mathring{A}_i)$ for planned vehicle	=	Current model's actual function-specific costs (A_i)	=	function-specific cost fluctuation component $(\pm\, e_i)$ for planned vehicle

The following steps use the estimated cost $(\mathring{A}_i)$ for each functional element in the planned vehicle to determine which functional elements must be subjected to cost reduction efforts.

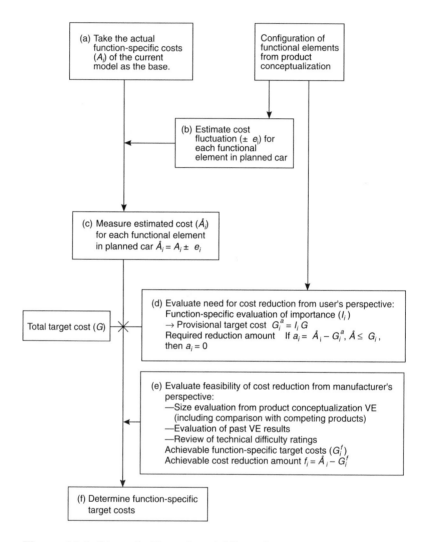

Figure 11-2. Steps in Functional Allocation of Target Costs

(d) First, evaluate the need for function-specific cost reduction from the user's perspective. To do this, evaluate the importance I_i (or contributing share or degree of necessity) of each functional element based on the product conceptualization, then use these importance rankings to calculate the allowable target cost G_i^a ($= I_i\,G$) for each functional element and the required cost reduction amount a_i ($= \mathring{A}_i - G_i^a$).

If $\mathring{A}_i > G_i^a$, then a_i ($= \mathring{A}_i - G_i^a$) > 0.

However, if $\mathring{A}_i \leq G_i^a$, then $a_i = 0$.

This is an application of the function-specific importance evaluation method (described later).

(e) Next, evaluate the feasibility of cost reduction from the manufacturer's perspective. The method for this is described below.

- Evaluate sizes in product conceptualization VE. This is an application of the competing products comparison method (described later) for cost evaluations.
- Evaluate past VE results for the current model of the planned vehicle.
- Evaluate the VE's technical difficulty estimates.

Use the above to calculate the manufacturer's achievable function-specific target costs G_i^f and achievable cost reduction amounts f_i ($= \mathring{A}_i - G_i^f$).

(f) For each functional element, compare the required cost reduction amount a_i calculated at step (d) with the achievable cost reduction amount f_i calculated at step (e). After making these comparisons, the product manager meets with various designers to work out a final list of function-specific target cost reduction amounts that will enable them to achieve the planned vehicle's total target cost reduction amount ($\Sigma\,\mathring{A}_i - G$). As a result, they can determine the function-specific target cost ($=$ function-specific estimated cost $-$ function-specific target cost reduction amount) and the adjusted function-specific target reduction ratio.

Step 5

If, during this cost allocation process, the parties concerned are not able to agree upon an achievable allocation of function-specific costs, the product manager may decided to set slightly lower achievement (performance) levels for certain functions to facilitate an agreement.

Step 6

Although the adjusted function-specific target reduction ratios may differ from one functional element to the next, these ratios should be about the same for similar functions among the planned vehicle line's various model numbers.

Step 7

This cost allotment process takes about six months to complete and is scheduled to start after body style authorization (at P minus 30 months) and end by P minus 24 months.

Departments Responsible

The product manager (engineering planning department) has the right to allocate the total target cost per vehicle unit among the relevant design departments. However, the process for determining this cost allocation is not controlled by the product manager alone. Instead, it is a matter to be negotiated by the product manager and the staff of the design departments so that a consensus-based agreement can be reached on specific cost allocations.

Each design department drafts detailed structural drawings for the sections corresponding to its assigned function and also formulates various cost reduction proposals (VE proposals) that may include ideas ranging from adopting new mechanisms or technologies to making small improvements in existing ones. They receive various kinds of assistance in making these VE proposals, such as from groups that study clay models of the planned vehicle or that disassemble and study other companies' vehicles.

At about this time the manufacturing and assembly plants submit their improvement plans for the planned model's design, based on cost-reduction activities carried out for the current model. They pay particular attention to DFM (design for manufacturing) methods for making the planned vehicle easier and less costly to manufacture.

The staff of this division present their vendors with the product manager's suggestions concerning major parts and then ask for VE proposals from the vendors.

Supplement 1: Methods for Determining Function-Specific Target Costs

The following methods can be used to determine function-specific target costs. These methods fall into two general categories: (1) methods that take the manufacturer's perspective in determining achievable minimum costs and (2) methods that take the user's (or customer's) perspective in determining target costs based on the relative importance (or contributing share or necessity) of each function.

Two types of methods from the first category are introduced below: the *value-based method* and the *competing products comparison method*. As for the second category, the DARE (decision alternative ratio evaluation system) method is described below as an example of the function-specific importance evaluation method, a typical method in this category.

The function-specific importance evaluation method is based on the VE-oriented idea that the user's need for a function takes precedence over the manufacturer's need for achievable target costs.

Target costs are not simply costs that are predicted as being achievable but are allowable costs based on basic necessity. They must be desired targets whose achievement presents a challenge. However, the fact remains that such target costs must be recognized by the project team members not only as necessary cost levels but also as achievable costs.

Value-Based Method

Two types of value-based methods are described below: one based on actual costs of similar functional elements (an actual-value-based method) and another based on engineering theory (a theoretical-value-based method).

Actual-value-based method

This method requires searching through information on products, subassemblies, or parts that serve similar functions in order to find actual costs that can be used in establishing a cost standard for new items. The steps in the method are as follows:

(a) Collect information on as many similar products or parts as possible (classify the items into in-house items, purchased items, and items made by other companies).

(b) Study and compare each product's function achievement level and relevant quality characteristics (such as performance, reliability, maintainability, and operability).

(c) Next, adjust the product's actual cost as required (for example, costs may have to be adjusted to reflect current market demand, materials costs, or other factors such as the plant's operating rate, lot sizes, etc.).

(d) Establish relationships between function achievement levels or quality characteristics and adjusted actual costs, then plot these relationships on a graph. Draw a line connecting the lowest cost points on the graph and make this the actual-value standard. (See example shown in Figure 11-3.)

The above example shows how a scatter diagram can be used to establish a cost standard, but other statistical methods can also be used, such as simple regression analysis or multiple regression analysis. The cost estimation system described in Part III of this book uses basically the same scatter diagram method. Although this method is useful for measuring function-specific estimated costs, to be useful for determining target costs it would have to include a cost allotment scheme based on contributing shares of estimated costs. In other words:

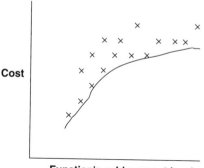

**Figure 11-3. Cost Estimates Determined via
Actual Value-Based Method**

$$\begin{array}{l} \text{Target cost} \\ \text{of function } i \end{array} = \begin{array}{l} \text{total target} \\ \text{cost of} \\ \text{product} \end{array} \times \frac{\text{estimated cost of function } i}{\text{total function-specific estimated costs}}$$

Theoretical-value-based method

This method is applicable only in cases where scientific theorems using physical laws (such as the law of dynamics) can be used to establish relationships between function achievement levels and costs.

For instance, the following formula shows the relation between C (cost per cm of metal rods) and T (torque, such as the rotational strength of a gear).

$$C = K \bullet T^{2/3}$$

$$\text{Where } K = \frac{\pi}{4} \rho p \left(\frac{16}{\pi S_t} \right)^{2/3}$$

ρ = relative weight of materials (kg/cm^3)

p = material price per kg

S_t = maximum allowable shear stress (kg/cm^2)

By applying this formula to every kind of material, we can clarify the minimum cost for each function achievement level (in this case, torque strength) for each material. However, this method can only be applied for certain types of functions, such as torque transfer, load support, and horsepower transfer.

Competing Products Comparison Method

This method requires searching in a particular functional category for products that appear to have roughly similar function levels, then comparing costs among those products and taking the product with the lowest cost as the target-cost indicator (see the example in Figure 11-4).

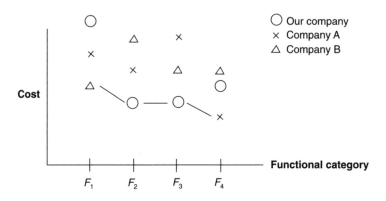

Figure 11-4. Competing Products Comparison Method

Function-Specific Importance Evaluation Method

Using this method, the project team evaluates the importance (or contributing share) of each function among the group of functions in a particular product. They then break down the product's target cost into functional elements based on each element's relative importance (or contributing share). The steps in this method are as follows:

    (a) Draw a functional block diagram for all of the functions in the product or part.

(b) Adopt the perspective of user needs in evaluating the ratings given to each functional category. Each member of the project team makes such an evaluation, applying the Delphi method.

For example, suppose that a product has three functional categories, F_1, F_2, and F_3. The most easily understood functional category (F_1, for instance) gets a rating of 10, and the project team members must each rate F_2 and the other functional categories relative to F_1's rating. The team members submit their individual ratings, then together review the results, explaining the approach or evaluation criteria they used in determining their ratings. After this discussion, they carry out another round of ratings and then work out a consensus on the relative importance of each functional category.

(c) Evaluation using the Delphi method is applied to each functional category in order. The end result is a set of function-specific ratings.

(d) Given that all functions add up to an importance rating of 100 percent, the importance rating (i.e., function-specific importance level) of each functional category is calculated based on the ratings obtained at steps (b) and (c) above. In other words:

$$\text{Function-specific importance level (\%)} = \frac{\text{rating of each functional category}}{\text{total ratings for all functional categories}} \times 100$$

(e) Allocate the product's total target cost into functional categories using the function-specific importance levels calculated at step (d) to get provisional function-specific target costs. In other words:

$$\text{Provisional function-specific target cost} = \text{function-specific importance level} \times \text{product's total target cost}$$

(f) Compare each provisional function-specific target cost with each function-specific estimated cost. If the estimated cost is smaller, use it instead of the corresponding function's target cost. Thus, no improvement of values is needed for the corresponding functions.

(g) Given the function's total value i (= 1, ..., n), if functional category j (= 1, ..., m) has a function-specific estimated cost that is greater than the function-specific target cost, the final function-specific target cost for the remaining function k (= $m + 1$, ..., n) can be determined as follows.

$$\text{Target cost of function } k = \begin{pmatrix} \text{product's total target cost} - \Sigma \\ \text{(estimated cost of function } j) \end{pmatrix} \times \frac{\text{importance level of function } k}{\Sigma} \times \begin{pmatrix} \text{importance level of function } k \end{pmatrix}$$

Where $j = 1, ..., m$ and $k = m + 1, ..., n$

Figure 11-5 shows a numerical example of the above step's calculations.

Functional category	F_1	F_2	F_3	Total
Function rating (A)	10	30	25	65
Function importance level (B)	15.4	46.1	38.5	100%
Provisional function-specific target cost (C)	154	461	385	¥ 1,000
Function-specific estimated cost (D)	125	505	450	¥ 1,080
Function-specific target cost (E)	125*	477**	398***	¥ 1,000
Target cost reduction amount (= D – E)	0	28	52	¥ 80
Value share (= E / D)	1	0.94	0.88	—

*   125 = estimated cost for F_1 (125) (therefore, 125 < 154)

**   477 = [product's target cost (1,000) – F_1's target cost (125)] × [46.1% / (46.1 + 38.5)]

*** 398 = (1,000 – 125) × [38.5% / (46.1–38.5)]

Figure 11-5. Allocation of Target Costs Using Function-Specific Importance Evaluation Method

Allocation of target costs using the function-specific importance evaluation method results in setting target costs that are relatively high for relatively important functions, based on the premise that the market (i.e., customers) will support higher costs for more important functions. Conversely, costs should be kept as low as possible for the least important functions, and these functions should be the focus of the most strident cost-reduction efforts.

However, since the more important functions tend to account for a relatively high share of actual costs, their estimated costs will tend to be higher than their target costs set via function-specific allocation, which produces a larger target cost reduction amount. Consequently, a great deal of effort and ingenuity must be invested toward achieving the target cost reduction amount for important functions.

The author's function-specific importance evaluation method differs from the VE method for determining function-specific target costs (based on function-specific importance levels) in the following two respects:

1. *Author's method:*
   Provisional function-specific target cost = function-specific importance level × product's total *target* cost

   VE method:
   Provisional function-specific target cost = function-specific importance level × product's total estimated cost

2. In the VE method, the final function-specific target cost is either the provisional function-specific target cost (via the above formula) or the function-specific estimated cost, and step (g) above does not exist.

   Accordingly, the VE method fails to start from a total target cost for the product (determined based on the target price and target profit), and so fails to take profit management into account.

DARE Method

The DARE (decision alternative ratio evaluation system) method is one type of function-specific importance evaluation method. It is similar to the multiple characteristics effects analysis method and includes the following steps:

(a) Determine the comparative relationships between pairs of functions. For example, if there are five functions named A, B, C, D, and E, we might compare them in order as shown below.

$$A = 2.5B$$
$$B = 0.5C$$
$$C = 1.5D$$
$$D = 3E$$

(b) Let us say that the importance coefficient of the last function, E, is 1. If we add E = 1 to the above set of equations and work out the correlative values in reverse order, we can calculate the importance (weight) of each function, as shown below.

$$E = 1$$
$$D = (3 \times 1 =) 3.00$$
$$C = (1.5 \times 3 =) 4.50$$
$$B = (0.5 \times 4.5 =) 2.25$$
$$A = (2 \times 2.25 =) 4.50$$

(c) Determine the function importance shares according to the above importance coefficients. In other words:

$$\begin{matrix} \text{Function} \\ \text{importance} \\ \text{share (\%)} \end{matrix} = \frac{\text{specific function importance coefficient}}{\text{total function importance coefficients}} \times 100$$

Using the above example, the total function importance coefficients for A, B, C, D, and E are (1 + 3.00 + 4.50 + 2.25 + 4.50 =) 15.25. Therefore:

Importance share of function A = (4.50 ÷ 15.25) × 100 = 29.5%
Importance share of function B = (2.25 ÷ 15.25) × 100 = 14.7%
Importance share of function C = (4.50 ÷ 15.25) × 100 = 29.5%

Importance share of function D = (3.00 ÷ 15.25) × 100 = 19.7%
Importance share of function E = (1.00 ÷ 15.25) × 100 = 6.6%

Supplement 2: Functions and Components Included in Function-Specific Estimated Costs

The functions to be included when calculating the function-specific estimated costs are those in the top two levels of the functional block diagram (see also Figure 20-2 in Chapter 20). At these levels, the functions are major component units, and estimated costs should be made for each unit (such as the engine). These are function-field-specific estimated costs.

Although function field component units may each consist of several parts, each part performs a certain function. In turn, parts may include several subparts, and some of these subparts may serve various functions within the part. Conversely, we may also say that each function is supported by several subparts.

Figure 11-6 illustrates the calculation of function-specific estimated costs. In the "functions" section of the figure, the numbers

Component or part			Functions Importance (weight)/Allocated costs				
Code	Part name	Estimated cost	F_1	F_2	F_3	....	F_n
1	A	600	2/200		4/400	....	
2	B	1,200	2/400	1/200	1/200	....	
3	C	300	1/100				2/200
⋮	⋮	⋮					
m	F (assembly, etc.)	200		1/100	2/50	....	
Total		10,000	800	500	1,000	....	2500

Figure 11-6. Calculation of Function-Specific Estimated Costs (when certain functions are supported by several parts)

shown on the left side of the slashes ("/") are the function contribution rating that indicates the degree to which the part contributes to the particular function. This rating is used to make a function-specific allocation of estimated costs among subparts.

In the "part name" column, enter the assembly costs, inspection costs, and other costs in assembly subparts into parts and component units.

12
Part-Specific Breakdown of Target Costs

Definitions

After the engineering planning department sends the design departments target cost lists broken down into function-specific categories, the design departments break these lists down further into part-specific target costs.

Specifically, each design department first breaks target cost lists down by major-component categories, and then by more detailed parts categories. The following is an example of a major-component breakdown. A detailed, part-specific further description is included in this chapter's supplement.

- Breakdown of chassis functions: front axle, front brakes, rear brakes, etc.
- Breakdown of body functions: white body metal, bumpers, window glass, trim, etc.
- Breakdown of interior functions: seats, air conditioning, interior panels, audio system, etc.

Next, a major-component category is further broken down into detailed part categories. For example:

- Breakdown of seat system: frame, slide rails, reclining mechanism, trim cover, etc.

For purchased parts, major components are broken down into parts based on the units in which the parts were purchased (i.e., either delivery units or freight-packaged units). For in-house parts, the parts breakdown is based on the smallest units of in-house parts.

Detailed parts breakdowns include all parts contained in the planned vehicles that are used as a basis for cost management, as well as the major parts constituting at least 80 percent of the cost area (total volume times unit cost) in other models related to the planned vehicles.

Objectives

1. Once the part-specific target costs have been determined, they function as the management units for long-term target costing activities (including the drafting of trial blueprints, etc.). Before each design department issues its part-specific trial blueprints, it must draft an implementation plan with realistic, achievable goals for each vehicle's part-specific list of target costs. As such, this implementation plan is a VE plan for part-specific target costs and specifications.

2. The design departments do not arbitrarily determine their part-specific target costs but must instead work with other related departments (such as production engineering, factory management, and purchasing) to make sure that their design work (trial blueprints, etc.) presents achievable goals.

3. The design departments must deploy (down to the level of individual parts) the concepts and performance characteristics envisioned for the planned vehicles in the product manager's product conceptualization and detailed development plan. They also bring VE planning into this process to make for higher reliability.

Input and Output

Input

- Function-specific target cost outline
- Actual costs of interior parts in current model
- Current costs of purchased parts in current model
- Part-specific conceptual drawings and concept manuals (showing that the planned vehicle's specifications meet the functional goals and requirements from the perspective of quality function deployment)
- Part-specific comparison of specifications for current model and planned model
- Planned volume of vehicles (commonization of parts within the same model series or among different model series may increase the volume and lower the per-unit cost)

Output

- Part-specific target costs of in-house parts
- Part-specific target costs of purchased parts
- Part-specific target costs listed by model number (see Figures 12-1 and 12-2)

	Function-specific target cost	Part-specific target cost	In-house	Outside
Seat system	30,000			
├ Frame				◯
├ Slide rails		1,000		◯
├ Reclining mechanism		2,000		◯
├ Trim cover		2,000		
		10,000	◯	
⋮		⋮	⋮	⋮
⋮		⋮		
		30,000		

(Source: Kimura 1991, p.39)

Figure 12-1. Part-Specific Target Costs (for Seats)

Function: _____   Subassembly No.: _____   Name: _____

| Part section | Part No. | Part Name | No. of parts | Process | Model No. | | | Materials costs (Yen) | Purchased parts costs (Yen) | Direct labor costs | | |
					A	B	C			Processes	Processing time (minutes)	Cash value (Yen)

| Variable indirect costs | | Fixed processing costs | | | Special fixed costs | | | | | | |
| Processes | Processing time (minutes) | Cash value (Yen) | Processes | Processing time | Cash value (Yen) | Equipment costs | | | Prototype development costs (Yen) | Other development costs (Yen) |
						Processes	Processing time	Cash value (Yen)		

Figure 12-2. Part-Specific Target Costs for Specific Model Numbers

Steps

The process of determining part-specific target costs is partly a process of seeking agreement and cooperation from all of the departments that will be striving to achieve the target costs set at the design stage. Such agreement and cooperation is essential for motivating and facilitating these efforts. This process includes the following steps.

Step 1

First comes the drafting of the part-specific conceptual drawings and concept manuals, which are needed before the various design departments (categorized by functions) can establish their function-specific target cost outline. These materials also include information concerning the detailed part functions and performance characteristics, structure, weight, materials, fabrication methods, equipment, and cost reduction plans. They document the deployment (down to the level of individual parts) of the product manager's concepts about the planned model's performance characteristics, structure, and so on. Accordingly, the VE plan that was used in breaking down target costs into functional categories is also taken into consideration as cost reduction targets are set at this next breakdown level.

Step 2

Referring to the part-specific conceptual drawings and concept manuals, the various design departments get together with the purchasing department (for purchased parts) and/or the production engineering department and factory managers (for in-house parts) to work out the preliminary cost estimates. They also revise the part-specific conceptual drawings from a VE perspective to keep the part-specific concepts within the function-specific target cost outline while proposing provisional part-specific target costs.

The steps in proposing provisional part-specific target costs are almost the same as those (described in Chapter 11) for establishing function-specific target costs (see Figure 12-3).

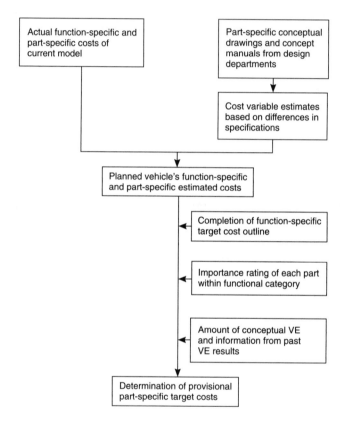

Figure 12-3. Steps in Design Departments' Determination of Provisional Part-Specific Target Costs

Step 3

The engineering planning department's product manager consults with various design department staff concerning their part-specific concept manuals to make sure that the product manager's planning concepts have been deployed, especially concerning the functions, structures, and marketing appeal of the listed parts. He or she also confirms that the function-specific target cost outline is achievable.

Step 4

After the above meetings with the product manager, the various design departments determine their provisional part-specific target costs along with the consent of the other relevant departments (purchasing, factory management, production engineering).

Step 5

The part-specific target costs are broken down as shown in Figure 12-4.

1. The target cost per part is first broken down into the broad categories of "in-house parts costs" and "purchased parts costs" at the part-specific level.
2. Next, the total target cost for purchased parts is broken down into (1) design function categories, (2) part-specific categories, and (3) supplier categories in that order.
3. The total target cost for in-house parts is broken down into (1) the cost categories of direct materials costs, direct labor costs, proportional processing costs, new direct fixed costs, existing direct fixed costs, prototype development costs, and other development costs, and then into (2) job categories (departmental categories) and process-specific categories. The allotment of fixed costs is based on the following:
   (a) Estimated costs of the typical model numbers in the planned vehicle series
   (b) How the planned vehicle's budget fits in with the company's overall budget
   (c) Results from previous similar models, commodity price fluctuations, etc.

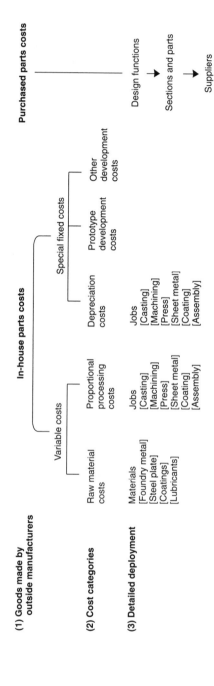

Figure 12-4. Flow of Per-Unit Target Cost Breakdown

Step 6

After selecting its suppliers, the purchasing department asks them for provisional target costs for parts to be purchased and the design departments deploy their provisional target costs for in-house goods down to the factory level (under job categories such as casting, machining, press working, sheet metal fabrication, coating, and assembly).

Step 7

At the part-specific level, these provisional target costs represent considerable challenges requiring strong cost-reduction efforts. To achieve these targets, the entire company, centered on the design departments but also including the factories, purchasing department, cost accounting department, and other departments, must cooperate in carrying out VE planning and activities to produce a plan for achieving these targets (including not only cost targets but other targets such as for specifications and manufacturing). For the purchasing department, that means including suppliers in VE activities. Through this kind of process, the various relevant departments eventually reach agreement on the target costs.

Step 8

The implementation plan for achieving part-specific target costs is presented to top managers at the costing cross-function meeting, where the plan must receive their approval.

Figure 12-5 illustrates this process from Step 3 to Step 8.

Departments Responsible

Although the various design departments are the chief agents behind the part-specific breakdown of function-specific target costs, the engineering planning department's product manager is

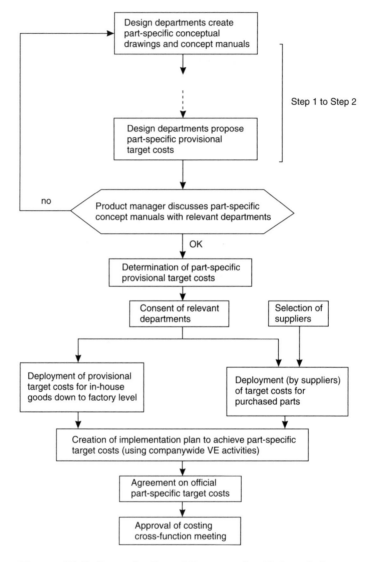

**Figure 12-5. Organizational Process for Determining
Part-Specific Target Costs**

the one who controls the concepts being considered by the design departments. In addition, other relevant departments such

as the production engineering department, the management departments at each factory (under job categories such as casting, machining, press working, sheet metal fabrication, coating, and assembly), and the purchasing department take part in VE planning of the parts' concepts. Determination of the official part-specific target costs is based upon a consensus reached among all of the relevant departments. Figure 12-5 illustrates this process.

Supplement: Typical Specific Automobile Components

Typical components under various functional categories are listed below. The lists are for illustrative purposes only and are not necessarily categorical or absolute.

- *Engine*
  Cylinder heads and cylinder block
  Combustion chamber
  Valve system
  Pistons
  Piston rings
  Connecting rods and piston pins
  Bore
  Camshaft
  Crankshaft
  Push rods and rocker arms
  Flywheel

- *Lubrication system*
  Oil pump and oil pressure regulator
  Oil filter and oil strainer

- *Cooling system*
  Radiator
  Thermostat
  Water pump
  Cooling fan

- *Fuel system*
  Fuel tank and fuel pipe line
  Fuel pump and fuel filter
  Carburetor
  Fuel injection system

- *Intake/exhaust system*
  Air cleaner
  Intake manifold and exhaust manifold
  Muffler and exhaust pipe
  Crankcase emission control system
  Supercharger
  Turbocharger

- *Electrical and ignition system*
  Ignition coil
  Distributor
  Solid-state ignition system
  Spark plugs
  Battery
  Starter motor

- *Power train*
  Clutch
  Transmission
  Synchromesh mechanism
  Shift mechanism
  Torque converter
  Automatic transmission
  Continuously variable transmission
  Propeller shaft
  Front axle
  Rear axle
  Differential gear
  4WD

- *Steering system*
  Steering gears

Power steering system
4WS
Steering wheel and steering column

- *Suspension system*
Front suspension
Rear suspension
Shock absorbers
Toe control suspension

- *Brake system*
Foot brakes
Parking brakes
Drum brakes
Disc brakes
Booster
Antiskid, antilock brakes

- *Tires and wheels*
Tires
Wheels

- *Body*
Body shell components
Bumpers
Doors and windows
Headlamps
Windshield wipers and washers

13
Product Design and Cost-Setting Activities

Definition

The activity of setting costs in product design consists of making product design drawings that meet the part-specific quality requirements of the various design departments while achieving the given part-specific target costs.

Objective

From the perspective of target costing, the objective of product design is to create design drawings that are conducive to part-specific target costs. This is known as designing to cost. From a companywide perspective, products are designed to meet three kinds of targets: the planned vehicle's functions (quality), delivery schedule, and cost.

Input and Output

Input

- Part-specific target costs
- Part-specific required quality, functions, and performance characteristics
- Estimated costs based on trial blueprint
- VE plans

Output

- Final blueprint
- Estimated costs based on final blueprint

Steps

The various design departments carry out their design and cost-setting activities via the following four steps (see Figure 13-1).

Step 1

The design departments hold several VE study group sessions to devise ways to met their allotted part-specific target costs. This type of VE activity is improvement planning, which lies at the heart of VE activities.

In general, VE efforts to meet target costs are generally channeled in two directions: lowering direct materials costs and lowering processing costs. Methods used to reduce direct materials costs include the following:

(a) Reduce the number of parts
(b) Design smaller, lighter parts
(c) Use less expensive parts
(d) Design parts that do not require highly precise or otherwise expensive fabrication methods

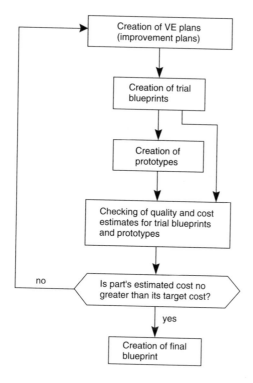

**Figure 13-1. Design Process from the Perspective
of Target Costing**

Methods used to reduce processing costs include the following:

(a) Raise weight allowances
(b) Reduce plant investment requirements
(c) Increase productivity
(d) Implement process design with a view toward minimizing
     costs

Step 2

Next, the departments draft trial blueprints based on their VE
plans (for further description of VE activities, see Chapter 20).

Step 3

The departments then make prototype parts based on their trial blueprints.

Step 4

The departments carry out another round of VE activities while studying the prototype parts' quality, limitations, and estimated costs.

In addition to these VE-oriented studies, prototype models are subjected to a variety of tests and evaluations, and designers consider tradeoffs among technical characteristics.

The above process is repeated during the development of first-, second-, and third-generation prototypes. Thus, this cycle of "trial blueprints → prototype parts → cost estimation of prototype parts → VE studies" is repeated three times during a period of about 16 months (from P minus 24 months to P minus 8 months). Once the targets for both functions (quality) and costs have been achieved, design activities are concluded and the production drawings (i.e., final blueprints) are drafted.

As for purchased parts, which typically account for 60 to 70 percent of total costs, the design departments send the trial blueprints and part-specific target costs to the suppliers. The supplier companies then apply their own specialized engineering skills and knowledge in presenting VE plans.

- *Special parts:* These are ordered from high-tech domestic suppliers (a.k.a. approved blueprint manufacturers). The automobile company not only presents its own VE plans for such parts based on the detailed development plan but solicits VE plans from parts suppliers. They consider both sets of plans as they devise improvements to help achieve the target costs so that they can go on to the final blueprint stage.
- *Standard general-purpose parts:* Drawings are sent to suppliers (a.k.a. borrowed blueprint manufacturers) along with production orders. The automobile manufacturer also helps such suppliers to improve their technological capacity by training them in target costing and VA/VE techniques.

- *Parts from overseas suppliers:* As automobile manufacturers continue to buy some parts from these sources, they extend technology transfers to help overseas parts suppliers improve their technology levels.

While the first prototype vehicles are being made based on the first-generation blueprints, cost estimates are also being made. The following departments are involved in this cost estimation process.

- Cost estimation of in-house parts: cost estimation managers from the production engineering department and target costing managers from the accounting division
- Cost estimation of purchased parts: purchasing department (while referring to estimates made by the target costing department at the product conceptualization stage)
- Compilation of cost estimates: accounting division's target costing department

The cost estimation results are then checked to make sure they will reach the target costs. If there is a gap between the two, the various relevant departments jointly implement additional VE activities to close the gap. These VE results are used as feedback for subsequent trial blueprint revisions.

Cost Management of Design Revisions

It takes about three years to develop a new vehicle from product conceptualization to the full-production stage. Various changes can occur during this time, such as in competitor trends, user needs, and economic conditions. The product planning process must be able to respond to such events with revisions that go all the way back to the design concept stage (the detailed development plan). These revisions are called design revisions.

Making revisions midway through the development period naturally tends to incur higher costs, and the company may choose to deal with such cost variables in one of the following ways:

(a) Raise the sales price if the product's merchandise value is being raised by the revisions.

(b) Allocate cost reserve funds from within the target cost per vehicle unit.

(c) Absorb the extra costs by cutting costs elsewhere.

The product manager and design department managers decide which method to use after studying the design revisions in detail to determine their impact and the need for cost/price adjustments. If they select option (a) or (b), they revise the target cost per vehicle unit, the function-specific target costs, and the part-specific target costs accordingly. If the designers are somehow able to revise their designs to make option (c) possible, there is no need to adjust target costs. Figure 13-2 illustrates this process.

Departments Responsible

Design Division

Among the design division's various design departments organized by product functions, the design managers responsible for certain parts within their respective functional category act as project team leaders in responding to design revisions.

Production Engineering Department

Staff from this department take part in VE activities for both in-house and purchased parts.

Manufacturing Department

Staff from this department take part in VE activities for in-house parts.

Purchasing Department

Staff from this department take part in VE activities for purchased parts.

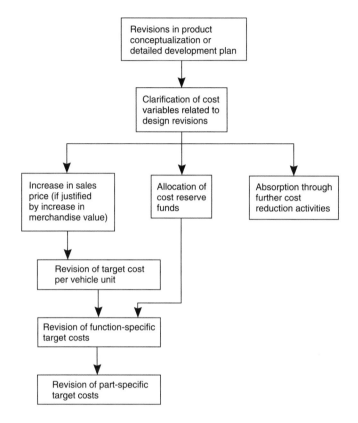

Figure 13-2. Cost Management Process in Response to Design Revisions

Suppliers

Suppliers participate in VE activities for the purchased parts that they supply. Concerning major parts and new products in particular, they take part in a project team comprising mainly staff from the automobile manufacturer's design, purchasing, engineering, and clerical departments, so that suppliers can be kept informed early on regarding design and manufacturing issues, process sequences at (process design) secondary suppliers, distribution issues, and so on. Figure 13-3 shows how such project teams are organized.

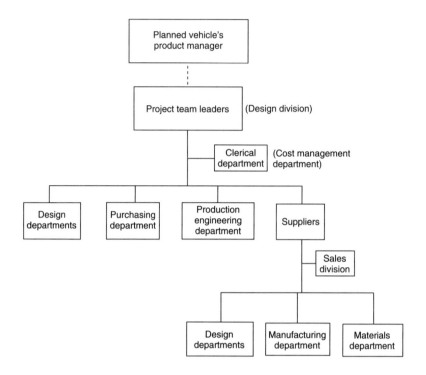

**Figure 13-3. Target Costing Project Team for
Purchased Parts**

As the project team strives to achieve the part-specific target costs, team members study many issues, such as variety reduction, parts commonization, design structures, quality, weight/size reduction, fabrication methods, plant investment, dies, jigs, distribution, and packaging.

Product Manager

The product manager exercises overall control of the design revision process.

14

Cost Estimation at the Design Stage (Using Cost Tables)

Definition

Cost estimation at the design stage entails estimating the costs of planned vehicles at the product-specific, function-specific, and part-specific levels based upon the design drawings. First, the cost estimators set standards for the various cost elements (materials, fabrication processes, fabrication equipment, processing cost rate, etc.). They then set up an outline of steps for calculating costs, which they use to determine the standard costs. At this point, they are ready to make detailed estimates for three categories of costs within the overall cost configuration: direct materials costs, direct processing costs, and direct operating costs.

Production cost	=	direct materials costs	+	direct processing costs	+	direct operating costs

Objectives

The primary objective of cost estimation at the design stage is to select the most cost-effective (cost-reducing) VE plan from among the VE plans that have passed the various prototype-based technical tests. These tests include tests to determine whether or not the product meets the functional and performance levels required by users as well as the levels of reliability, durability, maintainability, and safety required by the manufacturer.

The second most important objective is to estimate the cost of the planned vehicle based on the specifications from the planned vehicle's blueprints or prototype models and to compare this cost to the vehicle's target cost set for when full production begins some 30 months later.

If the estimated cost is greater than the target cost, VE activities are continued. If the estimated cost is less than or equal to the target cost, VE activities are concluded.

Input and Output

Input

- Cost tables
  Cost tables are cost references that are made for use in estimating costs as part of the process for determining manufacturing specifications (blueprints, etc.), the production setup schedule, production methods and steps, and so on. As such, they provide database information on direct materials costs, direct processing costs, and direct operating costs.

  Although computers are not necessary for using cost tables for all processes, bringing cost tables into a computer system makes estimating costs much faster and more accurate and makes maintaining cost tables easier. Figure 14-1 outlines the computer-based cost table system used by a large automotive parts manufacturer. The cost management department at the company's head office developed and maintains

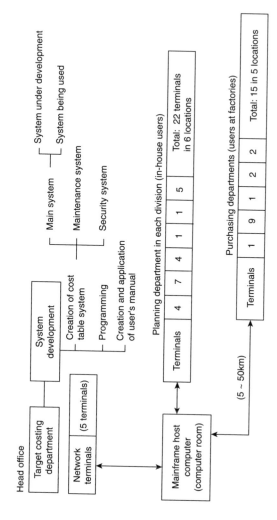

Figure 14-1. Example of Computer-Based Cost Table System

this computer-based system, which operates from the head office's mainframe computer. Each division's planning department has network terminals via which they communicate with the mainframe host computer as they make cost estimates for new products. The purchasing division's various purchasing departments are also part of this network.

- Estimated costs for new technologies (new devices or equipment)
- Development directive

Output

Cost estimates for planned vehicle: product-specific, function-specific, part-specific cost estimates

Steps

Step 1. Creation of Cost Tables and Cost Estimates

Cost estimates are done using separate cost tables for in-house part material costs, purchased part costs, processing costs, and direct operating costs. These cost tables are similar to the standard cost tables for the current vehicle model (which is different from "standard costs" as defined in conventional accounting), but they are updated once or twice a year to incorporate the results of cost improvements carried out each year, commodity price trends, and (predicted) changes in the operating rate. Figure 14-2 outlines the cost table configuration used by a large parts manufacturer.

The following steps are used by an automobile manufacturer when making cost estimates with the aid of cost tables. Detailed information is included under each of those steps.

(a) Direct materials costs

Direct materials costs include materials costs for in-house parts and costs of purchased parts.

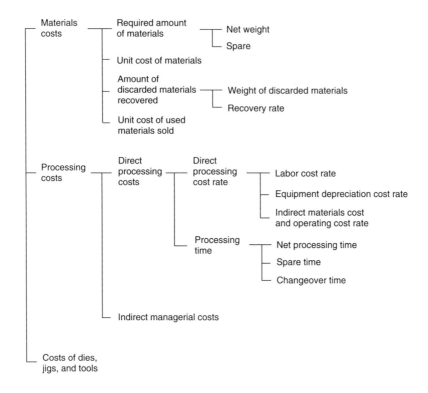

Figure 14-2. Example of Cost Table Configuration

1. Materials costs for in-house parts, categorized by type of material:
   - Foundry metal
   - Steel plate
   - Coatings
   - Lubricants

Direct materials costs such as primary material costs (the prices at which materials are purchased) and secondary material costs (in-house clerical costs for processing of materials purchases, acceptance inspections, and storage) are then added to the above to get the direct materials cost.

$$\begin{array}{ccc} \text{Standard} \\ \text{materials costs} \end{array} = \begin{array}{c} \text{standard} \\ \text{amount (kg) used} \end{array} \times \begin{array}{c} \text{standard} \\ \text{unit cost} \end{array}$$

The standard amount used value is revised based on the amount calculated using the drawing specifications, while the standard unit cost is based on the actual unit cost of purchased parts as of the end of the previous term. The standard amount used is also revised as needed based on the latest cost improvements. Other types of data are also kept, such as depreciation-rate and yield-rate data.

2. Cost of purchased parts

The cost of purchased parts accounts for the majority of direct materials costs. The standard cost per purchased unit is determined based on the supplier-specific and part-specific lists of primary and secondary materials costs. Parts manufacturers are divided into borrowed blueprint manufacturers and approved blueprint manufacturers.

Borrowed blueprint manufacturers are contracted manufacturers who receive parts production orders from their automobile company clients but have little involvement in designing the parts—their main responsibility is to process and assemble ordered parts. Typically, a borrowed blueprint manufacturer will be selected to supply the small pressed parts in the auto body, such as the bumpers, or the molded plastic components in the vehicle's dashboard. By contrast, *approved blueprint manufacturers* are involved in both the design and manufacture of certain parts, and they are called "approved" because their part designs must receive the client automobile company's approval. Typically, they produce electronic parts, batteries, carburetors, brakes, tires, bearings, seats, and other specialized parts.

Borrowed blueprint manufacturers share their cost tables for ordered parts with the client (specifically, the client's purchasing department). In addition, such suppliers also tend to share their information on production equipment, production capacity, factory labor capacity, and the like with their clients. For example, the supplier may share the following types of purchase price information with the client concerning pressed parts:

- Materials costs
- Most of purchased parts
- External processing costs (direct operating costs)
- In-house processing costs (direct labor costs + indirect manufacturing costs)
- Die costs (die depreciation costs)
- Sales costs and administrative costs
- Target profit
- Savings through improvement proposals

On the other hand, approved blueprint manufacturers generally do not share all of their cost table data with their auto company clients because they have developed some of the ordered parts themselves. However, many parts manufacturers fall between these two types (borrowed blueprint manufacturer and approved blueprint manufacturer), and in many cases the supplier and client jointly design and develop certain ordered parts.

The automobile company keeps and updates a parts master file that includes bills of materials and parts costs tables for each level of the bills of materials.

(b) Processing costs

Separate cost tables of processing costs are prepared for each manufacturing section (based on each kind of manufacturing process), and within each section are various job-specific groups that are categorized as cost centers based on types of processes.

1. Cutting	2. Molding
1-1 Lathe turning	2-1 Pressing
1-2 Drill press	2-2 Cold-pressing
1-3 Milling machine	2-3 Hot-pressing
1-4 Broaching machine	2-4 Header pressing
1-5 Cylindrical grinder	2-5 Rolling
1-6 Surface grinder	2-6 Pipe fabrication
1-7 Internal grinder	
1-8 Centerless grinder	

3. Casting
   3-1 Aluminum die casts
   3-2 Aluminum dies
   3-3 Steel dies
   3-4 Sintered metal
   3-5 Carbon brushing
   3-6 Injection molding
   3-7 Blow molding

Four approaches for creating processing cost tables are described below. Use the one that is most appropriate for the range of cost items under each type of process.

a) Direct labor costs and indirect manufacturing costs (= indirect materials costs + indirect labor costs + indirect operating costs) are added up for each process to establish a cost table showing the process-specific processing cost distribution rate. At the same time, process-specific cost drivers based on various driver data from the design drawings can be used to estimate the standard process equipment operating time per design part or the standard time per vehicle unit. Accordingly:

$$\text{Process-specific predicted processing cost distribution rate} = \frac{\text{process-specific estimated annual processing costs}}{\text{process-specific estimated annual operating rate}}$$

$$\text{Process-specific processing costs per part or vehicle unit} = \text{process-specific estimated processing cost absorption rate} \times \text{process-specific standard equipment operation time or production lot size}$$

Automobile manufacturers typically divide their manufacturing division into sections such as casting, machining, press working, sheet metal fabrication, welding, coating, and assembly, and within each section they have process- or job-based groups for which the cost per part or cost per vehicle unit is estimated using one of the above formulas.

In the numerical example given in Figure 14-3 (converted here at ¥100/$1):

	(a) Fixed costs	(b) Variable cost rate	(c) Monthly estimated operating rate	(d) = (b) × (c) Variable costs	(e) = (a) + (d) Monthly budget
	(Unit = ¥10,000)	(¥/Hr)	(Hours)	(Unit = ¥10,000)	(Unit = ¥10,000)
Direct labor costs		1,000 ×	10,000 =	1,000	1,000
Indirect materials costs					
Supplementary materials costs	80.2	150 ×	10,000 =	150	230.2
Consumable tools, jigs, and equipment	20.8	70 ×	10,000 =	70	90.8
Other consumables	15.4	80 ×	10,000 =	80	95.4
Indirect labor costs					
Indirect wages	150.0	500 ×	10,000 =	500	650.0
Salaries	170.2				170.2
Bonuses and allowances	30.8				30.8
Provision for accrued retirement allowances	15.0				15.0
Legal welfare costs	5.0				5.0
Indirect operating costs					
Welfare costs	10.0				10.0
Depreciation costs	160.5				160.5
Rental/lease costs	20.0				5.4
Insurance costs	8.0				8.0
Repair costs	90.1	500 ×	10,000 =	500	140.1
Gas	34.0	100 ×	10,000 =	100	134.0
Water	13.0	40 ×	10,000 =	40	53.0
Taxes and public dues	8.5				8.5
Travel costs	6.0				6.0
Miscellaneous costs	4.5				4.5
Supplemental costs absorbed by section					
Plant office costs	47.0				47.0
Power department costs	180.0	50 ×	10,000 =	50	230.0
Material warehousing costs	55.0	35 ×	10,000 =	35	90.0
	(Unit = ¥10,000)	(¥/Hr)	(Hours)	(Unit = ¥10,000)	(Unit = ¥10,000)
Total	1,124.0	2,525 ×	10,000 =	2,525	3,649.0

Note: The above numbers are all hypothetical

Figure 14-3. Monthly Variable Cost Budget for Processing Costs at Cutting Process

$$\begin{matrix} \text{Estimated} \\ \text{processing cost} \\ \text{rate for} \\ \text{cutting section} \end{matrix} = \frac{\text{monthly budget amount (\$365,000)}}{\begin{matrix}\text{monthly estimated operating rate} \\ \text{(10,000 hours)}\end{matrix}} = \begin{matrix}\$36.50 \\ \text{per hour}\end{matrix}$$

Where:

$$\begin{matrix} \text{Monthly} \\ \text{estimated} \\ \text{operating rate} \end{matrix} = \frac{\text{annual estimated operating rate}}{\text{12 months}}$$

$$\begin{matrix} \text{Annual} \\ \text{estimated} \\ \text{operating rate} \end{matrix} = \begin{matrix}\text{actual production} \\ \text{capacity per year}\end{matrix} \times \begin{matrix}\text{operating rate based} \\ \text{on sales potential}\end{matrix}$$

$$\begin{matrix} \text{Actual} \\ \text{production} \\ \text{capacity} \\ \text{per year} \end{matrix} = \begin{matrix}\text{theoretical} \\ \text{production capacity} \\ \text{per year}\end{matrix} - \text{idle time per year}$$

$$= \begin{matrix}\text{8 working} \\ \text{hours} \\ \text{per day}\end{matrix} \times \begin{matrix}300 \\ \text{working} \\ \text{days} \\ \text{per year}\end{matrix} \times \begin{matrix}51 \\ \text{persons} \\ \text{or 51} \\ \text{machines}\end{matrix} - \begin{matrix}\text{total} \\ \text{of 2,400} \\ \text{hours of} \\ \text{machine} \\ \text{downtime} \\ \text{per year}\end{matrix} = \begin{matrix}120,000 \\ \text{hours}\end{matrix}$$

Note: *The above numbers are all hypothetical.*

Alternatively:

$$\begin{matrix} \text{Monthly} \\ \text{estimated} \\ \text{operating rate} \end{matrix} = \begin{matrix}\text{average standard} \\ \text{operation time} \\ \text{per product}\end{matrix} \times \begin{matrix}\text{average production} \\ \text{output per month}\end{matrix}$$

$$= \begin{matrix}\text{(average} \\ \text{takt time}\end{matrix} \times \begin{matrix}\text{no. of line} \\ \text{operators)}\end{matrix} \times \begin{matrix}\text{average production} \\ \text{output per month}\end{matrix}$$

b) Direct labor costs and indirect manufacturing costs are categorized by process (or job) and are then added up.

Direct labor costs are allotted for parts or vehicle units based on the direct operation time per part or per vehicle unit. Indirect manufacturing costs are used to establish the indirect cost absorption rate per process and to estimate the standard machine operation time per part or per vehicle unit.

This method is also used for other manufacturing sections, such as press working, coating, and assembly. Accordingly:

$$\begin{array}{c}\text{Process-specific direct}\\\text{labor costs per part}\\\text{or vehicle unit}\end{array} = \begin{array}{c}\text{standard wage}\\\text{rate per process}\end{array} \times \begin{array}{c}\text{standard}\\\text{direct operation}\\\text{time per process}\end{array}$$

In addition:

$$\begin{array}{c}\text{Process-specific indirect}\\\text{manufacturing costs per}\\\text{part or vehicle unit}\end{array} = \begin{array}{c}\text{process-specific}\\\text{indirect cost}\\\text{absorption rate}\end{array} \times \begin{array}{c}\text{process-specific}\\\text{machine operation}\\\text{time or}\\\text{production output}\end{array}$$

c) For companies that use direct cost calculations, the processing costs that go into production costs consist only of variable processing costs. They also regard direct labor costs as variable costs and include them among the variable processing costs.

Indirect labor costs and equipment-related costs account for most of the fixed processing costs.

Per-process budgets are established for variable and fixed processing costs. In Figure 14-3 above, the budget for variable processing costs includes the items in columns (b), (c), and (d), while the items in column (a) are included in the budget for fixed processing costs. These form the basis for establishing an hourly rate of variable processing costs and an hourly rate for fixed processing costs.

According to the numbers given in Figure 14-3, the hourly rates at this process are:

$$\begin{array}{c}\text{Variable}\\\text{processing}\\\text{cost rate}\end{array} = \begin{array}{c}\$25.25\\\text{per hour}\end{array}$$

$$\begin{array}{c}\text{Fixed}\\\text{processing}\\\text{cost rate}\end{array} = \frac{\$112,400}{\text{monthly estimated operating rate (10,000 hours)}}$$

$$= \$11.24 \text{ per hour}$$

d) Based on the method used in "c)" above, if we exclude only the depreciation costs from the group of fixed processing costs, we have a method for establishing a separate machine-specific equipment cost rate. This method is used in the cost estimation system described in Part III.

(c)   Direct operating costs

These are newly incurred operating costs that can be traced to the planned vehicle. For example, they might include:

- Depreciation of new equipment, dies, and tools
- Prototype development costs
- Other development costs
- Patent-related costs

The equipment depreciation costs are often directly traceable to the particular manufacturing process where the equipment is used. Although some direct operating costs are incurred by initial investments made at the product design and development stages, it is better to amortize these costs (using the fixed installment method) over the four-year development period leading up to the start of full production in the case of major model changes or the two-year development period in the case of minor model changes, as is done in the long-term profit plan. New engine units are an exception, as they are amortized over two model cycles, i.e., over an eight to ten year period.

Given that the initial investment costs are handled as an amount to be paid in full, such payment will not correspond to the periods during which the product's return-on-sales profits are generated.

(d)   Factory management costs

These costs are incurred by all sections that are involved in managing the factory in general. They can primarily be traced to the following centers of management activity:

- General affairs section
- Accounting section
- Production planning section
- Process management section
- Quality control section
- Production engineering section

The management costs traced to these sections are absorbed by the various production-related sections based on a specified absorption rate.

Step 2. Cost Table Updates

The cost table of process-specific processing costs is usually updated once or twice a year, by either the accounting division or the target costing department. Each cost table update seeks to reflect changes that have occurred in inflationary factory and kaizen costing since the previous update.

The purchasing department meets with suppliers every six months to renegotiate the prices of purchased parts. Consequently, the purchasing department updates its cost tables every six months. The purchasing department also updates its supplier data files based on information (bids, etc.) it has received from potential suppliers. For example, an automobile manufacturer that shares its information on part features, performance characteristics, specifications, and prices with a parts manufacturer may occasionally visit prospective parts manufacturers to view their facilities, and such visits may provide information that can be used to update the auto maker's cost tables and/or supplier data files.

By keeping various kinds of cost table data, companies can analyze cost trends (such as via regression analysis) and determine how successful past improvement efforts have been. Although design department engineers do not update cost tables, they still maintain data concerning the in-house parts for which they are responsible.

Step 3. Various Ways to Use Cost Tables

1. Cost tables for part-specific processing costs can be used in the following ways:
   (a) Estimating costs for planned vehicles or planned parts
   (b) Estimating costs for new technologies
   (c) Predicting profitability at the manufacturing stage

2. Cost tables for purchased parts can be used in the following ways:
   (a) Setting price targets for parts to be purchased
   (b) Checking market-competitiveness of purchased parts
   (c) Presenting VE-related concepts to suppliers
   (d) Negotiating reductions in purchased parts prices at the manufacturing stage

Departments Responsible

The purchasing department is responsible for updating cost tables and estimating costs for the planned vehicle's parts and materials that are provided by outside suppliers.

The production engineering department and the accounting division's cost management department are responsible for updating cost tables and estimating processing costs for the planned vehicle's parts that are manufactured in-house.

The engineering planning department's target costing office is responsible for compiling cost estimation results for each model series. The accounting division's cost management department is responsible for updating the cost tables.

15

Production Transfer Plan

Definition

The production transfer plan is concerned with preparing the equipment, materials, and purchased parts needed to achieve the target profit and target costs at the production stage. This plan includes two parts:

(1) making sure that the company's factories and outside suppliers have prepared their production equipment and that the materials and parts are being delivered on schedule and are within their target costs; and

(2) setting standard values for the finished model series' sales prices, parts prices, materials consumption, and labor-hours.

Objectives

One objective is to achieve the target profits and target costs at the production stage as these profits and costs relate to the company's factories, outside suppliers, and the market.

Another objective is to check that costs for parts purchases, new production equipment, and processing have not gone far beyond their target levels as a result of the various lateral and vertical relationships among in-house departments. This task is a basic part of cost management. It means checking who, what, and when: whether someone actually did what they were supposed to do by the deadline. It refers to the PDC cycle of quality control, in which "P" (Plan) corresponds to the "who, what, and when," "D" (Do) is the action of doing the work, and "C" (Check) is the manager's checking of the results.

Input and output

Input

- Blueprints and corresponding prototypes
- Estimated costs of prototypes
- Final blueprints and corresponding pilot production vehicles

Output

- Determine purchases of various equipment
- Determine purchases of materials and outside parts
- Determine domestic and export sales prices
- Determine standards for part-specific consumption of materials and coatings, direct labor-hours, etc.
- Determine part prices

Steps

Step 1. Request and Approval of Various Equipment Purchases

The production engineering department carries out process design for in-house products at the prototype development stage and makes estimates of equipment, staffing, and labor-hour requirements for each production process (as part of the process design manual). These estimates must receive the approval stamps (or signatures) of the persons in charge (not the people who are using the cost tables and other data but rather the persons responsible for the process designs). Particularly important items must be approved by the top person responsible within the production engineering department.

New plant investment is required for products subjected to target costing. The target costing department chief must check and approve (stamp or sign) all equipment installation requests (proposals) that are submitted by the production engineering department for production equipment needed to manufacture planned products. Relatively inexpensive equipment requests can be approved by target costing managers, but large and expensive equipment requests may require authorization from the president or other top managers.

Such top managers may or may not approve requests that have been stamped or signed by the target costing department chief, but they will definitely reject requests that have not been approved by that chief. When reviewing such requests, the target costing department chief checks that the requested amount of plant investment money for the production line in question is less than the ceiling amount (for example, $2.2 million) proposed in the target costing plan. Thus, approval would be granted if the requests for that production line came to only $1.9 million, for instance.

Although the production engineering department is the requesting department in this case, such checking is still necessary to prevent problems that would arise if the production engineering department's actual plant investment disbursements were to exceed the planned amount. Unless cost control is carried out in detail for various types of cost items, it will be difficult to keep costs within their target amounts. This kind of checking seems natural enough, but it is easily neglected and must therefore be implemented thoroughly.

Step 2. Final Blueprint Completion and VE Activities

The final blueprints should be completed and submitted by about six or seven months before production starts. This allows prototype developers to begin putting together all of the components to make the pilot production vehicle (full-production prototype). VE activities (improvement plans, etc.) are implemented at the same time.

Although the target costs are usually achieved, when they cannot be achieved even after repeated application of VE techniques, it is time to consider tradeoffs. Tradeoffs involve coordinated adjustments among technical performance features (that affect the function achievement level), the development schedule, and costs. Tradeoffs may also be made among technical characteristics.

When even tradeoffs are not enough to achieve the target cost, cost reserves must be used. These cost reserves are set aside as a certain percentage of the vehicle's target cost, which is subtracted before breaking down the remaining percentage into function-specific and part-specific target costs. Having such cost reserves set aside makes the broken-down target costs a little stricter, but it also provides a buffer to make up for target costs that cannot be achieved.

If even the cost reserves are not enough to achieve all target costs, the design stage is concluded anyway and the project is transferred to the production setup stage.

Step 3. Final Cost Estimates

Final cost estimates are made after the first-generation and second-generation pilot production vehicles are manufactured and tested based on the final blueprints. At this point, the cost estimators can begin to consider the depreciation costs of newly installed production equipment.

The production engineering department is responsible for making final cost estimates for in-house parts, while the purchasing department makes the final cost estimates for purchased parts. Afterward, the accounting division's target costing department compiles the results.

Step 4. Determination of Final Sales Price

The target costing department submits the final cost estimates to the sales division as a reference when setting final sales prices for domestic and export markets.

The production engineering department studies the final cost estimates in tandem with the factories' pilot production (test line) results, determines standard values for various levels of parts costs, and submits these standard values to the factories.

Step 5. Determination of Final Cost of Purchased Parts

The purchasing department uses the final estimated cost of purchased parts as a basis for negotiating with suppliers to set the final cost of purchased parts. Generally, these negotiations are concluded before production starts.

The purchasing department submits its proposed purchased parts unit price agreement to the target costing department chief, who checks the suitability of the negotiated prices, approves the document, and returns it to the purchasing department. The purchasing department considers any comments that the target costing department chief has added and then concludes the process of determining purchased part costs. For example, the agreement might propose a unit price of $10 for a certain purchased part. After reviewing relevant estimated costs and target costs, the target costing department chief might suggest, "This unit price should be cut to $8." The purchasing department then responds by looking for ways to get the unit price down to $8.

Departments Responsible

See Steps 3, 4, and 5 above.

16

Evaluation of Target
Costing Process

Definition

The evaluation of the target costing process measures the results of the target costing process and reviews this process when the planned vehicle has finally reached the production transfer stage and production and parts delivery have begun.

Objectives

There are two main objectives:

1. Evaluate the achievement of target costs set during the process of drafting the detailed development plan and clarify where responsibility lies for target costs that have not been reached. In other words:
   (a) Responsibility lies at the design stage when the blueprints do not provide achievable targets.

(b) Responsibility lies at the production stage (purchasing and/or factory management departments) when the target shortfalls are due to problems in production activities.

2. Evaluate target costing activities: Determine whether target costing activities were timed well in coordination with the development schedule, whether they used appropriate methods, were effective enough, and so on. The results of this evaluation are provided as feedback for planning the next model series.

Input and Output

Input

- Target costs and actual costs (results for new-vehicle production in months following the first three months)
- Target prices and actual prices for purchased parts
- Target labor-hours and actual labor-hours

Output

- Causal analyses concerning gaps between target and actual costs
- Clarification of departments responsible for target shortfalls
- Evaluation of the timing and effectiveness of target costing activities

Steps

Abnormal values, such as for labor-hours, tend to appear frequently during the first three months of production due to the learning curve. Therefore, the results to be evaluated are taken from the fourth and subsequent months when normal values are expected. In the evaluation of the costing process:

- Target prices and actual prices for purchased parts are compared and evaluated.

- Target labor-hours and actual labor-hours are compared to evaluate direct labor costs.

Certain kinds of changes typically occur during the development process. For example, changes are made in part specifications or design as a result of measures undertaken to improve the product's marketability and/or quality. Also, costs revisions may occur due to market price trends. The amount of cost variation per vehicle is continually monitored to gauge changes in specifications or market prices that have occurred since target costs were set and to see how well actual costs match with target costs after subtracting the cost variation amount. Following this procedure makes it easier to maintain achievable targets.

Step 1. Review Target Costing Activities for Current Version of Same Model

Such a review might include the following:

(a) Consider whether target costing became too design-centered and failed to become a systematic, companywide activity.
(b) Review the adequacy of the timing and cost indications in the part-specific breakdown of target costs.
(c) Check whether or not the target costs were fully incorporated into the design drawings: When the design departments drafted the drawings, did they cover every process? How many design units did they use?

Step 2. Discuss and Determine Key Points for New Products

A target costing meeting should be held by the relevant clerical departments (target costing department, etc.) right at the start of target costing activities for the planned vehicle, in order to discuss and determine what the priority areas will be in the target costing activities. After the initial list of target costing priorities is made, the target costing meeting should reconsider the list to make sure no important points have been omitted and no unimportant points have been included. Specifically, they might consider the following kinds of issues when determining their list of priority points:

(a) Early development of a detailed plan for companywide target costing activities

(b) Prompt implementation of part-specific breakdown of target costs

(c) Deployment of part-specific target costs into design units

(d) Possible need for more study group sessions devoted to reducing plant investment costs

(e) Possible need for thorough VE activities to offset cost increases caused by design changes during the period of target costing activities

Departments Responsible

The accounting division's target costing department is responsible for compiling the data for studying actual costs of the current model and for determining the target costs of the planned model. However, the engineering planning department, design departments, purchasing departments, and factory management departments are also involved in analyzing gaps between target costs and actual costs.

Part II

Details of Target Costing

"A penny saved is a penny gained."

—*Thomas Fuller*

17
Target Costing Organizations in Division-Based Companies

Today, some companies that have divisions centered on product types are organizing company sectors, each of which comprises several product divisions for related product types. These company sectors function as strategic business units.

Such division-based companies usually have the following kind of target costing organization:

- The company's head office establishes a cost management department (sometimes called a target costing office or kaizen costing office) for promoting and coordinating the entire company's target costing efforts.
- Each sector establishes its own organizational unit (such as a planning office) that promotes target costing activities in the various divisions under the sector's jurisdiction.
- Although target costing activities are principally carried out independently by each division, the company's head office

target costing department lends support as needed for such activities. The target costing department also monitors the results of the various departments' target costing activities by conducting follow-up activities and keeping top management informed of the results.

• In addition to the sources of target costing support mentioned above, support also comes from the project leaders (product managers), generally the chief engineers of the departments within each division, who are responsible for managing the development of the division's new products. They are the front-line leaders in implementing target costing activities. Each manufacturing division also has its own production engineering department or production department, and there is usually a single purchasing department for an entire division. All of these departments lend support in various ways to their division's product development department. The project teams that include the project leaders and members from various departments may also include staff from the company head office's cost management department. Figure 17-1 outlines the membership of these project teams.

• A single product development department may have several projects under way at the same time, each managed by a

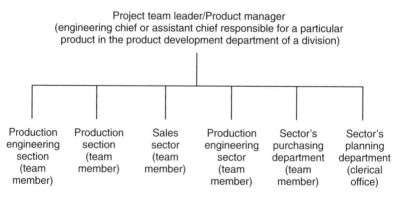

Figure 17-1. Membership of Project Teams in Division-Centered Company

project leader who is an engineering department chief within the product development department. These project teams are usually disbanded once the design of the product (or part) is completed. However, the project teams are not separate from factory-floor activities. Instead, they are an extension of factory-floor activities in that they provide additional layers of management support as needed for each new product or model change.

Figure 17-2 shows how the above organizational units fit into the entire company's organization (the shaded areas in Figure 17-2 correspond to the departments shown in Figure 17-1).

Role of Divisions within Each Sector

In Figure 17-2, the head office's corporate planning division is responsible for drafting the company's medium- and long-term profit plans. The head office's cost management department drafts and coordinates budgets for target costing and kaizen costing. The cost management department is mainly concerned with target costing and VE activities, so many more of its employees are involved in these activities than in budgeting. In some companies, the cost management department is divided into a target costing department and a budget management department.

The head office's information systems department operates the computer services for the entire company. If computers are used to calculate cost tables, this is the department that carries out the system design and programming for such tasks.

The head office's accounting division is responsible for financial accounting, settlement of accounts, and tax accounting.

Role of Planning Department in Each Sector

The planning department in each sector includes budgeting staff who draft budgets, predict demand trends, and perform profit planning-related calculations, as well as planners who

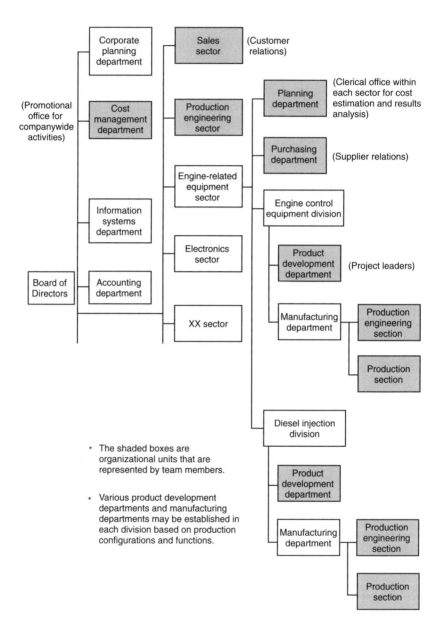

Figure 17-2. Organization of Target Costing-Related Departments in Division-Centered Company

work with sales staff. About half of the planning department employees are involved in planning estimated costs and calculating actual costs. In making cost estimations, they rely on VE activities for new or next-generation products as well as cost information based on customer orders. They use cost tables in these projects, and if a project concerns an entirely new kind of product for which there are no relevant cost tables, they usually seek assistance from the head office's cost management department.

Role of Head Office's Cost Management Department

The cost management department has five major functions to perform. The remainder of this chapter delineates those functions.

1. Implement Companywide Target Costing Promotion and Follow-up

- Establish criteria for selecting target costing themes
  Each division uses certain criteria to select and register target products ("themes") for target costing with its sector. Example of theme selection criteria:

  1. The target product's sales are at least $xx per month.
  2. The target product requires at least $xx.
  3. The target product is a "system product" that requires coordination among several divisions.

- Establish guidelines for target profits and target costs
- Coordinate promotional activities
- Implement lateral deployment of successes achieved by individual divisions
- Monitor progress toward target achievement and report to top management (these reported results are evaluated by the panel that awards the President's Prize and other achievement awards)

2. Prepare and Improve Tools for Promoting Target Costing

- VE methods
Using the function designs as a basis, VE methods are ways of economizing the design process starting from the earliest design and development stages.

- Cost tables
Included here is the drafting of standard cost estimation criteria for each type of manufacturing process (such as cutting, press working, and molding processes). These criteria can then be used to predict the effectiveness of VE activities, to manage prices of purchased goods, and to draft sales price proposals. Japanese automobile companies draft one set of cost tables for vehicles manufactured domestically and another set for each foreign country where they manufacture vehicles.

- Computerized cost tables
Use of a computer system to assist in the creation of cost tables for various manufacturing processes offers the following advantages:

  (a) Greater speed and efficiency in cost estimation work
  (b) Greater speed and efficiency in cost table revision work
  (c) Enables various kinds of simulations

- Product design manuals
Product design manuals are made to help implement minimum-cost designs. Taking the DFM (design for manufacturing) perspective, the writers produce manuals that present all of the design-related caution points concerning parts processing, welding, and assembly processes.

- System for management of purchased part prices
This system constantly monitors price trends for purchased parts so as not to miss any opportunities to negotiate lower prices for such parts.

3. Set up a Training System for Target Costing and VE

Because target costing requires cooperative efforts among staff from various related divisions and departments, some staff will need to acquire specialized knowledge and skills in the use of VE, cost tables, computerized cost tables, DFM manuals, and so on. Such training can be organized around three skill ranks: beginner, intermediate, and advanced ("veteran") trainees.

For example, Company N organized its training system as shown in Figure 17-3. Here, the advanced VE training includes three- or four-day seminars held at facilities that include lodging for seminar members. Such seminars provide trainees with intensive hands-on training that is considered part of their on-the-job training.

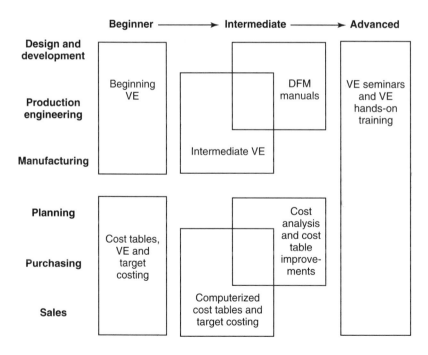

Figure 17-3. Training System for Target Costing and VE

4. Participate in Groups That Carry Out Actual Target Costing Activities

Head-office target costing experts may directly participate in various divisions' target costing activities and may especially help with lateral deployment of successes achieved in other divisions. These target costing activities generally include the following:

• Drafting plans for target costing activities
• Presenting cost improvement proposals
• Performing cost evaluations of improvement proposals
• Performing cost analyses of other companies' products
• Evaluating target cost achievement rates
• Helping suppliers make improvements

5. Respond to Requests from Projects in Each Division

If the project teams in individual divisions find themselves at a standstill with no recourse, they can ask for special assistance from head-office or outside experts (for example, they may need to obtain information from a different company).

18
Semi-Concurrent Target Costing by Parts Manufacturers and Product Manufacturers

Semi-Concurrent Target Costing

This chapter describes specific, systematic methods by which the target costing activities of automotive parts manufacturers can be made to proceed concurrently with the target costing activities of vehicle manufacturers.

For example, a parts manufacturer that produces items such as seats and door trim components must work very closely with its client vehicle manufacturers so that their products suit the design and style of the target vehicles. Consequently, parts manufacturers cannot be completely independent of their clients when implementing target costing and cost maintenance/improvement activities. They must instead work with such clients in a steady relationship of coordinated efforts.

Approved Blueprint Manufacturers and Borrowed Blueprint Manufacturers

Approved blueprint manufacturers follow the target purchases set by their automaker clients. Target purchases refers to the target prices for purchased parts that are set by the vehicle manufacturers early on. The vehicle manufacturer informs its parts manufacturer of the target prices it has set, after which the parts manufacturer designs the (approved) blueprints for the ordered parts with the target prices included as a design objective. The vehicle manufacturer then reviews and approves the blueprints and later purchases the parts at the target price.

It is very difficult, however, to set accurate target prices for some kinds of parts, such as interior components. In some cases, target costing activities for such parts may yield unexpectedly low parts costs that make the target prices too high; conversely, target costing activities may run into unforeseen difficulties that make it impossible to reach the target prices.

Among the borrowed blueprint parts manufacturers, who produce parts based on parts design blueprints borrowed from their vehicle manufacturer clients, many work on a design consignment basis (whereby the vehicle manufacturer is a parent company that pays the parts manufacturer to do the parts design work) or on a design assistance basis (whereby the vehicle manufacturer sends designers to assist in the parts manufacturer's design efforts). Thus, many so-called borrowed blueprint parts manufacturers are essentially approved blueprint parts manufacturers.

Development of Major Unit Components

In their development schedule, vehicle manufacturers put development of unit components even before development of the vehicle body. Unit components such as new engines and new transmissions have very long development lead times. In many cases, a new engine will be used in several different vehicle models, which makes the engine development process somewhat independent of the vehicle model development process. This is also why unit components such as engines must be developed even before the vehicle body. In addition, if the new engine has more horsepower than the previous engine, developers must determine how the greater horsepower will affect the vehicle's market value, which is an important factor in vehicle model planning.

On the other hand, development of such components for ordinary vehicle model changes can often be scheduled during or after vehicle body development. For example, seats and other components can often be incorporated into the development schedule for the vehicle body.

The targets set during early development of unit components are set not by the product managers but rather by the person responsible for the target component. If the unit component is the engine, for instance, the person in charge of engine design would propose and promote a development plan and estimate target costs for the engine, i.e., the engine's conceptual design.

Even when the engine is to be manufactured by an outside company, the outside company is not yet involved at this stage. However, the outside engine manufacturer does take part in the merchandising meetings and cost meetings that are held to help determine the target engine's target costs.

Stages in Target Costing by Parts Manufacturers

Target costing activities by parts manufacturers can be generally divided into three stages.

The first stage begins when the vehicle manufacturer sends the parts manufacturer a parts survey containing questions about cost levels for various parts. The parts manufacturer responds with price proposals for the parts in the survey.

The second stage starts when the vehicle manufacturer officially sets target costs for parts (the parts manufacturer regards these target costs as the target prices for its parts). The parts manufacturer then uses these target costs to set its own target costs for each part.

The third stage occurs when the parts manufacturer implements VE activities to achieve the target costs it set at the second stage.

Of these three stages, the first stage is where concurrent engineering (also known as simultaneous engineering) is most important. Both of these terms refer to a process whereby the parts manufacturer does not wait until the vehicle manufacturer has completed a target costing step before starting the same step, but instead starts the same step as soon as possible after the vehicle manufacturer has started it. To be precise, this is called a semi-concurrent approach (see Figure 18-1).

Figure 18-2 shows a target costing schedule that includes the three stages, which are further broken down into 13 steps.

First Stage: Response to Cost Survey (Launching the Vehicle Manufacturer's Target Setting Activities and Work Toward Achieving Goals)

Step 1. The parts manufacturer sends the vehicle manufacturer its response to the cost survey.

The cost survey is sent from the vehicle manufacturer's design department to the parts manufacturer's design department. The survey might explain that a certain new style is being considered for the front seat frame and then ask how much it would cost to produce the new seat frame design. Similarly, if new door trim components are being considered, it might ask how much those new components would cost.

The parts manufacturer responds to all questions by presenting a parts proposal to the vehicle manufacturer. Such a proposal might contain the following with regard to structural design:

- The parts manufacturer's proposal for DFM (design for manufacturing) parts structures
- The parts manufacturer's proposal for structural design that enables idle equipment or new equipment to be put to good use in manufacturing the target parts

Sequential approach

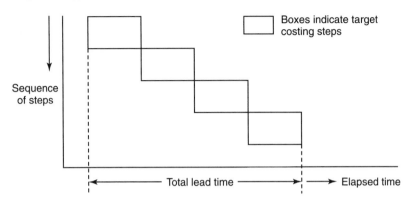

Semi-concurrent approach

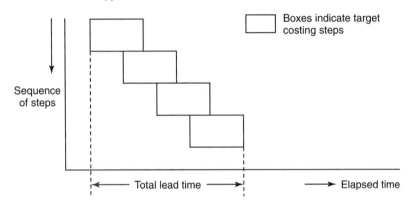

**Figure 18-1. Conceptual Diagrams of Sequential
and Semi-Concurrent Approaches**

The parts manufacturer carries out a pre-design check of costs (PDC) early on in the development process. For model changes, this check occurs at the very beginning of the development process (over 30 months before the new model enters production). The old (current) model's estimated costs are thoroughly analyzed to pinpoint problems that must be resolved lest they be

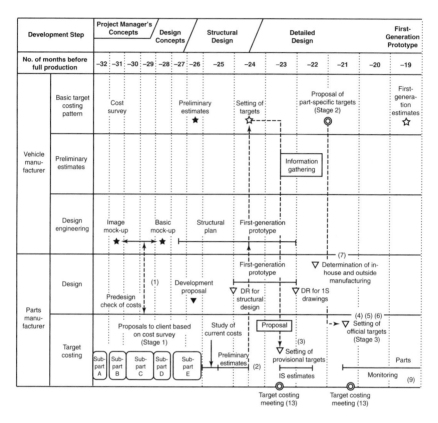

Figure 18-2. Parts Manufacturer's Target Costing Schedule

passed on to the new model. For example, such problems might involve a process that was designed poorly from the DFM perspective, or part specifications that are out of compliance with the relevant standards, or a requested variety reduction in parts that is not feasible.

After the product manager issues a request (via the cost management department) for cooperation from various divisions in identifying problems in current products and processes, the product manager receives a list of such problems from the cost management department. He or she then organizes a group to study

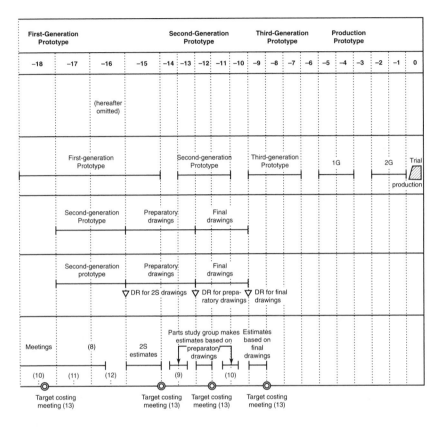

Figure 18-2. Contd.

the problems. This study group typically includes some top managers. They apply their findings as follows:

- Current-model improvements that can be made right away are implemented. Such improvements become part of the company's kaizen costing activities.
- Current-model improvements that cannot be made in the current model (perhaps because the improvement would require changes in the vehicle manufacturer's product catalog or new equipment investment) are still presented to the vehicle manufacturer to prevent the occurrence of similar

problems in the new model. The parts manufacturer also takes steps to ensure that these problems are not present in their own design drawings.

Step 2. The parts manufacturer makes preliminary estimates based on the structural design drawings to identify design problems as early as possible.

If the parts manufacturer sends design support staff to the vehicle manufacturer, the parts manufacturer will have more detailed access to the vehicle manufacturer's structural drawings. The parts manufacturer's target costing staff use these structural drawings as a basis for making preliminary cost estimates for their new parts.

The results of these preliminary cost estimates may reveal cost-raising problems for the parts manufacturer, such as new parts that will be difficult to manufacture or that will leave a lot of production equipment idle. To lower such costs and ensure profitability, the parts manufacturer must identify and correct such problems as soon as possible.

Step 3. The parts manufacturer gets an early start in parts design through early establishment of target costs and provisional target costs.

Having exchanged information during the first two steps, the vehicle manufacturer is able to estimate the target cost per vehicle by about P minus 24 months (i.e., 24 months prior to full production). However, the parts manufacturer is very busy at this time and cannot begin its part-specific target cost setting activities until P minus 23 months.

Even though the vehicle manufacturer's product manager (product-specific development leader) has not yet received the figures he needs to set part-specific target costs, he or she attempts to anticipate these costs and makes an in-house list of provisional target costs at about P minus 23 months.

Meanwhile, the parts manufacturer starts its first-generation prototype at P minus 24 months and completes it about a month later. Once the first-generation prototype is finished, the parts manufacturer uses it as a basis for making first-generation proto-type estimates (called 1S estimates for short). Before making these 1S estimates, they establish in-house provisional target prices that each relevant department in the company uses when designing cost factors into the first-generation prototype and working out their 1S estimates.

Figure 18-3 provides an outline summary of this process.

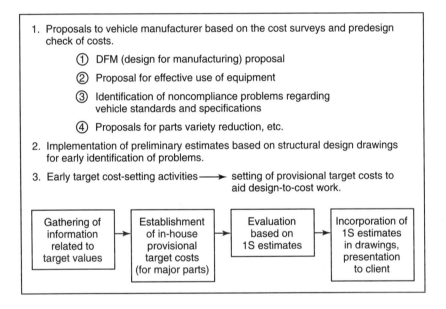

1. Proposals to vehicle manufacturer based on the cost surveys and predesign check of costs.

   ① DFM (design for manufacturing) proposal

   ② Proposal for effective use of equipment

   ③ Identification of noncompliance problems regarding vehicle standards and specifications

   ④ Proposals for parts variety reduction, etc.

2. Implementation of preliminary estimates based on structural design drawings for early identification of problems.

3. Early target cost-setting activities ⟶ setting of provisional target costs to aid design-to-cost work.

Gathering of information related to target values	Establishment of in-house provisional target costs (for major parts)	Evaluation based on 1S estimates	Incorporation of 1S estimates in drawings, presentation to client

Figure 18-3. Semi-Concurrent Target Costing by Parts Manufacturer

At this point, a target costing meeting is held. Target costing meetings for new products are chaired by the senior manager responsible and include other department heads and their assistants. These cost study meetings are held monthly. For example, suppose that the 1S estimate reveals a gap between the estimated cost and target cost for a set of seats to be produced for a new planned vehicle model. The target costing meeting investigates the possible causes of this gap, such as underestimation of design costs or processing costs, so that the points requiring improvement can be selected, discussed, approved, and acted upon.

Second Stage: Receipt of Official Target Prices and Deployment within Company

Step 4. When the official target prices are presented by the parts manufacturer, the vehicle manufacturer confirms their suitability, clarifies the target costing issues, and begins the systematic process of determining in-house target costs.

By the end of month P minus 22, the vehicle manufacturer has broken down its target costs into various part-specific target costs, which it then presents to the parts manufacturer. At this point, both companies work to clarify the following kinds of matters.

- Clarify the cost variables produced by differences in part specifications.
- Apply the pre-design check of costs to clarify what aspects of the current model are unprofitable, so that similar aspects in the new model can be specifically considered when establishing in-house target costs.
- Clarify cost-reduction targets to be achieved through VE activities. For example, the vehicle manufacturer might say, "The drawings show this part to have a target cost of $10, so we need to set a $1 cost reduction target for this part in our VE activities." Cost reduction targets must be clearly set in this way for numerous parts.
- Clarify target plant investment costs.
- Clarify target profits.

Once these matters have been clarified, the in-house target costs are officially established. In Figure 18-2, this is the "setting of official targets" that is scheduled at P minus 21 months.

The parts manufacturer establishes its in-house target costs in the following way. Using the target prices for purchased parts, set by the vehicle manufacturer's product development department or purchasing department, the parts manufacturer calculates a per-unit profit margin based on the target profit rate in its medium-term profit plan to determine its in-house target costs. As a formula, this may be expressed as follows:

Target cost = target price − (target price × medium-term target profit rate)

The parts manufacturer sets these target costs for each of the parts that it will produce and then begins target costing activities to achieve the targets. A separate program of target costing activities is carried out for each vehicle model for which the client has ordered parts. (For further description of the methods used by parts manufacturers to set target prices, see the supplement to Chapter 9.)

Step 5. The vehicle manufacturer also sets and deploys in-house target costs for large components and key parts that are not included in ordinary target costing activities. Here, the vehicle manufacturer does not try to set target costs for all models within each model series but instead selects one or two representative models.

However, the parts manufacturer must set in-house target costs and carry out design-to-cost work for all large components and key parts, including some parts for which the vehicle manufacturer has not provided target prices.

Step 6. Unit breakdown (deployment) is made of cost items in design.

The conventional approach to this has been that, for example, if the target cost for the vehicle seats is $1,000, then the cost for the seat covers is set as a portion of this amount, such as $100. However, this approach tends to create problems for design-to-cost work and the evaluation of design-to-cost results.

To facilitate the design-to-cost approach, costs must be broken down in more detail. To use the same example, more specific detailing might mean finding out what kind of sewing machine will be needed to sew the seat covers and how many press processes or other processes are involved.

Third Stage: VE Activities to Achieve In-House Target Costs

Step 7. The vehicle manufacturer determines which parts are to be produced in-house and which purchased from outside suppliers.

It is important to make this in-house/outside breakdown of parts production as early as possible to gain the cooperation of parts manufacturers in VE activities.

Step 8. Study meetings are implemented for each category of parts.

At this point, the parts manufacturer has received drawings and target costs from the vehicle manufacturer as well as from its own departments. The next step is to implement VE activities to determine how the targets can be reached. To be effective, these activities include the following study meetings and coordinated scheduling:

- DR (design review) of parts designs
- Study meetings for processing costs (production engineering) and design costs (design and purchasing)
- Study meetings for plant investment
- Study meetings for parts supplier negotiations
- Study meetings for production facilities

Step 9. Designers implement cost breakdown and self-evaluation.

At Step 6, the detailed units of cost breakdown may be provided by the designers themselves, which in effect means that such units are generally those that the designers are responsible for. The designers determine when extra costs have been designed in, such as when the target cost is premised upon a three-process production layout but the design calls for a four-process layout. Such discrepancies must be analyzed to identify their causes, which may or may not stem from design errors.

Step 10. Ongoing VE activities take place in response to higher costs created by design revisions.

Design revisions inevitably occur at various stages in the development process, and because such revisions tend to raise costs, VE activities are needed to keep such cost rises to a minimum.

Step 11. Cost rises due to design revisions imposed by vehicle manufacturer are clarified and costs are thoroughly retrieved.

Step 12. Hourly wage rates and labor-hours are reviewed and clarified.

The standard values used in cost tables are influenced by changes in the operating rate which result from changes in the market environment. Therefore, these standard values must be reviewed and revised frequently. At the very least, they must be monitored to readily identify problems as they arise.

Step 13. Systematic monitoring is carried out via target costing meetings.

- Detailed clarification and monitoring of causes for target shortfalls and responses taken
- Periodic review of progress in target costing implementation

Lastly, clear guidelines must be established for how staff responsibilities are assigned in various areas, down to the level of detailed scheduled tasks.

19

Companywide Approach to
Parts Reduction

Let us begin this chapter with a table that shows the kinds of costs incurred in the making of an automotive part (see Figure 19-1). Almost all of the costs in this table are fixed costs.

As can be seen in the table, the addition of one new part creates a variety of costs at each stage of the vehicle's life cycle. Therefore, parts reduction plays a very important role in companywide cost-cutting activities.

Ordinarily, one would think of part reduction and commonization as being the responsibility of the part designers and developers. For example, in a case where radiator types A and B are similar, discontinuing type B and replacing it with type A is an example of parts commonization. In this case, different parts are compared, and those whose functions include the functions of other parts are used to replace those other parts. This approach to part function comparison is called the tear-down method. Specifically, there are several types of tear-down methods, including the matrix tear-down method, in which the part numbers of similar parts are arranged vertically in a matrix and the parts' functional levels are arranged horizontally in the same matrix to facilitate comparison. Other methods include the static tear-down method and the GET method for group management.

Costs \ Stage	Survey	Merchandising planning	Design	Prototypes	Testing	Production setup	Production	Sales	Spares
Development									
Design costs		O	O						
Prototype development costs			O	O					
Prototype research and testing costs			O	O	O				
Management costs		O	O	O	O				
Production setup									
Tooling design costs						O			
Production prototype costs				O		O			
Tool fabrication costs						O			
Management costs				O		O			
Production									
Parts management costs (in-house and outside)							O		O
Equipment management and depreciation costs							O		O
Cost of losses due to reduced efficiency							O		O
Sales									
Management costs	O	O							
Catalog costs								O	
Advertising costs								O	
Parts storage costs (including sales co.)								O	O
Parts disposal costs (including sales co.)									O

Source: Yoshihiko Satō 1993, p.38.

Figure 19-1. Costs Incurred by One Part

However, all of these are methods to reduce the variety of existing parts by making improvements, which is a rather inefficient approach. Such an approach requires a lot of time and yields only modest results. Moreover, it does not prevent increases in the variety of parts.

Instead, there needs to be an approach that reduces the number of parts as early as possible in the design/development process. It is also important to make this approach a companywide approach, in part because the design/development staff would feel overly burdened if it were entirely their responsibility.

In view of these factors, the best approach is to make parts reduction a program that encompasses every company division. In particular, divisions concerned with processes that tend to increase the number of parts should be deeply involved in parts reduction activities. In automotive companies, the flow of work begins when the sales division informs the design/development divisions of current and emerging market needs. The design/development divisions then design and develop new products to suit those needs, after which the production division manufactures these new products (and the purchasing division buys parts to be supplied from outside vendors), and the replacement division stocks spares for buyers of the new products. Each of these divisions has its own role in reducing the number of parts. (The author is indebted to Mr. Yoshihiko Satō for much of the following explanation).

Parts reduction starts with devising ways to minimize parts early on, at the merchandise planning and product development stages. We might call this an industrial version of "birth control."

Next, at the production and sales stages, ways must be found to smoothly accommodate an eventual shift toward small-lot production during the latter part of the vehicle's model life, when an increasing share of parts are sold as replacement parts rather than new-product parts.

When the model life has ended and all of the model's parts are sold as replacement parts, cost-efficient ways to phase out the parts are also needed. One way is to avoid strict functional specifications and instead set standards that are conducive to parts commonization. In any case, it is important to consider the total cost of phasing out parts: Even though warehousing costs are eliminated, there are still other costs, such as for disposing of obsolete production equipment and unneeded spare parts.

The key is to retain profitability even as the number of parts and products shrinks. Just as birth control avoids the expense of rearing too many children, industrial parts reduction saves the expense of extra parts and allows the company to operate in a leaner and more profitable way. This all comes down to a series of tradeoffs between greater variety for the sake of customer satisfaction and reduced variety for the sake of profitability.

Deliberating such tradeoffs is the responsibility of a task force called the special council on parts reduction that is chaired by a company vice president and that oversees parts reduction subcouncils established within various divisions. Figure 19-2 illustrates the configuration of subcouncils and the types of work they do to reduce the number of parts. The following description is based on the information shown in the figure.

Sales Division

Establishment of Promising Products

The variety of product (vehicle) models increases as sales division staff report what type of product buyers want. The sales division staff must learn how to sort out orders to determine which products are likely to have the best sales potential. Consequently, the company tries to improve its methods for establishing such promising products at the merchandise planning stage.

Conversely, about every six months they also make a list of least promising products and consider whether any of them should be dropped.

Development of Menu-Based Sales

When automotive companies sell engines as separate products, customers may ask for specific features, such as a certain kind of oil filter. This practice also tends to increase the variety of product types. Rather than customizing each order, manufacturers can respond by offering a "menu-based" product line wherein customers buy a basic product and then choose among a number of options.

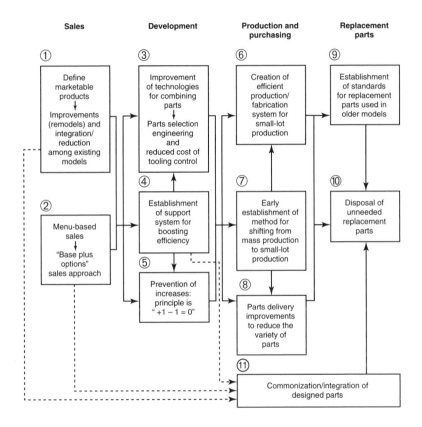

Figure 19-2. Parts Reduction Tasks Carried Out by Division-Based Subcouncils

Development Division

Establishment of Efficiency Support System

Development divisions are now using sophisticated CAD (computer-aided design) systems and other computer-based systems to boost development efficiency. For example, using a CAD system, an engineer can call up a drawing for a 60-liter fuel tank on the computer's display screen. Then, using a screen-pointing device such as a light pen, he or she can select "80-liter" as an option, after which the computer will automatically revise the drawing to show an 80-liter fuel tank. These kinds of automated tasks are especially useful when there is a wide variety of product models. In other words, CAD systems enable engineers to expand the selection of models much faster than the conventional method of finding similar parts or revising drawings manually. Such systems also make it easier to achieve an optimum design configured of parts having just the functions (such as liter size) needed to create the desired product.

Although CAD systems are useful as an efficiency booster, they are not without their problems. To make them truly useful and as unproblematic as possible, CAD systems need to be carefully studied, evaluated, and reconfigured to suit the specific needs of the user. Rarely would this need for fine-tuning make a CAD system more trouble than it is worth, though.

Specifically, CAD users in automotive development divisions need to have CAD systems that make it easier to find and use similar parts for new models. When similar parts are easier to find, they can be more easily integrated or commonized.

Parts are searched using code numbers assigned to each part. Another code is assigned to parts to enable parts to be displayed in lists when carrying out selective or modular design (described in the following section).

Combination of Parts through Selective Design

In selective design (also known as modular design), parts are listed in tables, where they can be categorized into module groups according to their varying features and functions. A designer at any departmental computer terminal can then call up a list of parts that meet the functional requirements and select specific parts for the design.

To achieve an optimum design, the designer must sometimes mix two grades of modules to produce an intermediary-grade module. For example, a higher-grade module configured of parts with more extensive functions ("big" parts) can be mixed with a lower-grade module configured of parts with less extensive functions ("small" parts) to produce an intermediary-grade module (a type of parts commonization). Such intermediary-grade modules will inevitably be more expensive than lower-grade modules by virtue of their more sophisticated parts, and therefore a cost limit should be set before mixing higher- and lower-grade modules in this way.

Such cost-limit standards for parts commonization should be different at different product life stages (merchandise planning, design, full production, replacement parts production).

However, if we seek to account for each individual cost incurred by commonization, the process of commonization will be made unnecessarily difficult. Therefore, it is best to establish a cost-rise standard for commonization that is lenient enough to facilitate this process rather than hinder it.

The Anti-Cost-Rise Principle of "+ 1 − 1 = 0"

First, the company sets a limit on the total number of new parts, most likely by limiting the number of drawings submitted for new parts. Once the limit has been reached, one new part can be produced only when it enables the elimination of another part. This is the principle of "+ 1 − 1 = 0."

To get an idea how reducing and commonizing parts will affect costs, the product planning department's target costing department categorizes the types and unit costs of parts and makes careful estimates of the various kinds of costs listed in Figure 19-1. The target costing offices receive the support of their respective product manager when making these cost estimates.

At the development stage people begin to look at whether the estimated costs will stay near the target cost levels. However, parts commonization, particularly the making of intermediate-grade modules, tends to raise costs so that estimated costs for newly designed vehicles may go beyond their target levels.

For instance, making part A available in two types requires two kinds of dies. This requirement doubles the plant investment cost (the depreciation cost of a die) for the dies used for this part compared to when there is only one type available. Simple parts commonization would reduce the types of dies to just one, thereby halving the plant investment cost. However, the parts commonization principle of having more sophisticated parts replace simpler parts tends to incur higher-than-estimated costs due to the higher plant investment cost for manufacturing sophisticated parts.

There is a way to manage this rise in fixed costs (such as costs for dies, jigs, and tools, plus design and management expenses) so that excess costs will be canceled out even when the cost rise goes beyond the target cost. This method is summarized in the following formula.

Amount of reduction in die appreciation cost per part unit

$$= \frac{\text{Total depreciation of two types of dies}}{\text{Total production amount of two types of parts}} - \frac{\text{Depreciation of one type of (commonized) part}}{\text{Total production amount of commonized part}}$$

Net cost reduction = Amount of reduction in die depreciation costs
– Higher costs due to use of more sophisticated parts for parts commonization

Production and Purchasing Divisions

Building an Efficient Production/Fabrication System That Supports Small-Lot Production

The production phase of a product life cycle starts out with large lots, and then lot sizes gradually shrink after production reaches the saturation point and the product gets older. The product's sales also decline until the next model change takes place. After the next model change, production of the previous model is discontinued for all of its parts except for replacement parts. When production enters this small-lot phase, it becomes necessary to reconstruct the way replacement parts are manufactured.

For instance, various kinds of dies and concrete molds may be needed for press molds in small-lot production. In some cases, the concrete molds can continue to be used even after the metal dies are discarded.

The variety of parts can be optimized by improving the way parts are delivered. The approach to parts delivery should be different for small-lot production than it was for full-scale production.

Replacement Parts Department

Although user's manuals for electrical products typically warn that replacement parts will no longer be produced after a certain number of years, automobile replacement parts are produced indefinitely; only rarely does an automobile company discontinue a part number. However, it is still advisable to establish standards for recognizing when some parts are no longer needed so that such parts can be properly eliminated.

Also, the replacement standards can change over the years. For example, vehicles sold in Hokkaido, Japan's northernmost large island, are equipped with more powerful heaters than are vehicles sold in Honshu, Japan's main island. Thus, vehicle models that are exactly the same except for their heaters may continue to have two types of heaters produced as replacement parts up to a certain time, after which it saves money to produce only the more powerful heaters for all vehicles in that model. Thus, vehicle owners in Honshu who receive the more powerful heaters as replacement parts will tend to use their new heaters less than their old ones. Also, the optimum design range of the replacement-part heaters will be exceeded somewhat by the extra-powerful heaters.

Likewise, optimum design calls for a wide variety of springs, some only slightly stronger than others, for various new vehicle models. In later years, when such springs are made as replacement parts, this wide array may be reduced to enable the discontinuation of some types and thereby cut costs.

Relation between Parts Reduction and Customer Satisfaction

Effects of commonization

Parts commonization almost always adheres to the principle of having more sophisticated parts replace simpler parts, and therefore it tends to raise customer satisfaction levels. Rarely does it replace more sophisticated parts with simpler parts.

For example, let us say that deluxe vehicles are equipped with a rearview mirror (type A) that has a lever to switch betwe n two types of mirrors, one for daytime and one for night, while the basic models have only a daytime-type rearview mirror (type B). If at a certain point only type A replacement parts are made for both deluxe and basic models, then basic-model drivers who receive such replacement parts will also get the night-time mirror setting to reduce headlight glare. Thus, in this case parts commonization tends to increase customer satisfaction.

However, if it costs $10 to make one type A mirror and only $8 to make one type B mirror, it costs $2 extra to replace type B parts with type A parts. Therefore, there must be a standard as to how much of a cost rise parts commonization can tolerate and still be cost-effective. If type A mirrors cost $24 each to produce, we might easily conclude that it would not be cost-effective to replace all rearview mirrors with type A mirrors.

Suppose that, for the sake of customer satisfaction, the automobile company wants to equip both basic and luxury models with the $10 day/night rearview mirror. For fear of losing sales, however, they decide not to raise the sales price of the basic model to cover this $2 difference. This means an extra $2 in variable costs for the mirror, but it also means that more $10 (type A) mirrors can be produced, which should lower the production cost somewhat thanks to economy of scale. Having only one type of rearview mirror to produce also reduces management costs.

Effects of option choices

Customer satisfaction also comes into consideration when implementing menu-based sales. For example, consider the types of buses that are sold. Some have bigger windows than others and some have entry/exit doors in various front/middle/back configurations. Each customer (i.e., bus company) has its own needs for a certain type of design. Similarly, prefabricated housing is built in various models, designed around the concept of "base model plus menu of options." Obviously, not all customers' wishes can be met with a menu of options, and designs that seek to ensure 100 percent customer satisfaction will require a wide variety of new parts, thereby incurring higher tooling costs that must be passed on to the customers.

As another example, suppose that certain customers have requested that they be able to externally check their oil level as part of engine maintenance without having to manually pull out the dipstick. This feature would require the design and installation of a device for this purpose (as well as related quality control costs, etc.). The designers must therefore consider whether this should be made a factory-built option that gets added to the sales price of the vehicle or whether it should be sold separately as a custom part that vehicle owners can buy at auto supply stores and install themselves.

Thus, customer satisfaction is only one factor that must be balanced against other factors to serve the ultimate objective of marketability. The concept of parts reduction is basically oriented toward higher sales and profits, and customer satisfaction levels may therefore decline in some cases. However, "cheaper" ceases to become "better" when "cheaper" reduces sales due to loss of customer satisfaction. Also, adding customer-pleasing functions may in some cases cause a slight loss of sales and a slight loss of profits due to higher costs. The bottom line is that customer satisfaction is indeed an important consideration, but it cannot be pursued without also ensuring profitability.

20

VE: The Core of Target Costing

Value engineering (VE) constitutes the very core of target costing. The VE concept of "activities that build cost in at the design stage" is a key determinant of cost reduction. However, VE is just one of several subsystems that go into the establishment of a target costing system.

As will be explained later in this chapter, VE activities as practiced by Japanese automotive companies include many methods and subsystems that were not part of the original VE methods developed in the United States. Examples include long-term profit planning, methods for determining target sales prices, and methods for determining target costs with a view toward reaching target profits. In short, this chapter presents an outline of VE activities in Japan.[1]

Definition of VE

The Japan Value Engineering Association defines VE as "organized efforts to implement functional analysis of products and/or services to reliably achieve all required functions at the lowest possible life cycle cost."

Let us briefly examine the different parts of this definition.

"The lowest possible life cycle cost" means minimizing all of the costs incurred during the life of a product or service (for products, this includes the development, manufacturing, sales, use, and disposal stages). It is best to include all of these costs, even those borne by the consumer (use and disposal costs).

"Reliably achieve all required functions" means meeting users' requirements for product or service functions (i.e., functional requirements). To do this, designers must identify and satisfy the various functional requirements indicated by users, including reliability, maintainability, and safety, as well as the various legal and regulatory requirements.

In addition, the VE approach lowers costs by identifying and eliminating functions that are not required.

"Functional analysis" means breaking down and meticulously investigating the product or service functions that are targeted by VE activities to determine whether each function is necessary. Having sorted the necessary functions from the unnecessary ones, the next step is to determine whether the necessary functions are being implemented at appropriate levels.[2]

Thus, the objective of functional analysis is to improve product or service functions so that all functions are both necessary in nature and appropriate in degree. Problems uncovered through functional analysis include unnecessary, inadequate, or excessive functions, and problems in implementation methods for functions.

We should avoid using the expression *reducing functions* when we speak of eliminating unnecessary functions or making excessive functions more appropriate.

Product manufacturers and service providers determine the levels to which functions should be implemented. Given the variety of users and their needs, it is impossible to provide a product or service that will completely satisfy every customer. Therefore, the manufacturer must identify its target users and then take their perspective in determining which functions are necessary and how they can be implemented to an appropriate degree in the product or service to be sold.

"Organized efforts" means teamwork among various kinds of specialists and general employees. This VE team is the project team that includes specialists from design, production engineering, purchasing, manufacturing, and cost management. Outside experts and specialists are also available for assistance with problems that cannot be resolved by the project team members. The VE approach thus pulls together the information, ideas, and expertise of various team members.

VE Job Plan

The VE job plan is a series of standardized steps for implementing VE activities. Figure 20-1 outlines the VE job plan, which includes three main steps:

1. Define functions
2. Evaluate functions
3. Draft improvement plans

These steps are described in more detail below.

Define Functions

In the context of VE, defining functions means thoroughly studying target functions to clarify their purposes and characteristics. As shown in the figure, there are three steps in defining functions:

1. Gather information
2. Define functions
3. Organize functions

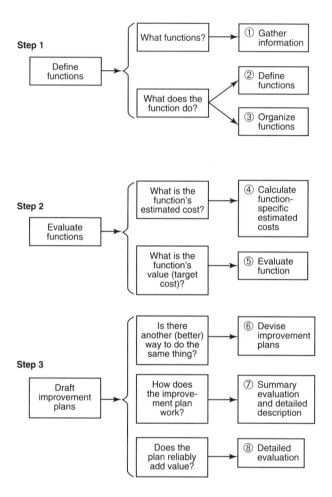

Figure 20-1. Configuration of VE Job Plan

Gather Information

Although the gathering of information is an indispensable part of every step in the VE job plan, this data-gathering step is given special mention because it is where we gather the information used to define the items to be targeted by VE activities. The main objective is to determine the latent needs of users for particular functions and to clarify which methods will best serve to meet those needs.

The information is also used to study the various types of requirements that occur during the entire life cycle (from planning and design to manufacturing and sales to use and disposal) of the product or service targeted by VE activities. These requirements generally include the following:[3]

- User requirements: Use objectives, use conditions, use environments, performance features, reliability, safety, durability, design, shape, color, etc.
- Sales requirements: Selling points, competitive performance features, competitive pricing, etc.
- Design-related requirements: Performance levels, added function levels, etc.
- Manufacturing-related requirements: Processing technologies, manufacturing processes and related labor-hours, materials, and purchased parts, etc.
- Distribution-related requirements: Packaging, loading, storage, transportation, etc.
- Cost-related requirements: Management of progress toward achieving target costs, etc.
- Legal and regulatory requirements: Patents and utility models, environmental protection laws, industry regulations and guidelines, etc.

Define Functions

Defining functions includes studying a product targeted for VE activities both as a whole and in terms of each of its elements (parts, etc.). Each definition should contain at least a noun and verb describing the function of the product or element.

This approach to defining functions enables us to clearly distinguish between necessary and unnecessary functions as well as between frivolous (or excessive) functions and important functions. Likewise, we can discern which functions are fundamental and which are secondary.

The output from VE activities consists mainly of improvement plans that raise the value of the target product. Therefore, VE requires the freedom to think beyond the product's current format or structure. The mechanisms and structure of previous products represent only some of the possible ways of implementing functions in products. We must go beyond the particular styles or configurations of current products to consider the functions that lie at the root of the product and to come up with new ideas that stem directly from a study of essential functions. As such, the purpose of defining functions is to clearly understand and describe functions so that new ideas and better methods can be devised.

Methodology of function definitions

Suppose that we must define the functions of a battery. Our definition might be: "A battery (= subject) supplies (= verb) electricity (= object)." Or, for brevity's sake, our definition might be simply "To supply electricity".

In each definition, the object indicates the product targeted by VE activities and the verb expresses what the function does. When the product has two or more functions (as is often the case), it is important to list a separate definition for each function so that, for example, the function definition for a switch lever should not be "to create circuits and pass current" but rather "to create circuits" and "to pass current."

Steps in formulating function definitions

1. Clarify the structure of the target item.

Specimens, drawings, specifications, and other reference sources should all be studied to determine exactly what the target item is. The project team members gather information on the item (its structure, nomenclature, etc.) and distribute it to others involved in VE activities for the target item.

2. Draft a product configuration drawing.

Products generally consist of one or more subassemblies, which in turn include several assembly parts. The product configuration drawing should indicate this configuration of product parts.

3. Define functions.

Define the functions of the parts (including assembly parts) shown in the product configuration drawing.

Organize Functions

It is not unusual for a product or service to be configured of many elements, each of which may serve several functions. "Organize functions" means systematically arranging the many separately defined functions in a way that helps clarify the interrelation of functions. Typically, a block- or tree-shaped diagram is created that indicates relations among the objectives and methods of various functions. Such drawings are called functional block diagrams or functional family trees.

Steps in creating a functional block diagram

As when using the KJ method, we start by making function cards from which we will systematically build relations among functional objectives and methods.

1. Make function cards

Make one function card for each defined function. These cards should include part names and, if possible, estimated costs.

2. Conduct searches for specific function objectives (higher-level functions) and function methods (lower-level functions).

Take all the function cards and randomly select one card. Ask, "How should this function be achieved?" Next, search through the function objectives written on the other cards to find cards that describe possible methods for achieving the function.

Figure 20-2 shows a functional block diagram for a small flashlight.

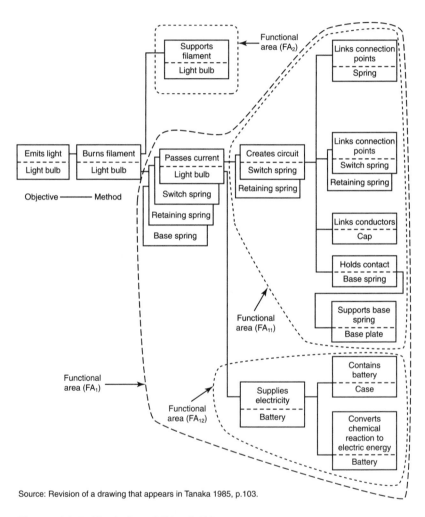

Source: Revision of a drawing that appears in Tanaka 1985, p.103.

Figure 20-2. Functional Block Diagram

Purposes of organizing functions

1. To distinguish between necessary functions and unnecessary functions

Creating a functional block diagram is one way to discover functions that have no defined objectives or that have no clear objective-method relationships. All of these are unnecessary functions. Functions should be sorted into necessary and unnecessary functions based on the user's perspective. Unnecessary functions can also be sorted more specifically into excessive functions, multiple functions, and redundant functions.

2. To distinguish between fundamental functions and secondary functions

When we create functional family trees (functional block diagrams), we can identify groups of fundamental (trunk) functions and groups of auxiliary (branch) functions. This tree enables us to recognize which functions are more important than others.

Fundamental functions are functions that are indispensable for realizing the user's use objective. Some fundamental functions pertain to the product as a whole, whereas others pertain to one or more of the product's elements (such as a subassembly or part). Secondary functions can be defined as functions that support the implementation of fundamental functions (they are also called auxiliary functions or subordinate functions). In the functional block diagram, the group of functions that most directly implements the highest-priority function is called the trunk function group, whereas the group of functions that supports this trunk function group is called the auxiliary function group.

3. To facilitate function evaluations that identify functional areas and thereby clarify improvement targets

Functional areas are the units by which functions in functional block diagrams can be grouped (see dotted lines in Figure 20-2). Each functional area can also include several of its own functional areas.

Once the functional areas have been identified, it becomes easier to calculate the target costs (F) and estimated costs (C) used for function evaluations (using the $V = F \div C$ formula described below). Functional areas that are evaluated as having a low value (i.e., a low "V" value in the $V = F \div C$ formula) can also be identified as likely targets for improvement efforts.

Evaluate Functions

The purposes of function evaluations are (1) to calculate a proportional value ($V = F \div C$) for each functional area to identify the functional areas having the least value; (2) to establish value improvement targets; and (3) to help motivate improvement efforts.

There are three steps in function evaluations:

1. Calculation of function-specific target costs (this by itself is the narrow definition of "function evaluation")
2. Calculation of function-specific estimated costs
3. Determination of functions needing improvement

The VE approach calculates a product's (broadly defined) value using the formula "Value = Function / Cost" ($V = F \div C$). In this formula:

$$\text{Numerator F (function)} = \begin{array}{l} \text{the value (evaluation result) of a functional} \\ \text{area in terms of cost, i.e., the target cost} \end{array}$$

$$\text{Denominator C (cost)} = \begin{array}{l} \text{the current cost of a functional area, i.e.,} \\ \text{the actual cost or estimated cost} \end{array}$$

If we know the values of F and C, we can calculate the proportional values (V) of each functional area. The functional areas that turn out to have the lowest proportional values are the areas most in need of value improvement.

The target for value improvement can be expressed either as a target cost reduction rate ($V = F \div C$) or as a target cost reduction amount ($C - F$). Presenting such specific targets for improvement efforts can help motivate VE team members to make value improvement efforts.

Draft Improvement Plans

Once we have completed the function definition and function evaluation steps, we have a clear indication of which functional areas most need value improvement efforts. Now it is time to devise improvement plans for this purpose. The drafting of improvement plans lies at the core of VE activities and is also a highlight of those activities. The function definition and function evaluation steps are preparations leading up to improvement planning, and at least half of the time spent in VE activities is spent in coming up with improvement ideas and plans.

The draft improvement plans step generally includes two steps of its own:

1. Presentation of improvement plans

At this step, VE team members devise ways to raise the value of the functions in the functional area targeted for improvement (usually, the functional area having the lowest value). This step is sometimes called devising alternative plans. Here it is not as important to produce a full-fledged improvement plan as it is to come up with ideas from which such a plan can be erected.

2. Evaluation and selection of improvement plan

First, evaluate several of the ideas that have been presented and use them to devise several improvement proposals. Next, broadly evaluate the improvement proposals to narrow them down to just a few. Finally, carefully evaluate these few proposals, applying appropriate tools such as technical tests and cost estimations in order to select the best proposal.

Enthusiasm: The Wellspring of Improvement Plans

- Presentation of improvement plans means coming up with basic ideas (basic concepts) that will lay the foundation for an improvement plan.
- The first step in generating such ideas is to correctly understand the target problems. Aside from avoiding the pitfalls of

overlooking problems completely or misunderstanding them, this also involves a step of evaluating functions, in which the object is to clearly identify any problem areas (functional areas) that require value improvements. It is no exaggeration to say that correctly understanding the problem is half the battle in finding a solution.

• The two key ingredients for success in problem solving are determination and enthusiasm. If a group enthusiastically adopts a whatever-it-takes attitude, their information-gathering efforts will be more productive and they will find it easier to get help from others. Only with such determination and enthusiasm can problem-solving efforts be truly concentrated and abiding until a solution is found.

• What is the source of this wellspring of determination, enthusiasm, energy, and diligence? The following incentives can help get enthusiasm started:

1. The participants must understand that solving the problem is for their own benefit. To make this so, the company must establish some means of evaluating the problem-solving performance of individuals or groups and should reward them for it.

2. It is important to get participants interested in the problem itself and to view finding a solution as a challenge—a goal worth achieving. Thus, in addition to external rewards such as money or special privileges, individuals can also enjoy internal rewards, such as taking interest in a puzzle to be solved and taking pride in finding a solution.

Methods for Generating Improvement Ideas

Several different idea-generation methods have been developed. These methods are briefly described below, along with a recommended method that mixes elements of each.

Step 1: Methods for Generating Ideas

The brainstorming method

A group of about 10 persons studies and discusses a problem from their various individual perspectives and then comes up with as many solution-related ideas as possible (this method was first proposed in 1941 by A. F. Osborne). This method has four rules:

1. No one is allowed to say anything negative about anyone else's ideas.
2. All ideas are welcomed—no matter how crazy or unconventional they sound.
3. The more ideas suggested, the better.
4. Ideas that are built upon or between other ideas are also welcomed.

The brainstorming session leader plays an important role. The leader should be someone who is good at generating and developing ideas. Before the brainstorming session, the leader must carefully study the problem and build up as much advance knowledge about it as possible. If the problem relates to VE, such a study might include looking into the role and relative importance of each functional area and identifying orientations (perspectives) for solving the problem.

A secretary is also needed to jot down all ideas that are suggested during the brainstorming session, so that they can be reviewed by other participants. The KJ method's idea card system for recording and referencing ideas is recommended for this purpose.

The Gordon method

This variation on the brainstorming method was proposed by W. J. Gordon. Whereas the brainstorming method attempts to start brainstorming sessions with a clear, detailed idea of the problem to be solved, the Gordon method starts with a more abstract theme and gradually defines the problem as ideas are generated. For example, a box of caramels might be abstracted as "candy," which might be made even more abstract as "sweets" or even as "food." Climbing this ladder of ever more abstract steps invites people to take increasingly broad perspectives in coming up with ideas.

When using the Gordon method, only the leader knows the actual problem at the start of the session. As ideas are generated at increasingly abstract levels, the leader makes note of ideas that seem promising as possible solutions to the problem. By noting these ideas, the leader gently guides the other participants in the right direction.

The checklist method

This method was first proposed as a method for individuals rather than groups, but it can also be effectively used in combination with the brainstorming method.

In any type of brainstorming approach, members will usually freely associate starting from an idea proposed by a member, which tends to limit the perspectives from which the problem is viewed. At an appropriate time, the leader should propose an idea or two from quite different perspectives to help broaden everyone's thinking. This is where the checklist method comes in.

The most famous feature of the checklist method is the "5W1H" approach. When considering a particular function, the group asks the "5Ws" (Why, Where, When, Who, and What), plus one "H" (How). Specifically, "Why" asks why the function is necessary, "Where" asks where the function is used, "When" asks when it is used, "Who" asks who uses it, "What" asks what the function does, and "How" asks how the function is used.

L. D. Miles, the inventor of VE, proposed 13 techniques that act as stimulants of VE success. These techniques can also be used as a checklist for generating VE-related ideas.

(a) Eliminate generalities
(b) Gather all usable costs
(c) Use only the best information sources
(d) "Blast, create, and refine" (let ideas burst forth freely, then refine them)
(e) Use truly creative thinking
(f) Identify and eliminate all obstacles
(g) Make use of available experts
(h) Convert major tolerances into monetary amounts
(i) Use similar-function products from outside suppliers
(j) Make use of outside suppliers' experience, knowledge, and information
(k) Make use of specialized manufacturing processes
(l) When possible, use standard parts
(m) Before deciding how to spend the company's money, ask yourself if you would invest your own money the same way.

Methods that break down and recombine problems

When the target problem is very large, often it must be broken down into more manageable parts, with countermeasures to be devised for each part. Once such countermeasures are determined, they are combined into an overall plan to solve the entire problem. Using the VE approach, we begin by making a functional block diagram (such as shown in Figure 20-2) to organize a breakdown and recombination of the entire system's functions.

The process of generating ideas is one of searching for methods (means) for achieving a certain objective. Various methods are suggested for reaching that objective, each starting from a different viewpoint. A functional block diagram that illustrates how functions relate to such methods serves as a guide to the methods that have been used to reach the objectives for existing products.

Since the point of generating ideas is to find better alternatives to previously used methods, the practice has been to begin generating ideas based on the higher-level functions in the functional block diagram. When it is possible to start at the higher level, the lower-level functions become restricted and improvement effects are greater. (However, ideas for upper-level functions take longer to work out and are generally more difficult to come up with. When top-level ideas fail to develop, it is best to go down to the functions at the next lower level and try again to generate ideas.)

After a certain amount of time and effort, giving up on ideas for high-level functions in favor of working on ideas for lower-level functions is a good way to shorten the lead time for generating ideas.

Step 2: Methods for Sorting and Coordinating Ideas

The following methods are recommended for coordinating ideas:

1. Sort ideas into categories based on design concepts. If individual ideas have been entered onto idea cards, they can be easily sorted into category-based groups.
2. For each group of cards, find a key word (also called a design index) that describes a common characteristic of the cards in the group. Write the key word for each group on a separate card and attach this as the title card for its group.
3. Ideas can be sorted not only based on similar design concepts but also based on other kinds of similarities and differences. For example, various methods for realizing high-level functions, various energy sources, and different materials and/or structures, shapes, and fabrication methods can all serve as criteria for sorting ideas.
4. Ideas can be developed and refined by combining them with other ideas and improving upon them.
5. Create an idea organization sheet (list) adding other ideas as necessary. When such lists are made and kept on file, they can collectively serve as an idea bank for future design proposals that address similar functions. Because each group of idea cards is marked with a key word describing the group's

similar characteristic, the groups of ideas are easier to use for technical and economic evaluations.

Evaluation and Selection of Improvement Plans

At this point, the improvement group (1) evaluates and selects ideas, then develops them into improvement plans; (2) performs a general evaluation of several improvement plans to narrow down the number of feasible plans; and (3) makes a second study, including a detailed evaluation, of plans that have passed the general evaluation and selects the final plan. This three-step method is described further below.

1. Evaluation of ideas

   • The group holds a brainstorming session to generate ideas. Next, they sort the ideas according to perspectives or other categories and develop and refine ideas to link them to specific needed improvements. At this point, the ideas are ready to be evaluated.

   • When evaluating the ideas, they sort them into three groups: technically feasible ideas, unfeasible ideas, and ideas requiring further study. Next, they evaluate them for economic feasibility. They then carry out extra research on ideas designated for further study and sort the ideas into usable plans and unusable plans. The evaluators conduct much of this general evaluation based on their own opinions and findings.

   In the case of automobiles, the economic evaluation here corresponds to the profitability check that is carried out during the product conceptualization stage.

   • Next, the group further refines ideas that have passed the general evaluation to draft improvement plans, which they sort into three groups, labeled Type A, Type B, and Type C:

   Type A: plans that can be implemented right away

Type B: plans that require detailed studies before they can be implemented, such as plans that require changes in large systems or structures

Type C: plans that call for a radical departure from current conditions and/or major changes in previous design concepts

2. General evaluation of improvement plans

- The general evaluation looks at improvement plans in terms of technical and economic feasibility and determines which of the proposed improvement plans merit a detailed evaluation.
- Evaluation points for technical feasibility:
  (a) Does it meet user needs in terms of functional level?
  (b) Does it meet requirements for reliability, maintainability, operability, and safety?
  (c) Does it fit in well with the rest of the system?
  (d) Does it pose any environmental or pollution problems?
  (e) Does it pose any manufacturing problems?

- Evaluation points for economic feasibility: At this point a profitability check is performed to see whether the improvement plan is economically feasible. The improvement plan's estimated costs are compared with the actual costs (of current products) to determine whether the improvement plan's costs are lower, equivalent, or higher. (If the improvement plan's costs are higher, the next question is whether the costs are higher than the function's value as determined by its evaluation.) This evaluation requires the use of a cost table based on costs of current products. It includes the following evaluation points:
  (a) How much of the product can be sold?
  (b) How much are the direct materials costs and processing costs?
  (c) How much are the direct operating costs (design costs, die/jig/tool costs, new equipment depreciation costs,

subcontracted processing costs, and other costs incurred by adopting the improvement plan)?

3. Detailed evaluation of improvement plans: The few improvement plans that passed the general evaluation are now subjected to a detailed evaluation that will determine the final improvement plan. This evaluation also considers the plan's technical and economic aspects.

  • Evaluation of technical aspects: All of the improvement plans to be evaluated, and especially those that are either Type B or Type C plans, must undergo prototype testing as well various technical and economic tests. The technical tests include (1) theoretical verification, (2) model-based testing, and (3) prototype testing. Also, when the final blueprints are completed, trial production tests must be done to determine suitability for full-scale production.
  • Technical evaluation points
    (a) Does the product provide user-required functions and performance features?
    (b) Does it meet requirements for reliability, maintainability, operability, and safety?
    (c) Does it fit in well with the rest of the system?
    (d) Can all of the materials and parts be readily acquired?
    (e) Can the number of parts be reduced and can any mechanisms be simplified?
    (f) Are there any problems concerning packaging, shipment, or installation?
  • Evaluation of economic aspects: This detailed economic evaluation is given only to improvement plans that have passed the detailed technical evaluation. The evaluation includes a comparison of the actual costs of the current product with the estimated costs in the improvement plan to calculate the cost savings offered by the improvement plan. (If the improvement plan's estimated costs are slightly higher than the current product's costs, that may be ac-

ceptable if the improvement plan raises the product's functional value as determined by VE analysis.)

- Economic evaluation points: The detailed evaluation includes calculation of detailed estimated costs, which requires the use of a cost table. The cost table must contain data for the current product's direct materials costs, process-specific processing (machining, etc.) costs, and direct operating costs. The following points are checked as part of the detailed evaluation:

  (a) How much of the product can be sold (or how much can be produced)?

  (b) What new costs are incurred by adopting the plan? (Such costs should be divided into related costs or incremental costs.) Also, what are the costs related to the existing product (unrelated costs or sunken costs)? Both of these types of costs should be defined separately as traceable costs or direct costs on the one hand and common costs on the other hand.

  (c) Separation and calculation of variable costs and fixed costs

  (d) The improvement plan's direct operating costs must be estimated. These include design costs, depreciation costs for dies, jigs, tools, and other new equipment, and prototype development and testing.

  (e) Calculation of recovery period for new equipment investment

  (f) Calculation of rate of return on invested capital (for accounting purposes)

  (g) Calculation of packaging and shipping costs

  (h) Cost comparison of in-house production vs. subcontracted production

  (i) Prediction of future cost fluctuations (price changes, etc.)

- Improvement plans that have passed these technical and economic evaluations are then evaluated as to whether they will lead to attractive products that meet user needs.

Evaluation points at this step include:
(a) What is the product's aesthetic value?
(b) Are there any sales-related problems?
(c) Are there any use-related problems? (use-related costs, etc.)
(d) Are there any problems related to after-sales service?
(e) Does the product fit in with the company's overall strategy?

Notes

1. The author is indebted to Mr. Masayasu Tanaka (see bibliographic reference for his work of 1985) for matters described in this chapter. In addition, other references can be found in Kurabayashi, Sugasawa, and Murata 1987 and Miles 1961, 1972.

2. The following definitions are provided for "function," "performance," "specifications," and "quality" (see also Masayasu Tanaka 1985):

   1) A function is an operation, use, or role that helps the target product (or subsystem or component) achieve the goals that have been set for it. Put more simply, it is the answer to questions such as "what does the product do?" or "what is the product for?"

   2) Performance is the level to which the target functions have been implemented.

   3) The JIS (Japanese Industrial Standards) define specifications as the particular shape, structure, dimensions, ingredients, capabilities, precision, performance, manufacturing methods, and/or testing methods required of materials, products, equipment, or tools. Accordingly, specifications include specific items or restrictions (including external restrictions such as legal regulations and in-house restrictions such as company regulations) that the manufacturer places upon its products to meet the specific requirements of customers (such as certain performance features, shapes, structures, etc.). When broadly defined, specifications includes the concept of performance (degree to which functions are implemented).

   Functions and specifications are different in that functions mainly concern abstract, qualitative items, whereas specifications mainly concern concrete, quantitative items. The VE approach seeks to make improvement plans easy to consider from a variety of perspectives, and qualitative "functions" are easier to consider in this way than are quantitative "specifications."

4) Quality consists of all of the performance features that are evaluated when determining whether the target product or service fulfills all of its use objectives. Specifically, quality is defined in terms of quality characteristics. For example, the quality of an ordinary fluorescent lamp (used for lighting) is typically based on quality characteristics such as power consumption, width, length, plug size and shape, starting characteristics, light flux maintenance, durability, clasp strength, light color, and appearance. Thus, quality is a general concept that refers to characteristics and performance features, and to study quality we must break this concept down into the above kinds of quality characteristics (also called quality elements). This breakdown and analysis of quality is called quality deployment. In everyday language, we tend to refer to certain quality elements (such as specific performance features or capabilities) as simply "qualities."

3. See also Masayasu Tanaka 1985, p. 65.

Part III

Cost Estimation System

"Which of you, desiring to build a tower, does not first sit down and count the cost, whether he has enough to complete it?"

—*Luke 14:28*

The cost estimation system described in Part III was created with reference to Hashimoto and Miyata (1988). However, the application software for this system was created by the author during the editing process, using a spreadsheet macro language.

21

Estimation of Direct Materials Costs

The formula "unit cost of materials × amount of materials consumed per product" can be used to estimate direct materials costs. To estimate this unit cost and the amount consumed, unit costs for each type of material must be gathered and prepared as basic data. Next, the types of materials required for the product are selected and their unit costs are checked, so that the amount consumed (also referred to below as the material investment amount or material supply amount) can be estimated. Below, we will see how a computer can be used to efficiently select from a wide array of materials to meet the design needs of a particular product.

Preparing Basic Data for Materials Cost Estimations: Material Unit Cost Master List Data

As a preliminary requirement for estimating materials costs, a *material unit cost master list* must be prepared (see the example shown in Figure 21-1). The steps for creating the material unit cost master list are described below.

Step 1: Establish material codes

• Register codes for categories of materials.

Use the same material categories as are used for accounting, namely: (1) raw material costs, (2) purchased part costs, (3) fuel costs, (4) factory consumable costs, and (5) costs for replacing worn tools, dies, etc.

• Register material codes and material names.

Material codes tend to get long when there is a wide variety of material types. Therefore, it is a good idea to devise ideographic

Material Unit Cost Master List (for Rods)

Material code	Material name	Purchasing code	Dimensions (mm)			Material unit cost (¥)	Scrap unit price (¥)	Relative density (kg)	Weight (kg)
			a	b	c				
1022020701	S20C	1	10.00	5500		100	10	7.85	3.39
1022020702	S20C	1	12.00	5500		100	10	7.85	4.88
1022020703	S20C	1	14.00	5500		100	10	7.85	6.64
1022020704	S20C	1	16.00	5500		100	10	7.85	8.68
1022020705	S20C	1	18.00	5500		100	10	7.85	10.98
1022020706	S20C	1	20.00	5500		100	10	7.85	13.56
1022020707	S20C	1	22.00	5500		100	10	7.85	16.40
1022020708	S20C	1	25.00	5500		100	10	7.85	21.18
1022020709	S20C	1	28.00	5500		100	10	7.85	26.57
1022020710	S20C	1	32.00	5500		100	10	7.85	34.71
1022020711	S20C	1	36.00	5500		100	10	7.85	43.92
1022020712	S20C	1	40.00	5500		100	10	7.85	54.23
1022020713	S20C	1	45.00	5500		100	10	7.85	68.63
1022020714	S20C	1	50.00	5500		100	10	7.85	84.73
1022020715	S20C	1	60.00	5500		100	10	7.85	122.01
1022020716	S20C	1	70.00	5500		100	10	7.85	166.07
1022020717	S20C	1	80.00	5500		100	10	7.85	216.91
1022020718	S20C	1	90.00	5500		100	10	7.85	274.53
1022020719	S20C	1	100.00	5500		100	10	7.85	338.92
1022020720	S20C	1	110.00	5500		100	10	7.85	410.10
1022020721	S20C	1	120.00	5500		100	10	7.85	488.05
1022020722	S20C	1	130.00	5500		100	10	7.85	572.78
1022020723	S20C	1	140.00	5500		100	10	7.85	664.29
1022020724	S20C	1	160.00	5500		100	10	7.85	867.64
1022020725	S20C	1	180.00	5500		100	10	7.85	1098.11
1022020726	S20C	1	200.00	5500		100	10	7.85	1355.70

Figure 21-1. Material Unit Cost Master List

material codes. For example, if we use the JIS symbols for material names in material codes, we can avoid having to register material names. Figure 21-2 lists various material symbols established in the JIS standards.

• Register material dimensions (and dimensional units).

Indicating material dimensions is important because unit prices differ among materials having different types of dimensional measurements, and only the most suitable and cost-effective materials should be chosen. Be sure to indicate the dimensional unit (mm, cm, m, etc.). The following formulas can be used to measure the dimensions of certain types of materials:

Coils: Thickness × width
Blocks and boards: Thickness × width × length

Step 2: Register unit costs

• Purchased part unit cost = purchased part unit price + handling costs (administrative cost of purchase + processing and shipping + cargo handling + insurance + tax).

Symbol for material type	Tensile strength	Tensile testing						Bending test		
		Expansion rate (%)						Bending angle	Inner diameter	
		Thickness: from 1.2 mm to 1.6 mm	Thickness: from 1.6 mm to 2.0 mm	Thickness: from 2.0 mm to 2.5 mm	Thickness: from 2.5 mm to 3.2 mm	Thickness: from 3.2 mm to 4.0 mm	Thickness: from 4.0 mm or more		Thickness: up to 3.1 mm	Thickness: 3.2 mm or more
SPHC	28 or more	27 or more	29 or more	29 or more	29 or more	31 or more	31 or more	180°	Adhesion	Thickness × 0.5
SPHD	28 or more	30 or more	32 or more	33 or more	35 or more	37 or more	39 or more	180°	Adhesion	Adhesion
SPHE	28 or more	31 or more	33 or more	35 or more	37 or more	39 or more	41 or more	180°	Adhesion	Adhesion

Figure 21-2. JIS Material Names

Material subcosts (purchasing office costs and costs for acceptance inspection, sorting, handling, storage, etc.) may have to be added in.

If the above handling costs and subcosts are not included in the purchased part unit cost, they are instead accounted for as processing costs.

• Register scrap unit costs.
• Register the unit of measurement (t, kg, g, piece, etc.) used for material unit costs.

Step 3: Update unit costs

Material unit costs and scrap costs tend to fluctuate frequently. Also, new materials appear on the market every now and then. Such changes can be entered on the material unit cost master list using (1) the batch update method, whereby all of the cost categories and purchasing categories affected by the changes are extracted as a batch and their unit costs are revised, or (2) the incidental update method, whereby revisions are made for specific unit costs as changes occur.

Step 4: Register relative densities of materials

Registering the relative densities of materials enables us to calculate their weights (see Figure 21-3).

Cast iron	7.21	Cast brass	8.10	Cast nickel	8.29
Wrought iron	7.71	6-4 brass	8.20	Nickel plate	8.69
Steel (average)	7.87	7-3 brass	8.30	Cast aluminum	2.57
Cast steel	7.85	Brass plate	8.45	Aluminum plate	2.68
Non-steel	7.78	Brass wire	8.56	Magnesium	1.74
Cast copper	8.62	Gunmetal (bronze)	8.74	White metal	7.32
Annealed copper	8.93	Cast lead	11.37	Electron (alloy)	1.82
Sheet metal	8.82	Lead plate	11.43	Duralumin	2.80
Wire	8.90	Phosphor bronze	8.60	Gold	21.52
		Aluminum bronze	7.79	Platinum	21.52
		Cast zinc	6.87	Silver	10.52
		Zinc plate	7.21	Mercury	13.60
				Tin	7.42

Figure 21-3. Relative Densities of Common Metals

Steps in Calculating Materials Costs

Step 1: Select the materials

Select the materials (substances) that best suit the product's type, functions, and quality grade.

Step 2: Calculate the product's area and volume per unit

Two methods for calculating this quantity are (1) combining various basic shapes and (2) mechanically (automatically) calculating the area on a computer after inputting the drawing via a scanner. With the second method, the computer reads the number of dots in the scanned reduced-image drawing and counts the dots to determine the area. This method can be employed when the scanner is linked to a CAD system.

In addition, the actual weight of a product that is still at the prototype testing stage can be measured to estimate the final product's weight or, even more simply, the material weight can be calculated in reverse by starting from the yield rate or scrap weight.

Step 3: Calculate the product weight

Product weight = product volume × relative density of materials

Step 4: Determine material shapes, sizes, and quantities.

Input the shapes (sheet, block, rod, pipe, etc.) of the materials to be used and calculate the quantity of materials.

For example, if the material is to undergo a blanking process (such as for pressed items), a blank layout must first be made for the sheets to be pressed. To make a blank layout, the outline of the product to be blanked is aligned upon a tie plate (made of coils or straps). The tie plate's width, feed-in rate, and angle of inclination must be adjusted to provide the best possible yield with minimal trim loss.

The blank layout can be done manually or via computer-based simulation. The simulation results can be used to determine the optimum material dimensions. For instance, a simulation could determine net material dimensions (thickness × width × length) with minimal trim loss from the sides and corners of the sheets to be pressed.

However, the amount of clearance between products when blanking materials in actual press processes must be considered, as must the amount of material consumed as chips in actual machining processes.

Step 5: Select materials for optimum yield

Example of method for calculating material use patterns:

Patterns for material types:
   three types of patterns of standard-size steel plates and 20 types of patterns of semi-standard sheets.
Patterns for shapes of purchased materials:
   three types of patterns for coils, standard-size plates, and semi-standard sheets.
Patterns for using materials:
   two types of patterns, one for using products vertically and one for using them horizontally.

Therefore, the total number of pattern types is

$$(3 + 20) \times 3 \times 2 = 138$$

We can now select the materials that will have the highest yield rate by arranging the material dimensions (width × length, etc.) that have been determined based on optimum yield via the above steps (i.e., steps to determine material shapes, sizes, and quantities) for each of the 138 types of material use patterns. Conventionally, the optimum materials have been defined as the least expensive materials based on the formula "material feed-in amount (weight used) × purchase price." However, it is also possible to use a simpler method by calculating the optimum materials based on optimum yield, as described above.

Figure 21-4 lists selections from three types of stock—semi-standard length coils (abbreviated as Semi CO), semi-standard

NO 2 Material Cost Estimations	LELEL ✳Low-level Item No. Value: 20 Target total: 1,800			
Item No. FPA110	Monthly volume: 208	Material weight	Product weight	Total material cost
Item Name: Flange A	Production lot: 1500			

NO	Cate-gory	Purchasing code	CODE	Material name and size	Unit	Yield	Feed-in and loss	Unit	Value
1	1	1							
			Products 1 piece per material unit	2.60 × 510 × 710	mm				

	Material	Products per material unit	Pieces/ months	Kg	Yield	
1	Semi CO	1524 × 510	2	104	1652	93%
2	Semi CO	1524 × 510	2	104	1652	93%
3	Semi CO	1524 × 510	2	104	1652	93%
4	Semi sheet	3200 × 1524	12	17	1728	89%
5	Semi sheet	2800 × 1524	10	21	1814	85%
6	Semi CO	1219 × 710	2	104	1840	84%
7	Semi CO	1219 × 710	2	104	1840	84%
8	Semi sheet	3048 × 1524	10	21	1975	78%
9	Semi CO	914 × 510	1	208	1982	78%

Coil (Slit width: 710)

1524

24 types of cut sheets and 12 types of coils can be used

Position = [↓↑ + < ↵]   Special size = [✳]   Material selection NO

Source: Hashimoto and Miyata 1988, p. 71.

Figure 21-4. Selection of High-Yield Materials

length sheets (Semi sheet), and standard-size steel plates (Std plate), starting with the highest yield rate so that the optimum-use material is listed first. (Actually, standard-size steel plates have such low yield rates that they are not included in this list.)

Step 6: Calculate material feed-in amount (weight)

The weight of steel-plate materials can be calculated as follows:

1. Basic weight = 0.785g (weight of piece 1 mm thick and 1 cm^2 in area [= 0.1 cm^3])

2. Unit weight = (1) × thickness (mm) × 0.01 ... rounded off to 4 significant digits
3. Steel plate area = width (mm) × length (mm) ... rounded off to 4 significant digits
4. Weight per piece = (2) × (3) rounded off to 3 significant digits
5. Weight per bundle = (4) × number of plates per bundle ... rounded off to nearest integer (kg)
6. Total weight = sum of bundle weights ... rounded off to nearest integer (kg)

JIS standard JIS Z 8401 was used as the basis for rounding off numbers in these calculations.

Step 7: Calculate cost for feed-in materials

Starting with the weight calculation shown as (6) in Step 6, calculate the material feed-in weight per product unit, also referred to as simply the material feed-in rate, to obtain the material feed-in cost.

For example, if two products can be obtained from one steel plate:

$$\text{Material feed-in weight per product unit} = \frac{\text{(weight of one plate)}}{\text{2 units}}$$

$$\text{Material feed-in cost} = \text{material feed-in weight} \times \text{material unit cost}$$

Step 8: Calculate yield rate and scrap value

The yield rate is defined as the amount of fed-in material that is actually transferred to (i.e., used in) products, as opposed to scrap material that is not used in products. There are several types of scrap:

• Operation-related scrap: trimmed-off materials and other scrap as specified in drawings

- Off-spec loss: trimmed-off materials and other scrap as generated in production processes when production does not follow specifications in drawings
- Reduction loss: Fed-in materials that are vaporized or liquefied and therefore do not get used in products

Use the following formulas for these calculations:

$$\text{Yield rate} \quad = \text{product weight} \div \text{feed-in weight}$$

$$\text{Scrap weight} = \text{feed-in weight} - \text{product weight}$$
$$= \text{feed-in weight} \times (1 - \text{yield rate})$$

$$\text{Scrap value} \quad = \text{scrap weight} \times \text{scrap unit cost}$$

Step 9: Calculate estimated materials costs

$$\text{Materials costs} = \text{feed-in material costs} - \text{scrap value}$$

Figure 21-5 shows examples of the above calculations. The numerical values in the figure were calculated as follows:

Yield rate
= part weight ÷ feed-in weight
= (8.04 ÷ 24.60) × 100 = 33%

Scrap
= feed-in weight − part weight
= 24.60 − 8.04 = 16.56

Estimated materials cost
= feed-in material cost − scrap value
= feed-in weight × material unit cost
+ additional material cost − scrap (weight)
× scrap unit cost
= (24.60 × 100.0) + 1,230.2 − (16.56 × 10) = 3,524.6

Materials Cost Estimation Form

Part code	3G1A6792	Feed-in materials	¥3,690.5
Part name	Bearing support	Scrap value	165.6
Function priority level	Low		

Production lot	20	Estimated materials cost	¥3,524.9

No.	Cost item category	Purchasing category	Material code	Material name	Material dimensions			No. of products obtained
					a (mm)	b (mm)	c (mm)	
1	1	1	1022020723	S20C	140.0	5,500.0	0.0	27

Left side

Feed-in weight (Kg)	Part weight (Kg)	Yield rate (%)	Material unit cost (Yen/Kg)	Scrap unit cost (Yen/Kg)	Feed-in material cost (Yen)	Material sub-cost (Yen)	Scrap value (Yen)	Quantity
24.60	8.04	33%	100.0	10.0	2,460.3	1,230.2	165.6	1

Right side

Figure 21-5. Form for Estimating Materials Costs

22

Estimation of Processing Cost Rates

Steps and Objectives for Estimating Processing Costs

Processing costs for products undergoing design and development can be estimated as follows for each type of product and for each process:

Product-specific or process-specific estimated processing cost	=	product-specific and process-specific processing cost rate per hour	×	estimated processing time for product or process

To enable such calculations, process-specific and equipment-specific processing cost rates must first be established along with other basic data. Establishing these rates is the theme of this chapter.

Before we can estimate process- and equipment-specific processing times, we must prepare a *table of standard times* for work elements concerning each process or equipment unit. The preparation of such time tables will be the theme of Chapter 23.

After carrying out process design based on these time tables, we can select the most appropriate production processes and equipment for the target product and can also estimate the processing time at each process. Process design will be the theme of Chapter 24.

Processing Cost Rate and Equipment Cost Rate

Processing Cost Rate Categories

Process-specific processing cost rates must be predicted for all processing costs except equipment depreciation costs, including direct labor costs and indirect manufacturing costs. In addition, equipment-specific equipment cost rates must also be obtained to enable estimation of equipment depreciation costs.

Why must equipment depreciation costs be handled separately in this way? The reason is that, as part of target costing, accounting practices dictate that cost estimations cannot use equipment acquisition costs based on existing equipment's depreciation value. Instead, cost estimations must use the reacquisition cost (the amount that must be spent to buy the same equipment now), which is based on the estimated depreciation value for the planned product. Even when the equipment acquisition cost is for the same equipment model, the cost can change over time and can also change depending on which accounting method is used (the fixed percentage method or the fixed installment method).

In contrast to this, financial accounting figures provide the basis for the cost items for processing costs not related to equipment depreciation.

The processing cost rate should be divided into process-specific variable costs and fixed costs.

The equipment cost rate naturally falls under the category of fixed processing costs. The purpose of separating variable cost rates and fixed cost rates is to enable simulation of the profit plan using breakeven analysis.

We can summarize the above as follows:

$$
\begin{matrix}
\text{Product-specific} \\
\text{or process-specific} \\
\text{variable} \\
\text{processing costs}
\end{matrix}
=
\begin{matrix}
\text{process-specific} \\
\text{variable cost} \\
\text{rate per hour}
\end{matrix}
\times
\begin{matrix}
\text{product-specific} \\
\text{estimated} \\
\text{labor-hours per} \\
\text{product unit}
\end{matrix}
$$

$$
\begin{matrix}
\text{Product-specific or} \\
\text{process-specific} \\
\text{fixed processing} \\
\text{costs}
\end{matrix}
=
\begin{matrix}
\text{process-specific} \\
\text{fixed cost rate} \\
\text{per hour} \\
\times \text{ product-specific} \\
\text{estimated} \\
\text{labor-hours per} \\
\text{product unit}
\end{matrix}
+
\begin{matrix}
\text{equipment-specific} \\
\text{equipment cost} \\
\text{rate per hour} \\
\times \text{ product-specific} \\
\text{estimated time} \\
\text{per product unit}
\end{matrix}
$$

Processing Cost Rate Absorption Standards

Product-specific processing costs are often calculated based on the formula "employee rate × labor-hours" where labor-hours = takt time per operator per workpiece × number of operators at process.

In other words, labor-hours are counted between two points in time: the time when the product or workpiece enters the process and the time when it leaves the process. To be precise, it includes any changeover time and idle time that occurs between these two points.

With recent advances in factory automation, machine hours (a.k.a. equipment time) have come to replace labor-hours in these calculations as machines have taken over operations that had been performed manually. Likewise, the number of machines is considered instead of the number of operators. However, even today many processing costs are proportional to labor-hours. In addition to labor-hours and machine hours, there are various other standards used to calculate the absorption of processing cost rates.

Rate Master List

The following items should be registered in a *rate master list* to be used for calculations of processing cost rates.

Process names and codes

The process units used to categorize processing cost rates correspond to the cost center units used in cost management. There are two kinds of cost centers: (1) sections of the organization that are responsible for cost minimization management and (2) sections based on function-specific activities. In factories, the organizational units are made up of teams led by supervisors.

Once the processes have been categorized in this manner, each process is assigned a code. Each process code should include a job category code. Figure 22-1 lists JIS-based codes for processing in metal machining processes. If we use a four-digit process code, we might use the JIS code as the first digit to indicate the job category (except for the two-digit code "RL" in this case).

Equipment names and codes

Equipment codes should be established separately from the job category codes described above. However, when selecting equipment during process design, the process designers need a simple way to determine what kinds of equipment are used at various processes, so in this case it is useful to draw a relation between the process and the equipment (a method for doing this will be described later). Basically, any type of code can be used as the equipment code.

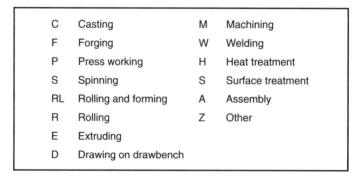

C	Casting	M	Machining
F	Forging	W	Welding
P	Press working	H	Heat treatment
S	Spinning	S	Surface treatment
RL	Rolling and forming	A	Assembly
R	Rolling	Z	Other
E	Extruding		
D	Drawing on drawbench		

Figure 22-1. Job Category Codes (based on JIS B0122)

Estimation of Department-Specific Processing Cost Rates

The method used to calculate the estimated rate for process-specific processing costs is the same as that used to calculate estimated rates for accounting purposes (for further description of this method, see Figure 14-3 in Chapter 14).

Process-specific estimated rate for variable processing costs

$$= \frac{\text{process-specific annual estimated rate for variable processing costs}}{\begin{array}{c}\text{standard values for absorption of process-specific} \\ \text{annual estimated processing costs} \\ \text{(labor-hours, time, weight, square meters, etc.)}\end{array}}$$

Process-specific estimated rate for fixed processing costs

$$= \frac{\begin{array}{c}\text{process-specific annual} \\ \text{estimated rate for fixed} \\ \text{processing costs}\end{array} - \begin{array}{c}\text{process-specific} \\ \text{estimated equipment} \\ \text{depreciation cost}\end{array}}{\begin{array}{c}\text{standard values for absorption of process-specific} \\ \text{annual estimated processing costs} \\ \text{(labor-hours, time, weight, square meters, etc.)}\end{array}}$$

Figure 22-2 shows an example of a rate master list for process-specific processing costs.

Estimation of Equipment Cost Rates

Equipment cost rates—i.e., the time-based depreciation cost of equipment—can be calculated as follows:

Equipment-specific equipment depreciation cost rate

$$= \frac{\text{reacquisition price of target equipment}}{\begin{array}{c}\text{use life of target} \\ \text{equipment (in years)}\end{array} \times \begin{array}{c}\text{operating time} \\ \text{per year}\end{array} \times \begin{array}{c}\text{no. of} \\ \text{shifts}\end{array} \times \begin{array}{c}\text{operating} \\ \text{rate}\end{array}}$$

The elements on the right side of this equation are described below.

Direct department	Process	Unit of measurement	Annual estimated rate for variable processing costs	Annual estimated rate for fixed processing costs	Estimated equipment depreciation cost	Unit for annual estimates	Estimated processing cost rates	
							Variable cost rate	Fixed cost rate
Team 1	Lathe	Labor-hours	56,683,000	37,580,000	16,793,000	20,000	47.2	17.3
Team 1	NC lathe	Labor-hours	57,533,000	35,980,000	15,853,000	20,000	47.9	16.8
Team 1	Vertical milling machine	Labor-hours	59,404,000	37,341,000	15,324,000	20,000	49.5	18.3
Team 1	Horizontal milling machine	Labor-hours	59,344,000	37,146,000	15,314,000	20,000	49.5	18.2
Team 1	NC vertical milling machine	Labor-hours	57,052,000	36,440,000	17,454,000	20,000	47.5	15.8
Team 1	NC horizontal milling machine	Labor-hours	59,288,000	39,608,000	18,291,000	20,000	49.4	17.8
Team 1	Drill press	Labor-hours	56,407,000	38,381,000	17,845,000	20,000	47.0	17.1
Team 1	Vertical boring machine	Labor-hours	57,747,000	38,827,000	16,544,000	20,000	48.1	18.6
Team 1	Horizontal boring machine	Labor-hours	56,691,000	36,406,000	18,388,000	20,000	47.2	15.0
Team 1	NC vertical boring machine	Labor-hours	58,614,000	38,677,000	19,478,000	20,000	48.8	16.0
Team 1	NV horizontal boring machine	Labor-hours	55,830,000	35,414,000	15,807,000	20,000	46.5	16.3
Team 1	Machining center	Labor-hours	56,610,000	39,872,000	18,589,000	20,000	47.2	17.7
Team 1	Cylindrical grinder	Labor-hours	58,453,000	37,825,000	17,146,000	20,000	48.7	17.2
Team 1	NC cylindrical grinder	Labor-hours	58,589,000	39,540,000	19,909,000	20,000	48.8	16.4
Team 1	Internal grinder	Labor-hours	58,741,000	36,567,000	19,436,000	20,000	49.0	14.3
Team 1	Surface grinder	Labor-hours	57,137,000	38,641,000	15,696,000	20,000	47.6	19.1
Team 1	Honing machine	Labor-hours	55,917,000	38,513,000	19,346,000	20,000	46.6	16.0
Team 1	Centerless grinder	Labor-hours	58,491,000	37,336,000	16,810,000	20,000	48.7	17.1
Team 1	Inspection proces	Labor-hours	56,219,000	38,217,000	15,986,000	20,000	46.8	18.5
Team 2	Cutting	Labor-hours	57,284,000	39,917,000	17,656,000	20,000	47.7	18.6
Team 2	Punching	Labor-hours	66,580,000	53,563,000	6,483,000	20,000	55.5	39.2
Team 2	Bending	Labor-hours	66,580,000	53,563,000	6,483,000	20,000	55.5	39.2
Team 2	Restricting	Labor-hours	66,580,000	53,563,000	6,483,000	20,000	55.5	39.2
Team 3	Lathe turning	Labor-hours	25,416,000	22,961,000	1,745,000	12,000	35.5	29.5
Team 3	Drilling	Labor-hours	25,416,000	22,961,000	1,745,000	12,000	35.5	29.5
Team 3	Boring	Labor-hours	25,416,000	22,961,000	1,745,000	12,000	35.3	29.5
Team 3	Milling	Labor-hours	25,416,000	22,961,000	1,745,000	12,000	35.3	29.5

Figure 22-2. Rate Master List for Process-Specific Processing Costs

Reacquisition price

As mentioned earlier, cost estimates made for target costing cannot rely on previous acquisition prices but must be instead based on the cost of repurchasing the target equipment. Moreover, the depreciation cost must be calculated based on the fixed installment method with a residual (scrap) value of zero.

Use life (in years)

The use life of equipment as defined by Japan's corporate tax laws for various types of fixed assets provides a close approximation of actual use life, and consequently many companies use this definition. However, when estimating costs as part of target costing, the exact use life of equipment is required. Specifically, the use life of production equipment is equivalent to the life cycles of all of the products manufactured by the equipment, so that, for example, equipment used to manufacture two generations (successive models) of a product would have a use life equal to the two product model lives.

Annual operating time and number of shifts

With overtime included, the annual operating time averages from 2,000 to 2,100 hours per year at most Japanese manufacturing companies. This is the average for single-shift manufacturing schedules. When there are two shifts, the annual operating time is multiplied by two.

Operating rate

In actuality, few if any companies have equipment operation times that equal their labor-based annual operating time, since that would require 100 percent breakdown-free equipment operation. If a factory has an annual total of 2,100 working hours, it is more realistic to estimate that equipment downtime due to low demand, faults, maintenance, and other causes will claim about 20 percent of those hours, which means an operating rate of about 80 percent. Therefore, the formula for estimating the equipment operating time rate must include "labor-based annual operating time × equipment operating rate."

Figure 22-3 lists equipment rate calculation elements and calculation results for various types of company departments and equipment.

Cost Estimations for Dies, Jigs, and Tools

Often, metal dies, jigs, and tools must be custom-made for particular planned products. Therefore, the depreciation costs of such devices are not included in either the processing cost rate or the equipment cost rate, but instead are directly tied to the planned product and depreciated as direct operating costs. Accordingly, their cost estimations are calculated as follows:

$$\text{Die/jig/tool costs per product unit} = \frac{\text{acquisition price}}{\text{estimated production volume during product's model life}}$$

Rate Master List for Equipment Costs

Team	Equipment code	Equipment name	Mo/Yr acquired	Acquisition price	Use life	Shifts	No. of units	Operating rate (%)	Depreciation cost	Equipment cost rate (2000)
1	1101	Ordinary lathe A	74/8	5,700,000	12	1	1	80	427,500	4.95
1	1102	Ordinary lathe B	74/7	5,700,000	12	1	1	80	427,500	4.95
1	1103	Ordinary lathe C	86/10	5,900,000	12	1	1	80	442,500	5.12
1	1104	NC lathe A	78/5	4,971,000	12	1	1	80	372,825	4.32
1	1105	NC lathe B	78/9	5,490,000	12	1	1	80	411,750	4.77
1	1106	NC lathe C	85/2	6,583,000	12	1	1	80	493,725	5.71
1	1107	Combined lathe A	80/6	9,460,000	12	1	1	80	709,500	8.21
1	1108	Combined lathe B	89/10	8,980,000	12	1	1	80	673,500	7.80
1	1109	Vertical milling machine A	77/11	7,657,000	12	1	1	80	574,275	6.65
1	1110	Vertical milling machine B	78/8	8,700,000	12	1	1	80	652,500	7.55
1	1111	Horizontal milling machine A	77/8	6,540,000	12	1	1	80	490,500	5.68
1	1112	Horizontal milling machine B	83/6	7,453,000	12	1	1	80	558,975	6.47
1	1113	Table-top drill press A	82/6	5,430,000	12	1	1	80	407,250	4.71
1	1114	Table-top drill press B	80/1	6,230,000	12	1	1	80	467,250	5.41
1	1115	Table-top drill press C	87/4	3,400,000	12	1	1	80	255,000	2.95
1	1116	Vertical drill press A	76/4	4,500,000	12	1	1	80	337,500	3.91
1	1117	Vertical drill press B	76/9	5,150,000	12	1	1	80	386,250	4.47
2	2001	150-T blank	71/7	15,000,000	12	1	1	80	1,125,000	13.02
2	2002	110 TLP	75/7	8,000,000	12	1	1	80	600,000	6.94
2	2003	200 T	85/6	24,260,000	12	1	1	80	1,819,500	21.06
2	2004	150-T coil	80/9	13,885,000	12	1	1	80	1,041,375	12.05
2	2005	75 T	78/11	3,800,000	12	1	1	80	285,000	3.30
2	2006	35 T	55/7	484,000	12	1	1	80	36,300	0.42
3	3101	150 PUL	87/4	9,300,000	12	1	1	80	697,500	8.07
3	3102	Lathe No. 1	71/5	1,800,000	12	1	1	80	135,000	1.56
3	3103	Lathe No. 2	75/6	3,000,000	12	1	1	80	225,000	2.60
3	3104	Lathe No. 3	75/10	3,100,000	12	1	1	80	232,500	2.69

Figure 22-3. Rate Master List for Equipment Costs

23

Time Tables for Estimating Labor-Hours

While cost estimations at the unit component level or product level are a necessary part of target costing, estimation of processing costs at the level of individual processes is a prerequisite for this, and to estimate processing costs, we must first have standard time tables for each process.

As explained in the previous chapter, processing costs are estimated using the formula "rate of processing cost × labor-hours (i.e., time)." However, labor-hours cannot be readily estimated unless we first have a time table, which is a database of time values.

Labor-hours are defined as the average amount of time consumed by operators who perform tasks using standard work methods. Such time amounts are called *standard times*. Standard times consist of the following elements:

$$\begin{array}{c}\text{Standard} \\ \text{time}\end{array} = \begin{array}{c}\text{basic} \\ \text{time}\end{array} + \begin{array}{c}\text{allowance} \\ \text{time}\end{array} = \begin{array}{c}\text{basic} \\ \text{time}\end{array} \times \begin{array}{c}(1 + \text{allowance} \\ \text{time rate})\end{array}$$

261

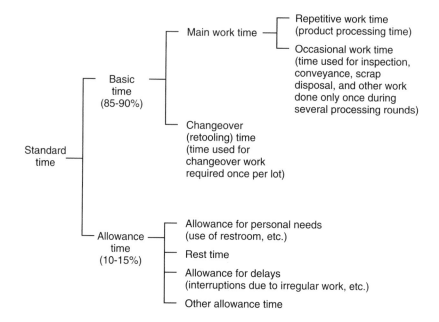

Figure 23-1. Elements in Standard Time

Figure 23-1 diagrams the elements that make up the basic time and the allowance time.

The following sections describe methods for creating data bases of standard times for specific processes and work elements.

Creation of Standard Time Data Bases

There are two methods for creating time tables.

IE-Style Combination Method

Using this method, we first use the PTS (predetermined time standard) method to obtain standard times at the "motion" level, then apply these times as a database from which we combine standard times for each work element. Next, we calculate the standard times for each process by combining the standard times for work elements at each process.

After that, we obtain the standard-time data for each intermediary product and then for each product.

Statistical Estimation Method

With this method, we conduct a multiple regression analysis of the time requirement values for the process's work elements and the factors (called *drivers*) that influence these values, to estimate their interrelations. Therefore, the resulting table of standard times is obtained using a regressive method rather than a tabular compilation method.

This method is described in more detail below.

Application Example of Multiple Regression Analysis

Take as an example a secondary press working process which is performed by one operator. The drivers for this process are the material's major dimensions (X_1), weight (X_2), applied pressure (X_3), and the degree of difficulty in processing (X_4). The standard time (or estimated processing time) Y for this one-operator secondary press working process can be expressed in a regression equation as follows:

$$Y = 0.04615X_1 + 2.59750X_2 - 0.04949X_3 + 9.07557X_4 + 76.43219$$

Reliability value = 0.95649

The reliability value in this regression equation is expressed as a coefficient of determination. As such, it is double the correlation coefficient between the actual data for the time value Y and the theoretical value obtained through regression analysis. Experience has shown that if this coefficient of determination is 0.85 or greater, there will not be any significant reliability problems.

The following are ways to ensure a coefficient value of at least 0.85.

(a) Effective selection of drivers (addition or deletion): Although drivers that are correlative should be selected, principal component analysis can be done to narrow the range of drivers.

(b) Deletion of abnormal values: Create a graph to compare actual values with estimated values and delete data that have large gaps between the two (these are indicated as relative errors, not absolute error).

(c) Addition of data

(d) Restriction of applicable range: When using linear regression analysis, the actual data for time values may change quickly if the driver data values exceed a certain range. In such cases, the driver data should be divided into at least two ranges and separate regression equations should be worked out for each range.

Steps in Creating a Standard Time Table Using Regression Equations

Step 1: Create a Table of Contents for the Standard Time Table

(a) Register processes: Register the codes and names of the target processes. For example, JIS codes can be used for the process codes.

(b) Register equipment: Register the codes and names of the target equipment. The JIS pictographic code can be used for these codes.

(c) Register work elements: Register the codes and names of the work elements that go into the standard times. It is best to divide the work elements into process-based groups before assigning their codes.

Step 2: Register the Relations between Processes and Equipment and between Equipment and Work Elements

Relations between processes and equipment

Register the names of the equipment used in each process in a matrix format. When certain processes are selected during the process design, a list can be made of the equipment used for the processes.

Relations between equipment and work elements

Register the names of the work elements used in each equipment in a matrix format. When certain equipment are selected during the process design, a list can be made of the work elements used for the equipment.

Step 3: Register the Drivers

Select and list the drivers that correspond to the time values for each work element registered at Step 2. A list of drivers must be obtained from the drawings before the time values for the work elements can be obtained during process design. The codes and names of these drivers should also be registered.

Step 4: Register Equipment Capacity Data

In Figure 23-2, the minimum and maximum dimensions—length, width, height, weight, etc.—for the material (steel plate) used in a press working process are registered on an *equipment capacity master list.*

Dept.	Team 1	Equipment name	150-T press

Code	Equipment capacity factor	Condition	Capacity value	Unit
101	Pressure	< =	150.00	t
102	Bolster dimension (vertical)	< =	900.00	mm
103	Bolster dimension (horizontal)	< =	1500.00	mm
104	Slide dimension (vertical)	< =	800.00	mm
105	Slide dimension (horizontal)	< =	1500.00	mm
106	Die height	< =	550.00	mm
107	Cushion pressure	< =	20.00	t
108	No. of strokes	< =	25.00	spm

Source: See Hashimoto and Miyata 1988, p.132

Figure 23-2. Equipment Capacity Master List

This kind of equipment capacity master list should be prepared in advance, since it enables us to automatically tell whether the equipment selected during process design can be used to process the target parts or products.

Step 5: Register Numerical Data for Drivers and Time Data for Work Elements

The time data for work elements can be measured using either the stopwatch method or the PTS method, or previous actual data can be used. Refer to the example shown in Figure 23-3, where actual data are listed concerning drivers for a press (major dimensions, weight, pressure, processing difficulty) and where data from past instances concerning press operation times have been registered.

In this example, data from results can be gathered for the time data and driver data during process design and when estimating labor-hours. Also, if there is a table of standard times for each work element that has already been made using the IE-style method, these times can be gathered as process-specific times to facilitate estimation of regression equations used as the basis for process-specific standard time tables.

Step 6: Create a Time Table

When we use the gathered time data and driver data in multiple regression analysis, we are able to create a time table based on regression equations. An example of this was described above in the section titled "Application example of multiple regression analysis."

Code No.	3G		Time unit			No. of data items	
Document name			No. of drivers		4		

Regression equation: $y = 0.04615X_1 \div 2.59750X_2 - 0.04949X_3 + 9.07557X_4 + 76.43219$

X*	Driver code	Driver name	Applicable range		Unit	↓ input
X_1	L	Major dimensions	40	900	mm	600
X_2	W	Weight	0.15	5	kg	4.1
X_3	PRS	Pressure	20	200	t	150
X_4	DIF	Processing difficulty	1	6	d	4
					Actual time	150
					Rate value	100%
					Basic time	150

Regression result:

Y specimen	76.43219			
Standard deviation of evaluation result for Y	4.328057			
$R \times 2$	0.95649			
No. of specimens	15			
Degrees of freedom	10			
X coefficient	0.0461534	2.597502	−0.04949	9.075574
Standard deviation of X coefficient	0.02213946	8.511906	0.037896	3.165982

Time data

No.	X_1	X_2	X_3	X_4	Actual time	Rate value	Basic time
1	900	4.6	20	5	177	100%	177
2	800	4.7	150	6	169.2	100%	169.2
3	700	4.5	150	5	157	100%	157
4	750	4.5	130	5	154	100%	154
5	600	4.3	150	4	145	100%	145
6	750	4.5	150	5	160	100%	160
7	800	4.8	150	5	165	100%	165
8	800	4.8	150	5	168	100%	168
9	550	4.2	100	4	145	100%	145
10	400	3.9	85	3	130	100%	130
11	500	4.3	100	4	145	100%	145
12	450	4.2	100	3	130	100%	130
13	350	3.5	50	2	115	100%	115
14	550	4.3	100	3	130	100%	130
15	600	4.1	150	4	150	100%	150

Figure 23-3. Table of Driver Data, Time Data, and Standard Time Data

24

Process Design, Labor-Hour Estimation, and Processing Cost Estimation for New Products

Role of Production Engineering Department and IE (Industrial Engineering) in Target Costing

VE (value engineering) is a methodology used when considering specific cost-cutting steps as part of target costing. In fact, the detailed steps used in the VE approach closely resemble those used in target costing.

In this chapter, we will examine how the product design department—a key player in VE activities—estimates direct materials costs, which are the biggest cost element among the various manufacturing-related costs. We will also see how they apply VE methods to find alternative materials and fabrication methods that are able to reduce costs.

We will also examine the handling of processing costs—another major cost element in manufacturing-related costs—to see how process-specific processing costs are estimated after the target product or part is designed and after the production engineering department has studied the drawings and carried out process designs to minimize processing costs. The estimated processing cost data are then provided to the product design department.

As they draft the product design drawings, the product design department staff work to achieve cost reduction targets by studying the estimated processing costs and considering various possible fabrication (i.e., manufacturing) methods. In addition, process design managers from the production engineering department seek to apply IE (industrial engineering) techniques to create process designs that minimize costs under the given conditions, and these process design efforts also help to reduce processing costs.

The IE approach seeks to create work systems that combine personnel, materials, and equipment as efficiently as possible.

The IE methods used by process designers include the method engineering techniques that form part of work study. The objective is to identify all operations that comprise the target work process and to eliminate those that are not strictly necessary. After that, they study the remaining operations in detail with a view toward selecting the most efficient work methods. As part of these efforts, they also seek to standardize the equipment, work methods, and working conditions for each work process. They often apply concepts from the just-in-time production system in doing this.

Figure 24-1 outlines how these product design and process design activities fit into the target costing process.

In this chapter, we will study the process design and labor-hour estimation methods that are used to estimate processing costs as part of target costing. Taking the IE approach, the goal is to lower processing costs by designing the most economical manufacturing system, i.e., one that requires the least possible number of processing hours and labor-hours.

The methods introduced in this chapter do not include process design automation techniques, such as the use of expert systems, but instead rely upon existing design staff to use existing computer systems to create process designs and estimate labor-hours.

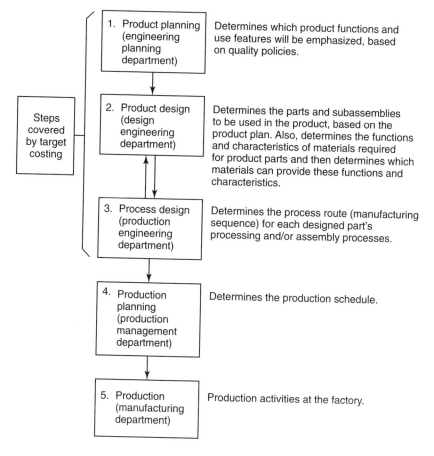

Figure 24-1. Process Design as Part of the Target Costing Process

Significance of Process Design

In process design, information from drawings drafted by the design department (information such as product or part configurations, technical requirements for product performance, etc.) is used as input data for the following activities:

1. Determining manufacturing methods and their sequence
2. Determining manufacturing processes and their sequence

3. Determining manufacturing equipment and their sequence
4. Determining manufacturing operations
5. Estimating operation labor-hours

Determining manufacturing methods involves deciding what kind of manufacturing process is needed for the target product or part (e.g., a cutting process, casting process, or welding and assembly process). In other words, it involves determining the type of process and the sequence of that process in the manufacturing system. Naturally, the next step is to determine what kind of equipment and/or tools will be needed for such a process. The data output from these process design decisions include the types of manufacturing processes, equipment, and tools and their sequence as well as the standard times for each process.

The production engineering department is responsible for process design, but the actual process design work is shared among the production engineering department, the design department, and the manufacturing department, where design data are converted into production data. The design department's chief responsibility in this endeavor is to produce information on the implementation of required performance features and required conditions in the process design for the target product or part. This information, however, does not take into consideration all details of manufacturing, such as relevant conditions or restrictions. It is the manufacturing department's responsibility to consider restrictions concerning the availability of production resources (personnel, materials, and money) and technology, and to produce information regarding how equipment and personnel can be best managed.

The production management department and cost management department can use the information output from process design as basic data for their management tasks. For example, using the information output from the process design, they can design the work processes, establish the work conditions and sequence of work operations, set a work schedule, and otherwise provide work instructions. The data on standard times at each process can also be used as basic data for cost improvement activities.

Their scheduling tasks include creating a manufacturing schedule that incorporates factors such as staff and equipment workloads, delivery deadlines, and work progress conditions. They must also produce an equipment plan that describes the equipment layout and design.

Steps in Process Design and Labor-Hour Estimation

Labor-hour estimates are an element required for estimating processing costs as part of target costing and are part of the output from process design. As mentioned above, how labor-hours are allocated helps determine the flow of manufacturing processes for the planned product or part. Figure 24-2 describes the sequences of steps in carrying out process design and labor-hour estimations.

In the figure, the steps differ depending upon whether the target product requires a completely new design (i.e., is completely unlike previous products) or can instead use a design similar to previous products. (The circled numbers in the figure correspond to the steps described below.)

Steps for New Designs

Step 1. Register Component Parts

Register all components in the product or part for which the process design or labor-hour estimate is to be made. The detailed parts lists should include all subassembly parts.

Step 2. Register Drawing Data

Using drawing data output by the CAD system, register all of the drivers that affect operation times. For example, register the names, codes, and numerical values for items such as the width, clearance, depth, and length (mm) for cutting processes, as well as the weight (kg), the number of stroke holes, and the finishing precision tolerances.

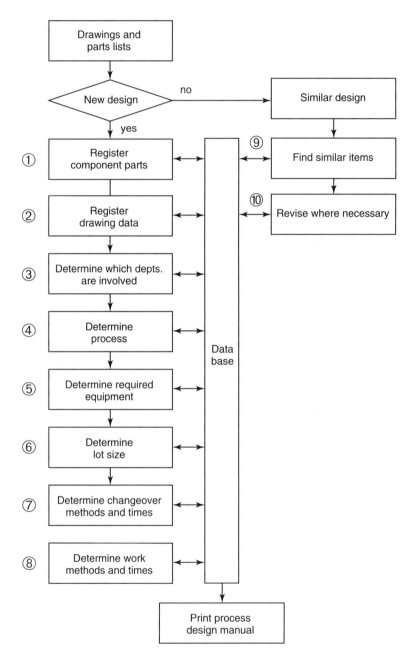

Figure 24-2. Steps in Process Design and Labor-Hour Estimation

Step 3. Select the Relevant Departments and Their Sequence

The "department" in this case is the organizational unit that includes the processes designated when establishing the processing cost rate. For parts manufactured by outside vendors, indicate the type of job (press working, welding, surface processing, etc.). The process designers use a department code or vendor job type code to indicate these organizational units on their drawings.

Step 4. Select Processes and Determine Their Sequence

The processes are under department-specific categories and are the cost centers used to calculate processing cost rates.

Step 5. Select Equipment and Determine the Processing Sequence

For each process selected at Step 4, select the equipment that most efficiently serves the needs of the process. At this point check the equipment capacity data (e.g., the available range of external and internal diameters and lengths) and the drawing data to select equipment that suits the various performance requirements.

Step 6. Determine Lot Sizes for Processes

Determine the production lot size for each process.

Step 7. Determine Changeover Methods and Times

Determine the type of changeover work required for each process, along with the requirements for basic changeover time, personnel, allowance time rate, etc.

$$\begin{matrix} \text{Changeover} \\ \text{time} \end{matrix} = \begin{matrix} \text{basic} \\ \text{changeover time} \end{matrix} \times \begin{matrix} 1 + \text{allowance} \\ \text{time rate} \end{matrix}$$

$$\begin{matrix} \text{Changeover} \\ \text{time} \end{matrix} = \begin{matrix} \text{basic changeover} \\ \text{time} \times \text{no.} \\ \text{of operators} \end{matrix} \times \begin{matrix} 1 + \text{allowance} \\ \text{time rate} \end{matrix}$$

Step 8. Determine the Main Operation Methods and Times

Determine the type of operations to be done at each process, along with the requirements for basic operation time, personnel, allowance time rate, etc.

$$\begin{array}{c} \text{Operation} \\ \text{time} \end{array} = \begin{array}{c} \text{basic} \\ \text{operation time} \end{array} \times \begin{array}{c} 1 + \text{allowance} \\ \text{time rate} \end{array}$$

$$\begin{array}{c} \text{Operation} \\ \text{time} \end{array} = \begin{array}{c} \text{basic operation} \\ \text{time} \times \text{no.} \\ \text{of operators} \end{array} \times \begin{array}{c} 1 + \text{allowance} \\ \text{time rate} \end{array}$$

The steps in determining standard times for main operations are as follows.

1. Use regression equations to estimate the labor-hours for the work elements (use the method for calculating standard times)

First, select the most suitable of the work elements that can be used for the equipment selected at Step 5. Next, perform the calculations to estimate the basic times for the selected work elements, using the driver data (e.g., diameter, length, etc.) from the drawings. These driver data can be selected from the drawing-based data list that was registered at Step 2.

When one process includes several work elements (i.e., several operator stations in one process), the above step must be repeated for each work element.

2. If the regression equations have not been specified, use IE techniques to estimate labor-hours based on actual (result) values.

In such cases, compile the figures for drivers and labor-hours (i.e., time values), and when a sufficient amount of such data have been accumulated, use multiple regression analysis to estimate the standard times.

If the labor-hours that were estimated based on actual values are fewer than expected, use the rate values for work efficiency to calculate revised time values (this is called rating). In other words:

$$\frac{\text{Work efficiency}}{\text{(rate value)}} = \frac{\text{allowable standard time}}{\text{actual time}}$$

Where

$$\frac{\text{Allowable}}{\text{standard time}} = \frac{\text{standard time}}{\text{per product unit}} \times \frac{\text{actual production}}{\text{volume}}$$

$$\frac{\text{Revised}}{\text{time value}} = \frac{\text{estimated}}{\text{time value}} \times \frac{\text{work efficiency}}{\text{(rate)}}$$

Steps 6, 7, and 8 above can be repeated for each of the several processes and equipment units selected at steps 4 and 5.

Similar Design

In this context, similar design is also known as similar item search method. It refers to a process design and labor-hour estimation method that simply compares the planned part or product with similar previous parts or products (using the process design results of previously manufactured products) to determine their similarities and differences. Only the differences (i.e., variants) then need to be addressed with revisions. This approach is also called the variant approach, and it is often used by process designers.

The steps in this search method are described below (note that the step numbers below do not correspond with those shown in Figure 23-2).

Step 1. Enter the Heading Items

Enter heading items related to the planned part or product, such as Part number, Part name, Production volume, Lot size, and Production period.

Step 2. Search for and Select Similar Items

Search for items most similar to the planned part of product among the items listed in the results from past process designs and labor-hour estimates (see circled number 9 in Figure 24-2). There are three ways to do this kind of search.

Search based on part numbers

Part numbers usually have certain digits specified to describe three elements:

- Type (model, mechanical structure, method, etc.)
- Size (capacity, functional performance, dimensions, etc./
- Grade (materials, precision, class, etc.)

Search based on part names

An obvious way to search for parts is by their names (nut, bolt, washer, etc.).

Search based on search codes for similar parts

Search codes for similar parts can be made by compiling lists of part names and part characteristics (shape, functions, etc.). This method takes the GT (group technology) approach.

The GT approach is a set of techniques for raising efficiency in wide-variety, small-lot production. The basic idea is to organize parts into groups based on similar characteristics, such as shape, dimensions, functions, and processing methods. Then, the best manufacturing methods are determined for each group to help raise production efficiency.

Using the GT approach, we can, for example, establish a 9-digit part code, wherein the part class is indicated by the first digit, the external shape by the second digit, the internal shape by the third digit, the type of surface processing by the fourth digit, the type of drilling and/or gear cutting by the fifth digit, the diameter or border length by the sixth digit, the type of material by the seventh digit, the material shape by the eighth digit, and the precision rating by the ninth digit.

This GT-style organization of parts has two main categories—geometric characteristics such as part sizes and dimensions, and manufacturing technology-related characteristics such as manufacturing methods and processes. The latter category tends to be more useful for process design.

Step 3. Revise Variant Points

Copy the process information—(1) department, (2) process, (3) equipment, (4) time values, etc.—to use process design and labor-hour estimation results for the planned product or part.

Next, only the variants (items that differ from previous items) need to be revised (see circled number 10 in Figure 24-2).

Step 4. Display the Results of Process Design and Labor-Hour Estimation

These results are displayed as a *process design manual*, in a format such as that shown in Figure 24-3. Process design manuals are useful not only for estimating processing costs as part of target costing, but also for designing work operations, equipment layout, and production schedules, as described at the start of this chapter.

Figure 24-3 should be read as follows. The part, a spindle bearing support, requires four processes for its manufacture, and is produced in a lot size of 20 units. The four processes are a lathe process, a horizontal milling process, a drill press process, and a vertical milling process. At the lathe process, for example, the changeover time is given as 10 minutes per lot. Adding a 6 percent allowance for error, we can calculate that:

Standard changeover time = $10 \times (1 + 0.06) = 10.60$ minutes

Similarly:

Standard operation time = $29.04 \times (1 + 0.06) = 30.78$ minutes

Process Design Manual

Part code	3G1A6792
Part name	Spindle bearing support
Functional position	Low
Production lot	20
No. of processes	4

No. 1	Dept.	Team 1	Process	Lathe		Equipment name
Changeover			Description	Replace cutting tool		
			Basic time		10	Operators
Operation			Description	Cutting		
			Basic time		29.04	Operators

No. 2	Dept.	Team 1	Process	Horizontal milling		Equipment name
Changeover			Description	Replace jig and tool		
			Basic time		10	Operators
Operation			Description	Groove processing		
			Basic time		4.58	Operators

No. 3	Dept.	Team 1	Process	Drill press		Equipment name
Changeover			Description	Replace jig and tool		
			Basic time		10	Operators
Operation			Description	Drilling		
			Basic time		7.44	Operators

No. 4	Dept.	Team 1	Process	Vertical milling		Equipment name
Changeover			Description	Replace jig and tool		
			Basic time		10	Operators
Operation			Description	Groove processing		
			Basic time		1.89	Operators

Figure 24-3. Process Design Manual

Calculations to Estimate Processing Costs

Once we are able to estimate labor-hours for each process based on the process designs, we can use those estimated values as shown below to calculate variable processing costs and fixed

Unit (minutes)	Labor-hours per unit	Labor-hours per production lot
Changeover	2.12	42.4
Operation	45.53	910.5
Total	47.65	

Ordinary lathe A	Lot	20		
			Basic	10.00
1	Allowance	0.06	Standard	10.60
			Basic	29.04
1	Allowance	0.06	Standard	30.78

Horizontal milling machine A	Lot	20		
			Basic	10.00
1	Allowance	0.06	Standard	10.60
			Basic	4.58
1	Allowance	0.06	Standard	4.85

Vertical drill press A	Lot	20		
			Basic	10.00
1	Allowance	0.06	Standard	10.60
			Basic	7.44
1	Allowance	0.06	Standard	7.89

Vertical milling machine A	Lot	20		
			Basic	10.00
1	Allowance	0.06	Standard	10.60
			Basic	1.89
1	Allowance	0.06	Standard	2.00

Figure 24-3. Contd.

processing costs for each process (see Figure 24-4). To do this, we must differentiate the fixed processing cost rate from the equipment depreciation rate and other unrelated fixed processing cost rates.

Processing Cost Estimation Worksheet

Part code: 3G1A6792
Part name: Spindle bearing support
Functional position: Low
Production lot: 20

Variable processing costs: ¥2312.6
Fixed processing costs: ¥1087.9
Estimated processing costs: ¥3400.5

No.	Team	Process	Equipment / Operation	Lot per process	Variable cost rate / Fixed cost rate	Equipment cost rate	Standard labor-hours	Work efficiency rate	Estimated labor-hours	Rate × labor-hours for variable and fixed costs	Equipment costs
1	1	Lathe	Lathe A	20	47.24	4.95	0.53	98%	0.54	1,509.3	158.1
			Cutting		17.32		30.78	98%	31.41	553.5	
2	1	Horizontal milling machine	Machine A	20	49.45	5.68	0.53	98%	0.54	271.7	31.2
			Groove processing		18.19		4.85	98%	4.95	100.0	
3	1	Drill press	Drill press A	20	47.01	3.91	0.53	98%	0.54	403.7	33.5
			Drilling		17.11		7.89	98%	8.05	147.0	
4	1	Vertical milling machine	Machine A	20	49.50	6.65	0.53	98%	0.54	128.0	17.2
			Groove processing		18.35		2.00	98%	2.04	47.4	

Figure 24-4. Calculation of Estimated Processing Costs

Calculations to estimate variable processing costs

$$\text{Standard labor-hours} = \left(\frac{\text{changeover labor-hours}}{\text{lot size}} + \text{main operation labor-hours}\right) \times (1 + \text{allowance rate})$$

$$\text{Estimated labor-hours} = \frac{\text{standard labor-hours}}{\text{work efficiency rate}} \times (1 + \text{allowance rate for training and small lots})$$

$$\text{Variable processing costs} = \text{estimated labor-hours} \times \text{variable processing cost rate}$$

Where:

$$\text{Allowance rate for training} = \text{rate for time losses due to training during the period until the product reaches full production}$$

$$\text{Allowance rate for small lots} = \text{rate for time losses (other than changeover time) due to changes in processing steps, methods, and in parts used to accommodate small lots}$$

Calculations to estimate fixed processing costs

$$\text{Standard time} = \frac{(\text{changeover time} \times \text{lot size})}{+ \text{operation time}} \times \frac{1 + \text{allowance}}{\text{rate}}$$

$$\text{Estimated time} = \frac{\text{standard time}}{\text{work efficiency rate}} \times \frac{1 + \text{allowance rate for}}{\text{training and small lots}}$$

$$\text{Fixed processing costs} = \frac{\text{estimated labor-hours} \times}{\text{fixed processing cost rate}} + \frac{\text{estimated time} \times}{\text{equipment cost rate}}$$

Figure 24-4 should be used as follows. Calculate the variable and fixed processing costs and the equipment costs for each process specified in the process design manual (Figure 24-3) by performing the following calculations (this example uses Team 1's lathe process):

Part code: 3G1A6792		Part name: Spindle bearing support	
No.	**Cost item**	**Material**	**Input material cost**
1	1	S20C	3,690.5
No.	**Direct dept.**	**Process**	**Equipment**
1	Team 1	Lathe	Lathe A
2	Team 1	Horizontal milling machine	Machine A
3	Team 1	Drill press	Vertical drill A
4	Team 1	Vertical milling machine	Machine A
Cost item		**Estimated cost**	**Target cost**
Material cost	Raw materials cost	3,524.9	3,500.0
	Purchased parts cost	0.0	0.0
Processing costs	Variable processing costs	2,312.6	2,000.0
	Fixed processing costs	1,087.9	1,500.0
Direct operating costs	Prototype costs	0.0	0.0
	Development costs	783.0	1,000.0
	Dies, jigs, tools	543.0	500.0
	Other	0.0	0.0
Total		8,251.4	8,500.0

Figure 24-5. Comparison of Estimated and Target Product Costs

$$\text{Estimated changeover labor-hours} = \frac{\text{standard changeover labor-hours per product or part unit (0.53 minutes)}}{\text{work efficiency rate (0.98)}}$$

$$= 0.54 \text{ minutes}$$

Where:

$$\begin{array}{c}\text{Standard changeover labor-hours per product or part unit}\\ (0.53 \text{ minutes})\end{array} = \frac{\text{standard changeover labor-hours given per lot in Figure 24-2 (10.60 minutes)}}{\text{lot size (20)}}$$

$$\text{Estimated operation labor-hours} = \frac{\text{standard operation labor-hours (30.78 minutes)}}{\text{work efficiency rate (0.98)}} = 31.41 \text{ minutes}$$

Functional position: Low		Production lot size: 20	
Scrap value	**Estimated material cost**		
165.6	3,524.9		
Process-specific lot	**Variable processing costs**	**Fixed processing costs**	**Equipment costs**
20	1,509.3	553.5	158.1
20	271.7	100.0	31.2
20	403.7	147.0	33.5
20	128.0	47.4	17.2

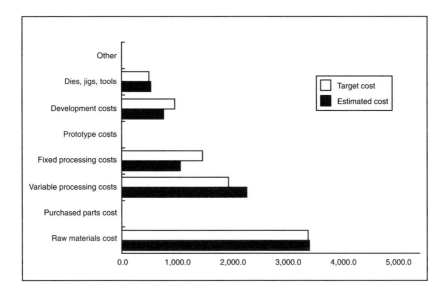

Figure 24-5. Contd.

$$[\$.47] \quad \begin{matrix} \text{Variable} \\ \text{processing} \\ \text{costs} \end{matrix} = \begin{matrix} \text{variable cost rate} \\ (¥47.24 \text{ per minute}) \end{matrix} \times \begin{matrix} \text{total estimated} \\ \text{labor-hours} \\ (0.54 + 31.41) \end{matrix} = \begin{matrix} ¥1,509.3 \\ (\$15.00) \end{matrix}$$

$$[\$.17] \quad \begin{matrix} \text{Fixed} \\ \text{processing} \\ \text{costs} \end{matrix} = \begin{matrix} \text{fixed cost rate} \\ (¥17.32 \text{ per minute}) \end{matrix} \times \begin{matrix} \text{total estimated} \\ \text{labor-hours} \\ (0.54 + 31.41) \end{matrix} = \begin{matrix} ¥553.5 \\ (\$5.54) \end{matrix}$$

$$[\$.05] \quad \begin{matrix} \text{Equipment} \\ \text{costs} \end{matrix} = \begin{matrix} \text{equipment cost rate} \\ (¥4.95 \text{ per minute}) \end{matrix} \times \begin{matrix} \text{total estimated} \\ \text{labor-hours} \\ (0.54 + 31.41) \end{matrix} = \begin{matrix} ¥158.1 \\ (\$1.60) \end{matrix}$$

Calculations to estimate product costs

Now that we have obtained estimated values for direct materials costs, processing costs, and direct operating costs, we can estimate the product costs. We can then compare the estimated product costs with target costs for specific cost items and specific products (see Figure 24-5).

Part IV

Kaizen Costing System

God helps those who help themselves.

— Benjamin Franklin

Light gains make heavy purses.

— George Chapman

25

What Is Kaizen Costing?

Definitions

Kaizen costing means maintaining current cost levels for currently manufactured vehicles and working systematically to reduce costs to desired levels.

There are two types of kaizen costing:
(a) Factory- or department-specific kaizen costing activities scheduled for each business term
(b) Vehicle model-specific kaizen costing activities carried out as special projects with an emphasis on VA (value analysis)

This chapter focuses on the first type of kaizen costing. The second kind will be described in Chapter 29.

A kaizen costing system encompasses the company's managerial accounting system and its program of factory floor-level kaizen activities (JIT, TQM, etc.). This chapter will focus mainly on the managerial accounting aspects of the kaizen costing system.

Objectives

The main objective of kaizen costing is the relentless pursuit of cost reductions at every stage of manufacturing to help close any gaps between target profits (budgeted profits) and estimated profits. This approach differs both conceptually and procedurally from cost management as practiced in a standard costing system.

Conceptual Differences

A *standard costing system:*
- Exercises control to make actual costs equal standard costs (objective is cost maintenance)
- Assumes that current manufacturing conditions will be maintained and not changed

A *kaizen costing system:*
- Is a cost reduction system that aims to reduce actual costs to below standard costs
- Exercises control to achieve target cost reductions
- Continually changes current manufacturing conditions to reduce costs

Procedural Differences

A *standard costing system:*
- Sets standard costs once or twice a year
- Conducts analyses of differences between standard costs and actual costs
- Carries out investigations and corrective measures when standard costs are not achieved

A *kaizen costing system:*
- Sets new cost reduction targets every month; these targets are designed to close gaps between target profits (budgeted profits) and estimated profits
- Conducts kaizen (continuous improvement) activities throughout the business year to achieve target cost reductions

- Conducts analyses of differences between target costs and actual costs
- Carries out investigations and corrective measures when target cost reductions are not achieved

Steps

The kaizen costing system established for each business term will be described in steps in the following three chapters:

1. Preparation of budget and determination of target cost reduction amounts (Chapter 26)
2. Factory-based kaizen activities (Chapter 27)
3. Measurement and analysis of gaps between target costs and actual costs (Chapter 28)

Let us begin by elaborating on these steps to establish a clear understanding of the context for the matters explained in the following three chapters.

Automotive parts manufacturers that have a division-based corporate organization use the following eight steps in carrying out kaizen costing activities with regard to their automobile manufacturer clients.

Step 1

Every business year, their business planning department reviews and revises the company's (or division's) medium-term business plan.

Step 2

Their cost management department plays a central role in this business planning by reviewing and revising the medium-term profit plan (and, consequently, the next annual profit plan).

Step 3

The starting point for the parts manufacturer's preparation of its annual budget comes in December, when it receives the annual production plan from its client (automobile manufacturer). Although the annual production plan typically includes many favorable figures, the parts manufacturer must make a careful study to determine whether the production plan is feasible and to request revised figures if necessary.

Step 4

Based on the final (revised) production plan, the parts manufacturer's sales department drafts the annual production plan for its company.

Step 5

Next, each department in the parts manufacturing company calculates its own cost estimates in line with the annual production plan. For example, if the design department wants to develop a particular item, it must estimate the development and testing costs and the operating costs required for such development. Likewise, if the production engineering department wants to develop new production techniques (and buy new equipment, etc.) in the coming year, it must estimate the costs involved, including the equipment depreciation costs. These estimates must be completed two or three months before the start of the next accounting (business) year, which is typically April 1 for Japanese companies.

Step 6

Each division's cost management department collects the departmental cost estimates and drafts a provisional profit/loss statement. The figures in this statement are then compared with the target profit figures in the medium-term profit plan, the gaps are measured, and the results (gaps) serve as a basis for calculating kaizen costing goals for the coming business year.

Step 7

Kaizen costing (cost reduction) targets are set for various cost items, particularly variable costs such as direct materials costs, indirect materials costs, and direct labor costs (labor-hours). Fixed costs for specific cost items are allocated to each division. These kaizen costing targets and fixed-cost budgets are taken into consideration when drafting the annual budget.

Step 8

After the new budget comes into effect (usually on April 1), follow-up studies are done monthly to determine whether the reduction targets for variable costs and the budgeted fixed costs are being achieved.

26
Budget Formulation and Determination of Target Cost Reductions

Definition

The determination of target reduction amounts as part of budget formulation starts with calculating the company's target profit improvement amount, defined as the difference between the target profit (budgeted profit) and the estimated profit. To achieve this target profit improvement amount, the company must determine its kaizen costing target amount, i.e., its target cost reduction amount. This amount must be factored into the budget for the next business term and plans must be made for achieving the budgeted profit.

The target reduction amount is broken down into amounts for individual factories and factory departments, where it is reflected in kaizen costing target values set for specific processes. This approach is illustrated in Figure 26-1.

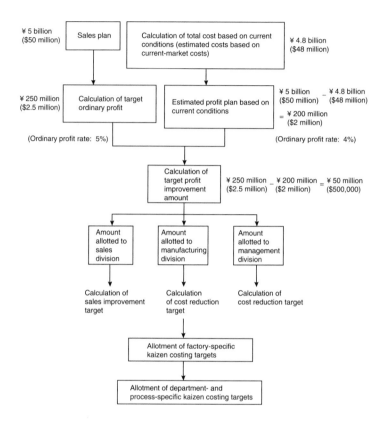

Figure 26-1. Approach to Calculating Target Cost Reduction Amount

Objective

The allocation of target reduction amounts to specific processes helps motivate staff in improvement activities that aim to reach targets for their own processes. It also helps the entire company achieve its budgeted operating profit.

Input and Output

Input

1. Project planning.
    (a) Sales plan for manufactured and delivered vehicles. This narrowly defined short-term profit plan is based on the direct cost calculation method. The previous term's variable cost results are used as the standard costs (i.e., standard variable costs) for this term. The predicted variable costs (based on these standard variable costs) are subtracted from the planned sales volume to establish a plan for contributing profits.
    (b) Price planning for parts and materials ... targets for procurement department.
    (c) Factory rationalization plan (manufacturing-related variable cost reduction plan). This plan forms the crux of kaizen costing activities in factories. Target reduction amounts are set for variable costs at factories.
    (d) Personnel planning (direct personnel planning and overtime planning for indirect departments). Because this area includes rationalization planning for direct and indirect labor costs, it is considered part of kaizen costing for factories.
    (e) Plant investment planning (including planning of depreciation costs).
    (f) Budget planning for fixed expenses (prototype costs, advertising expenses, sales promotion expenses, general management expenses, etc.).

2. Actual per-vehicle costs per cost item during previous term (see part 2 of Step 2 below). These costs are used as the standard costs for this term.

3. Actual number of vehicles produced during previous term and estimated production volume for current term (see part 3 of Step 2 below).

4. Target reduction rate for each cost item (see part 4 of Step 2 below).

Output

1. Sales profit in annual budget (see Step 1 below). The short-term general profit plan is drafted as part of the term's planning (a.k.a. period planning). To achieve the target profit set by the long-term profit plan for the first business year, the six project planning areas listed in the "Input" section must be factored in and adjusted based on the measurement standards of revenues, costs, and profits.
2. Profit budget for each sales-related department (see Step 1 below).
3. Monthly table of kaizen costing targets (see Step 2 below).
4. Allotment of kaizen costing targets at each stage (see Step 3 below).

Steps

Step 1. Formulation of Short-Term General Profit Plan—Strategy to Close the Gap between Target Profit and Estimated Profit

- The "Sales plan for manufactured and delivered vehicles" listed under "Input" forms the foundation for the short-term general profit plan. At this point, we plan the number of vehicles to sell in each model line, estimate their sales prices, and plan the contributing profits using standard variable costs (based on the previous term's cost results). Accordingly,

$$
\begin{matrix}
\text{Estimated} \\
\text{contributing} \\
\text{profit total}
\end{matrix}
=
\begin{matrix}
\Sigma \text{ product-specific vehicle-specific} \\
\text{estimated contribution rate} \\
\times \text{ planned number of vehicles to be sold}
\end{matrix}
$$

- In the short-term general profit plan, the planned sales profit is the planned profit for the first year in the five-year long-term profit plan. The six project planning tasks described in the "Input" section are introduced to help achieve the planned profit as the budgeted sales profit.

- Project planning tasks (b) "Price planning for parts and materials" and (c) "Factory rationalization plan" are incorporated as current-term cost reduction amounts for variable manufacturing costs.
- Although fixed-cost planning is done for specific cost items, it is also incorporated in the short-term general profit plan via three of the above project planning tasks: (d) "Personnel planning," (e) "Plant investment planning," and (f) "Budget planning for fixed expenses."
- These steps result in a sales profit budget such as that outlined in Figure 26-2.

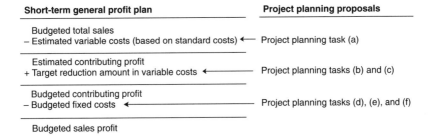

Figure 26-2. Annual Sales Profit Budget

- The companywide sales profit budget is then deployed into sales-department-specific sales profit budgets. Figure 26-3 illustrates how costs and revenues for products can be categorized into specific sales departments.
- As a calculation of results, we can use the standard per-vehicle cost for vehicles actually sold during the current term to calculate the result costs—in other words, the sales cost, which we then subtract from the total sales figure. Sales expenses and general management expenses should also be calculated as part of the product-specific cost/revenue account and sales department-specific cost/revenue account. For the purpose of profit management, the direct cost calculation method should be used for both the product-specific cost/revenue account and the sales department-specific cost/revenue account.

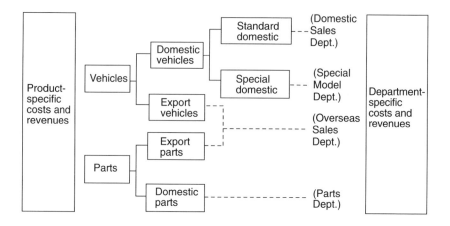

Figure 26-3. Example of Department-Specific Deployment of Costs and Revenues

Step 2. Determination of Companywide Target Reduction Amount—Targets in "Factory Rationalization Plan"

1. Calculation of companywide target reduction amount

The first step in calculating the companywide target reduction amount (the amount of cost reduction required of each factory, etc.) is to establish a target reduction percentage rate for each type of cost, relative to the per-vehicle cost results as of the end of the previous business term. We can then apply this percentage rate to the planned production volume for the current term (converted to figures for representative vehicle models). The formula for this is then:

$$
\begin{array}{l}
\text{Companywide} \\
\text{target} \\
\text{reduction} \quad = \\
\text{amount}
\end{array}
\begin{array}{l}
\overset{m\ n}{\underset{i\ j}{\Sigma\ \Sigma}} \text{(conversion to current-term production} \\
\text{volume for representative vehicle model } j) \\
\times \text{ per-vehicle standard cost for cost item } i \\
\times \text{ target reduction rate for cost item } i
\end{array}
$$

The method for determining the elements on the right side of this equation is described below.

2. Standard cost for cost item

This corresponds to the actual variable cost per unit as of the end of the previous term.

3. Conversion to current-term production volume

For this calculation, use the total number of vehicles converted to the specified representative model. The converted amount of vehicles will differ for each cost item due to the different basic units (labor-hours, money, etc.) that are used as measurement standards. Figure 26-4 describes the method for calculating the converted amount of vehicles.

Model	(1) Target labor- hours	(2) Production volume	(3) = (1) × (2) Total standard time	(4) Total actual time	(5) = (4) ÷ (2) Result per vehicle
A	30 min./unit	2,000 units	60,000 min.	57,000 min.	28.5 min./unit
B	50	800	40,000	40,000	50.0
C	40	200	8,000	12,000	60.0
Total		3,000 units	108,000 min.	109,000 min.	Achievement rate 99.1%

Calculation of converted vehicle amount for Model A:

$$\frac{108,000 \text{ min.}}{\text{(total standard time)}} \div \frac{30 \text{ min./unit}}{\text{(basic unit for Model A)}} = \frac{3,600 \text{ units}}{\text{(converted vehicle amount for Model A)}}$$

Figure 26-4. Example of Vehicle Quantity from Labor-Hours

4. Determination of target reduction rate for each cost item

• The target reduction rate for each cost item is the proportion by which the vehicle-specific standard variable cost per cost item must be lowered. However, the target reduction rate relative to direct labor costs is not a reduction rate relative to per-vehicle standard direct labor costs, but instead is relative to per-vehicle labor-hours.

- The target reduction rate per cost item must be determined when costs must be adjusted to close the gap between the target's budgeted profit and estimated profit. However, in many cases, this rate changes only slightly from year to year. By contrast, other costs, such as transportation and energy costs, tend to vary more widely. There are also differences between factories in the cost reduction rates they set for themselves (see Figure 26-5).

Cost item	Evaluation standard	Annual target reduction rate (example)
Direct materials costs Basic materials costs (dies, steel plates, molded plastic materials, etc.)	• Monetary value per vehicle as of end of previous term	2%
Purchased part costs	• Monetary value per vehicle as of end of previous term	4%
Other direct materials costs (parts, thinner, gasoline adhesives, etc.)	• Monetary value per vehicle as of end of previous term	8%

Processing costs
  Variable rate
    Direct labor costs
	• Standard hours per vehicle as of end of previous term	6%

Variable indirect materials costs	• Monetary value per vehicle as of end of previous term	8%
Part transportation costs	• Value of suggested improvements	10%
Variable direct costs	• Cost per hour in same month last year	4%
Fixed costs: Direct labor costs	• Personnel and overtime costs as of end of previous term	*
Other fixed costs	• Results for same month last year	4%
Office-related energy costs (power, air conditioning, etc.)	• Budget for current month (total amount)	*
Supplemental departmental costs (maintenance, factory, depreciation, etc.)	• Budget for current month (total amount)	*

* Although no reduction target has been set for the cost items having this mark, differences from the budget (target amounts) can be considered as a result of rationalization efforts (the target reduction rates shown here are examples only).

Figure 26-5. Target Reduction Amounts per Cost Item

5. Management of fixed costs

Ordinarily, target reduction amounts are not set for fixed-cost items. Instead, the difference between the estimated (in the target total cost) and the actual fixed costs are compared to determine the amount to be saved through rationalization (see the asterisked sections in the lower part of Figure 26-5).

- Target values are set for the labor costs (indirect labor costs) for the general management departments and related departments based on estimated personnel costs, overtime costs, and the like. If rationalization can reduce these costs even slightly, it may be enough to meet the target reduction amount.
- As for allotted general management expense items, such as advertising, maintenance, and sales promotion, these are included in the budget as part of the total general management costs.
- Regarding energy costs, such as power and air conditioning for offices, a target reduction rate is set for the amount budgeted for such costs. Energy costs are the only fixed costs for which a specific target reduction amount is set.

6. Current-term kaizen costing target chart

The procedures described in (1) to (5) above pave the way for creating a chart that lists target reduction amounts to be achieved through kaizen costing at all factories during the current term (see Figure 26-6). The management organization improvement amount shown between the subtotal and total in this chart is a 20 percent reduction rate that is applied as an average reduction rate for all cost items (i.e., it does not mean that each individual cost item must be reduced 20 percent).

Step 4. Reconciliation of Target Profit Amount and Kaizen Costing Target Amount

In the "Definition" section at the start of this chapter (see also Figure 26-1), we learned that the company's target profit

Kaizen Costing Target Chart for 19_ Term (Unit: ¥100 million)

Cost item for kaizen costing	Standard amount	Target reduction rate (%)	Target reduction amount
Materials costs			
Basic materials costs	XXX		XX
Main materials costs	XXX	2%	XX
Indirect materials costs	XXX	4%	XX
Direct labor costs	XXX	8%	XX
Transportation costs	XXX	10%	XXX
Energy costs	XXX	4%	XX
Subtotal	XXXX	Average reduction rate	XXX
Management organization improvement amount		20% of subtotal	
Total	XXXX		XXX

Figure 26-6. Current-Term Kaizen Costing Target Chart

improvement amount is calculated by the accounting division's cost management department as the difference between the target profit (budgeted profit) and the estimated profit. These estimated profits are calculated based on market costs (estimated costs).

Next, the companywide target profit improvement amount is allotted into target profit improvement amounts for the manufacturing division (factories), sales division, management division, and so on. The sales division works to achieve its target profit improvement amount by raising its target for overall sales as well as by setting cost-reduction targets for sales and advertising costs. The management division manages overtime hours through budget management. The purchasing division sets reduction targets for its purchased part costs.

Using the method described in Step 2, the manufacturing division sets kaizen costing targets for its various manufacturing cost items at each factory while referring to previous target reduction rates.

In this way, the accounting division is able to gather estimates of the kaizen costing target values pursued by each of the company's functional divisions, which it then presents in a report to top management. Top management uses this information to judge how far these kaizen costing target values will go toward meeting the companywide profit improvement target. This process of kaizen costing planning and top management review is repeated until the company is able to determine a final set of division-specific kaizen costing target amounts.

Step 5. Target Management—Factory- and Department-Specific Breakdown of Target Reduction Amounts

Two allotment methods can be used to break down the companywide target reduction amount for factories into factory-specific target reduction amounts.

1. Using factory-specific manageable costs as the allotment standard (where "manageable costs" include direct materials costs, direct labor costs, variable indirect costs, etc. but not fixed costs such as depreciation costs)

$$\text{Factory-specific target reduction amount} = \text{companywide target reduction amount} \times \frac{\text{factory-specific manageable costs}}{\text{total manageable costs (for all factories)}}$$

2. Using previous-term actual costs at each factory as the allotment standard

$$\text{Factory-specific target reduction amount} = \text{companywide target reduction amount} \times \frac{\text{factory-specific previous-term actual costs}}{\text{total previous-term actual costs (for all factories)}}$$

The manufacturing division's senior managers (vice-president rank) are in charge of allotting these target reduction amounts among the various factories. They use and refer to both allotment methods before making their allotment decisions at a cost function meeting (attended by top managers).

As a third consideration, extra-large target reduction rates are set for factories that have just completed a model change and are turning out new-model vehicles. Conversely, factories that manufacture models near the end of their model life have already implemented round after round of improvements each year and have less room for further improvement. Therefore smaller target reduction rates are applied to such factories to help keep targets within attainable limits.

The managers of each factory are responsible for allotting reduction amounts for specific departments and cost categories within their factory.

In each factory, the target reduction amount for the entire factory is allotted into target reduction amounts for each department, then further broken down for each section, then each subsection, work team, and so on. This allotment system is called the *target management system*. Cost meetings are held at the various management levels to set reduction targets for each level based on evaluations of past kaizen costing results and application of target reduction amounts or target reduction rates. As the factory's top manager, the factory superintendent is responsible for providing support for these cost meetings.

Figure 26-7 illustrates the processes that constitute the target management system.

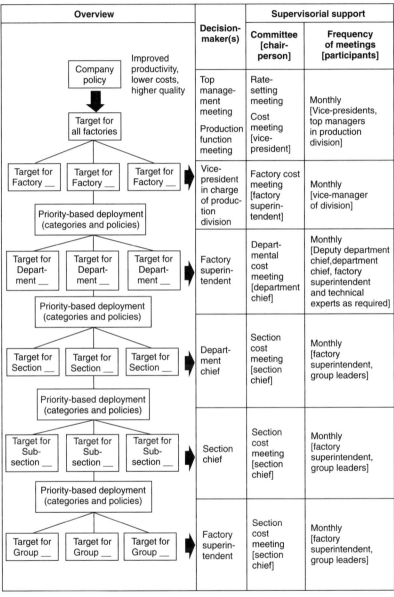

Overview				Supervisorial support	
			Decision-maker(s)	Committee [chairperson]	Frequency of meetings [participants]
Company policy → Target for all factories	Improved productivity, lower costs, higher quality		Top management meeting / Production function meeting	Rate-setting meeting / Cost meeting [vice-president]	Monthly [Vice-presidents, top managers in production division]
Target for Factory __ / Target for Factory __ / Target for Factory __ / Priority-based deployment (categories and policies)			Vice-president in charge of production division	Factory cost meeting [factory superintendent]	Monthly [vice-manager of division]
Target for Department __ / Target for Department __ / Target for Department __ / Priority-based deployment (categories and policies)			Factory superintendent	Departmental cost meeting [department chief]	Monthly [Deputy department chief, department chief, factory superintendent and technical experts as required]
Target for Section __ / Target for Section __ / Target for Section __ / Priority-based deployment (categories and policies)			Department chief	Section cost meeting [section chief]	Monthly [factory superintendent, group leaders]
Target for Sub-section __ / Target for Sub-section __ / Target for Sub-section __ / Priority-based deployment (categories and policies)			Section chief	Section cost meeting [section chief]	Monthly [factory superintendent, group leaders]
Target for Group __ / Target for Group __ / Target for Group __			Factory superintendent	Section cost meeting [section chief]	Monthly [factory superintendent, group leaders]

(Source: Tomo and Kimura 1986, p.18.)

Figure 26-7. Target Management System

27

Kaizen Activities at the Workplace

Kaizen Costing Activities at the Workplace

There are two kinds of term-specific kaizen costing activities: activities organized under the company's accounting system, and workplace kaizen activities (also known as shop-floor improvement activities or factory-based improvement activities). The latter kind is the type we speak of when discussing the Toyota production system or JIT (just-in-time) production—they are activities that seek to thoroughly eliminate waste from the factory or other workplaces. The former (accounting system) kind of kaizen costing system provides the division-specific cost reduction targets—in other words, the goals that help motivate kaizen activities.

In the context of the Toyota production system, waste occurs whenever resources such as labor, materials, money, space, time, and information are used inefficiently. In terms of organization theory, this definition corresponds to organizational slack that prevents the company from taking advantage of all available opportunities. It also refers to the kind of waste incurred by lax or complacent organizations.

Kaizen is the effort to eliminate waste. Specifically, kaizen deals with waste at up to four levels of cause and effect, known as primary, secondary, tertiary, and quaternary waste.

- Primary waste: An excess of production capacity elements, such as too many employees, too much equipment, or excess inventory. Such excesses incur unnecessary costs for labor, equipment depreciation, and capital interest.
- Secondary waste: Waste caused by producing too much or by working too far ahead. This is the worst kind of waste.
- Tertiary waste: Waste from excess inventory. This kind of waste incurs higher interest on capital (and higher opportunity costs).
- Quaternary waste: Waste from excess transportation (conveyance, etc.), excess warehouse inventory, excess warehouse management, and excess quality maintenance.

All these wastes lead to higher equipment depreciation costs and indirect labor costs.

Once we have identified waste from excess human resources (standby waste), we can reassign duties to reduce employee requirements and thus reduce labor costs.

If we can also somehow eliminate overproduction waste, we can greatly reduce tertiary and quaternary waste. To reduce overproduction waste, first determine the average daily sales rate within a given week or month (the average interval between sales of individual product units, also known as the *takt time*), then simply coordinate product output with this sales-based takt time. This method is a central part of the know-how behind the Toyota production system. Naturally, a company must implement many changes to rebuild its production system based on this know-how.

The Toyota Production System

Figure 27-1 illustrates the Toyota production system, which is briefly described in the following paragraphs. (For a more detailed description of this system, see the author's *Toyota Production System*, 2d edition, Industrial Engineering and Management Press, 1993).

The objective of the Toyota production system is to increase profits by cutting costs—which means thoroughly eliminating such things as excess inventory and excess labor capacity. To achieve such cost reductions, the company must get rid of the various kinds of waste ("slack") in the current production system and make the production system flexibly and rapidly responsive to market fluctuations. The JIT ideal is to manufacture just what is needed, just in the amount needed, and just when it is needed.

Toyota developed the kanban system as a means of processing monthly production data and managing JIT production. Basically, the kanban system requires that each later process routinely go to the previous process to withdraw required parts. In response to each withdrawal, the previous process manufactures just what is needed to replace the withdrawn parts. Such a manufacturing system is called a "pull" system.

To implement this kanban system, production must first be leveled, so that the final assembly line has a fairly even flow of withdrawn parts from hour to hour.

In turn, implementing production leveling requires a shortening of production lead time—the entire period between the start and completion of production. Many different kinds of parts must be manufactured daily and in rapid sequence. This system requires small lot sizes for certain parts—in other words, small-lot or one-piece flow production, and corresponding small-lot or one-piece conveyance. However, a factory cannot carry out small-lot production unless it first manages to shorten changeover (retooling) times, nor can it achieve one-piece flow production without multiprocess handling by each operator.

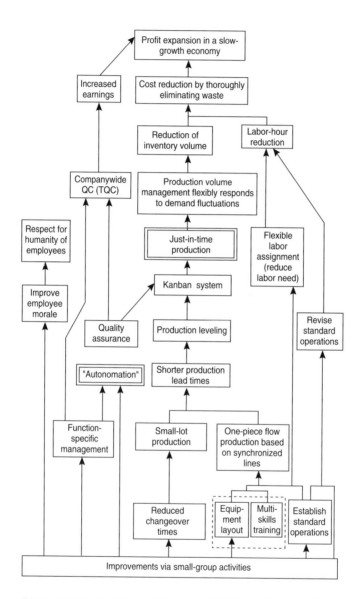

**Figure 27-1. Outline of Toyota (JIT) Production System:
Costs, Volume, Quality, and Human Resources**

By combining standard operations appropriately, all work required to produce one product unit can be made to fit within the product's takt time. The sales cycle—the average time in which one unit of the target product is sold—is therefore the same amount of time it takes each operator to complete the work for each product unit. JIT production also depends upon 100 percent nondefective production. The method for achieving zero defects is called "autonomation" (a method for automatically handling abnormalities).

Finally, at the bottom of Figure 27-1 we find kaizen activities. Kaizen activities refine standard operations and deal promptly with abnormalities to boost workplace morale and improve the processes where abnormalities occur.

Cost Drivers

Cost drivers are the factors that incur costs. Workplace-based kaizen costing activities take cost drivers as a starting point in carrying out cost reductions.

Cost Drivers and Department-Based (Process-Based) Activities at an Auto Plant

Here, we will examine the standard used to allocate process-specific costs among products.

Press process

- Direct operation time is a cost driver for direct labor costs associated with material handling activities such as conveying materials to the press process and removing the pressed parts.
- The punch rate (i.e., the stroke rate) is a cost driver for indirect costs related to press activities.

Casting process

The engine case casting process includes the following cost drivers:

- Among the processing costs for pig-iron casting, one "output figure" is the number of sand mold frames required. Therefore, the number of sand mold frames is a cost driver. If two engine cases can be made from one sand mold frame, then we have a per-case cost of 0.5 frames.
- For aluminum-cast engine cases, each shot of molten aluminum into the mold produces one aluminum case, and therefore the number of shots is taken as a cost driver.

Machining processes

Let us consider an automated machining (lathe working) line for engine cases. This machining line includes several NC (numerical control) machines linked by conveyors. The machine operation time at each machine station (i.e., each machine center cell) is regarded as a cost driver.

At each machine station, the processing costs (the sum of direct labor costs and indirect manufacturing costs) are incurred by machine operation time. The indirect costs are driven by indirect labor costs, such as for the person who retools the machines, the person who performs quality checks, the maintenance person, and the conveyance handler (work setter).

Heat treatment process

Machine operation time is also the basic cost driver for costs incurred by activities at this process.

Coating process

Two kinds of cost drivers are combined at this process:

- Direct labor costs (such as for people who set up and remove workpieces on hangers), for which direct operating time is the basic cost driver.
- The number of vehicles to be coated is the basic cost driver for the processing costs. Although there is some variation in the size of the vehicles, the coating time (i.e., the coating equipment operation time) is about the same for all vehicles.

Assembly process

As in the coating process, direct operation time is used as the cost driver for direct labor costs, while the number of units assembled is the cost driver for processing costs.

Welding process

Welding-related lines (side lines or under lines) that are placed closer to prior processes are regarded as specialized lines for certain vehicle models, and such lines are typically fully automated. Therefore, the number of welded vehicles can serve as the cost driver for welding line activities.

- The final line in the welding process, however, namely the shell body line, uses many operators and has a "multipiece flow" of several vehicles at once on the line. Accordingly, it is similar to the assembly line in that direct operating time can serve as a cost driver for direct labor costs while the number of welded vehicles serves as the cost driver for processing costs.

Cost Drivers for Cost Management by Cost Item, Department, or Level

Figure 27-2 lists these kinds of cost drivers, some of which were described earlier.

		Overall	Labor costs	Material costs	Energy costs
Section chief	Manufac-turing department	• Rationalization costs • Current status of improvement projects	• Total labor-hours per vehicle unit • GSPH (press)	• Value per vehicle unit • Defective rate (casting) • Value of consumed materials (press)	• Value of energy conservation measures
	Indirectly related departments	• Current status of improvement projects	• Overtime hours • No. of missing parts • Equipment stoppage rate and no. of occurrences	• Budget for fixed operating expenses	• Value of energy conservation measures • Feed-in amount
Group leader	Manufac-turing	• No. of study-group meetings	• No. of operators assigned to line • Attendance rate • Overtime hours • Availability rate	• Amount of high-priority items used • [Related to cost drivers] Coating: coating thickness, spray volume Casting: melting temperature, etc.	

Figure 27-2. Cost Drivers for Factory Cost Management by Cost Item, Department, or Level

28

Measurement and Analysis of Kaizen Costing Differentials

The Need for Differential Analysis

Just as differential analysis is an essential part of a cost maintenance system based on standard costs, differential analysis is
also required for a kaizen costing system that uses cost reduction targets.

Although some aspects of differential analysis for kaizen costing have not been fully developed, certain distinctions can be
recognized during evaluation of a department's performance results by analyzing operating rate differentials, budget differentials (or performance differentials), and "spec differentials" for
design changes resulting from current-term VA (value analysis)
activities (such spec differentials are regarded as part of the budget differentials).

This chapter examines the procedure for carrying out basic differential analysis for kaizen costing systems.

Steps

Step 1. Calculation of Monthly Kaizen Costing Differential

The following series of formulas can be used to measure each department's kaizen costing results for the prior month (also known as the "monthly rationalization value"), which we then compare to the month's target reduction amount. The illustration in Figure 28-1 provides a visual aid for learning these formulas and steps.

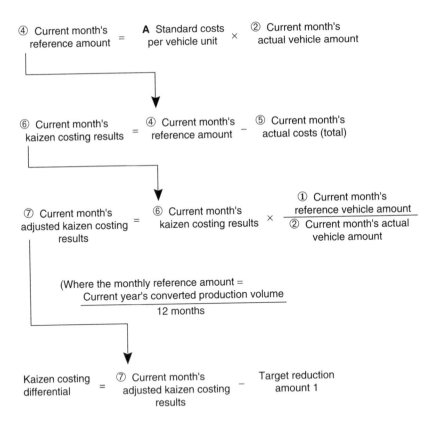

The results of these calculations are written onto a monthly kaizen costing results table (such as shown in Figure 28-2), which is sent to management for review. The "current month's adjusted

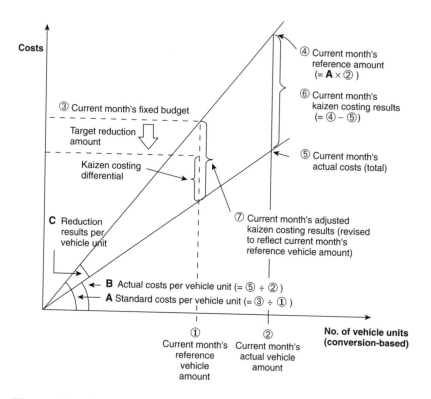

Figure 28-1. Calculation of Monthly Kaizen Costing Differential

kaizen costing results" is the same as the current month's kaizen costing results except that the operating rate differential has been removed from the equation.

The following is a simple method for calculating the current month's adjusted kaizen costing results:

$$\text{B Actual cost per vehicle unit} = ⑤ ÷ ②$$

$$\text{C Reduction results per vehicle unit} = \text{A} - \text{B}$$

⑦ Current month's adjusted kaizen costing results	=	C Reduction results per vehicle unit	×	① Current month's reference vehicle amount

Costs		Current Month (October 1994)			Cumulative, Apr-Oct 1994		
		Target	Result	Differential	Target	Result	Differential
Factory A	Direct labor	40	35	▲ 5	160	165	+ 5
	Indirect labor	0	▲ 5	▲ 5	0	▲ 35	▲ 35
	Materials	15	25	+ 10	60	75	+ 15
	Energy	10	15	+ 5	40	50	+ 10
	Transport	5	5	0	20	35	+ 35
	Total	70	75	+ 5	280	290	+ 10
Factory B	Direct labor	20	25	+ 5	80	75	▲ 5
	Indirect labor	0	5	+ 5	0	10	+ 10
	Materials	10	5	▲ 5	40	25	▲ 15
	Energy	5	0	▲ 5	20	15	▲ 5
	Transport	5	2	▲ 3	20	15	▲ 5
	Total	40	37	▲ 3	160	140	▲ 20

[Remainder omitted]

Note: Both the targets and the results indicate the target reduction amount. Solid triangles indicate negative or shortfall figures.

Figure 28-2. Monthly Kaizen Costing Results Table

Step 2. Reporting and Evaluation of Monthly and Cumulative Kaizen Costing Results

Each department reports and evaluates the monthly results, calculated as shown earlier, for its kaizen costing differentials. Departments that report especially good results receive bonuses. Even when the kaizen costing results for the month are positive, the evaluators are more concerned with whether the department is closer to achieving its target reduction amount.

Taking the information shown in Figure 28-2 as an example, we can see that the monthly evaluation for factory A shows a negative result for indirect labor costs, but the figure of 75 as the total value of the improvement results gives Factory A an overall improvement differential of +5.

Meanwhile, the monthly evaluation for Factory B shows 37 as the total value of improvement results, but this figure is still 3 points short of the target 40, as shown by the improvement differential of −3.

Step 3. Details of Kaizen Costing Differential Analysis—Mid-Term Revision of Target Reduction Rate and Target Reduction Amount

The target reduction rate and monthly target reduction amount are usually applied in linear fashion throughout the business year, but two factors disrupt such linear schemes.

The cost variables that are rooted in these factors as spec differentials must be subtracted and separated from "⑦ Current month's adjusted kaizen costing results" (a kind of budget differential) as calculated at Step 2.

1. Design changes during current term

There are generally two kinds of factors behind design changes:

- One factor occurs when design changes are required by quality measures taken in response to customer complaints. In such cases, costs rise and the basic labor-hours taken as the reference value must also be revised upward to maintain a fair evaluation of the factory's kaizen costing activities. This kind of revision is made on a monthly basis.
- Another factor occurs when design changes are recommended following value analysis. Today, almost all VA takes place during target costing, leaving little need for it during kaizen costing. However, at the planning stage, products tend to be somewhat overengineered for quality and safety. For example, cardboard packaging may be a little thicker than necessary. The slack contained in such safety-minded specifications can in many cases be trimmed away once the products are actually moving on the production line.

2. Increase in converted vehicle amount due to variable model production

Buyers' requests for the addition of certain optional features can cause a wide variation in the vehicle models put on the line each month. For example, when a particular month has an especially large number of vehicles that must be equipped with time-consuming options such as a sunroof or antilock brakes, there is a major fluctuation in assembly labor-hours. When there are many major changes in vehicle models, there must also be changes made in the converted vehicle amount, which was calculated based on a typical model. As a result, the monthly cost total and the target reduction amount changes according to the following formula.

$$
\begin{array}{c} \text{Monthly} \\ \text{standard} \\ \text{indirect costs} \end{array} = \begin{array}{c} \text{standard} \\ \text{wage rate} \end{array} \times \begin{array}{c} \text{monthly} \\ \text{standard} \\ \text{indirect costs} \end{array} \times \begin{array}{c} \text{monthly} \\ \text{converted} \\ \text{vehicle} \\ \text{amount} \end{array}
$$

Accordingly, the target reduction amount for labor-hours per vehicle (based on the target reduction rate) must be revised during the business term when there is considerable variation in vehicle models.

29

Product-Specific Kaizen Costing

Definitions

There are three types of product-specific kaizen costing.

1. Product-specific kaizen costing in which the objective is to make up the shortfall for target costing goals that have not been fully attained

Three months after a new product has entered into full production, the target costing results for that product are evaluated. If this evaluation shows that some of the target costing goals (target costs) were not reached, improvement plans are determined to make up the difference. This shortfall then becomes the target reduction amount for these further improvement activities. The new targets are to be achieved through value analysis (VA) activities carried out by the cost kaizen committee (the project team). This approach is sometimes called an "early warning system."

2. Product-specific kaizen costing in which the objective is to recover profitability for unprofitable models

When certain vehicle models become unprofitable due to factors such as a poor economy, rising oil prices, and/or unfavorable currency exchange rates, a cost kaizen committee is formed especially for those vehicle models. The committee undertakes a project to further cut costs for those models, setting a cost reduction target that will achieve the profit target for each vehicle model and carrying out companywide activities to achieve the cost reduction target.

3. Product-specific kaizen costing by unit-specific committees

These committees plan and implement kaizen costing for specified parts or subassemblies, such as a particular engine or turbocharger, using the steps outlined in the next two sections.

Formation of Cost Kaizen Committee and Planning of Activities

Committees, with titles such as the "Model X Cost Kaizen Committee," are the project teams that are formed to plan and implement the type of cost reduction projects described in (1), (2), and (3) above. Figure 29-1 illustrates the configuration of such committees. Specifically:

- The superintendent of the plant where the target vehicle model is manufactured or the executive in charge of cost management serves as the team leader.
- The product manager for the target vehicle model serves as the subleader.
- The cost management office (or kaizen costing office) serves as the clerical center.
- Division chiefs of related divisions serve as team (committee) members.
- Various subcommittees (or study groups) are organized under each division. For example, the manufacturing division chief establishes process-specific subcommittees or a

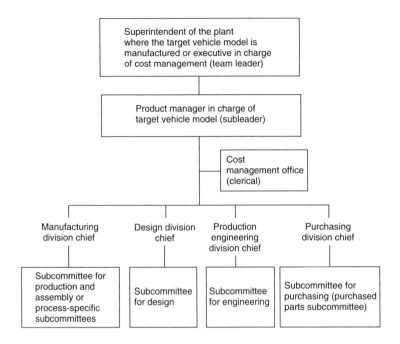

Figure 29-1. Typical Configuration of Model-Specific Cost Kaizen Committees

subcommittee for production and assembly. Likewise, the design division chief establishes a design subcommittee, the production engineering division chief establishes an engineering subcommittee, and the purchasing division chief establishes a purchasing (or purchased parts) subcommittee.

The cost kaizen committee and its various subcommittees carry out their activities for about six months. Their activities are centered on VA. (The Toyota group, the original source of the target costing/kaizen costing concept and methodology, defines value engineering (VE) as involving basic functional changes during the new product development stage and VA as the making of design changes related to cost reduction activities for vehicles already in production.)

Like new product development, VA activities require a process that includes presentation of drawings, prototype development, testing, and evaluation. This process requires the cooperation of the various subcommittees described above.

Once the cost kaizen committee and its subcommittees have been established, the process from presentation of drawings to evaluation focuses completely on the target vehicle model. This concentration enables a relatively short lead time and a quick payback in terms of recovered profitability.

Cost Analysis for Kaizen Costing of Specific Products

Almost all manufacturing companies have a wide variety of products that are manufactured simultaneously. Some of these products sell well and result in profits and others sell poorly and result in losses. The combined sales performance of these various products determines the sales figures reported in the whole company's profit-loss statements. The following are three methods for improving companywide sales profits:

1. Improve the profitability of current products.
2. Carry out model changes for certain current products.
3. Develop completely new products.

New product development concerns itself with the second and third method, but companies that are weak financially (i.e., unable to raise much capital) or are riding out a recession may concentrate on the first method. There are three ways to improve the profitability of current products:

(a) Turn money-losing products into moneymakers.
(b) Turn moneymakers into even bigger moneymakers.
(c) Combine methods (a) and (b).

Product portfolio management (PPM) is an approach for determining long-term strategies for new product development, including the methods described as (2) and (3) above. It generally does not concern itself with relatively short-term improvements for existing products. The first method (in both lists) is the one to emphasize when seeking to improve existing products.

The logic behind this approach to existing products is simple: If all of the company's existing products can be turned into moneymakers, then the company as a whole will surely be profitable.

The rule of thumb for kaizen of existing products is also simple: Clarify the various causes of poor profitability and then make improvements to eliminate the causes.

Steps

Step 1. Analyze the Products

Stratify existing products according to their degree of profitability, and analyze the biggest money losers first.

Step 2. Compare Product Sales/Costs to Target Values

Taking the biggest money losers as high-priority targets for improvement, draw a graph showing time-series trends for each product's sales, volume, and loss figures. Then draw another time-series graph for each product's cost elements. Compare those figures to the target values set during target costing (see Figure 29-2).

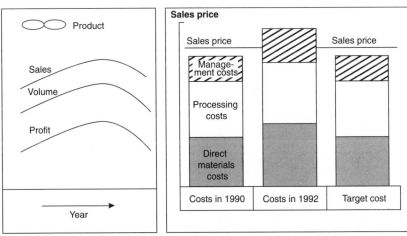

(Source: Nishiguchi 1993, p. 5.)

Figure 29-2. Cost Analysis for Product-Specific Kaizen Costing

Step 3. Search for Causes and Solutions

While referring to Figure 29-2, search for the basic causes of poor profitability among the items listed in the right column in Figure 29-3 (these items are possible causes for the cost categories listed in the figure's left column), and plan improvements to eliminate the selected causes.

Step 4. Plan and Supervise Improvement Targets

(a) Establish improvement targets and assign tasks to the departments in charge of implementing the improvements.
(b) Clarify improvement items and scheduling with the departments in charge of implementing the improvement.
(c) The department in charge of supervising these kaizen activities checks whether the improvement targets are achieved.

Improvement targets are assigned among cost kaizen committee members and improvement efforts are supervised in much the same way as for term-specific, department-specific kaizen costing systems.

Category		Cause of Poor Profitability
Sales price		Poor exchange rates adversely affect market prices
Volume		Past fluctuations and trends for the future
Design		Design changes which address improved performance, quality issues, new variations, greater variety of parts
In-house manufacturing costs		
	Labor	Processing time, higher wages
	Equipment depreciation	Currently planned equipment, additional equipment, equipment operating rate
	Indirect materials	Budgeted and actual costs of parts
Purchased parts		Division of in-house and outside parts manufacturing, price levels for purchased parts, unit price trends for materials

Figure 29-3. Causes of Poor Profitability

Allocation of kaizen costing activities, however, does not have to be part of a project such as this in which a cost kaizen committee is established. Instead, such activities can be assigned by workplace-based groups, who work to achieve department-specific kaizen costing goals in the same way that term-specific goals are pursued.

Case Study

In 1974, just after the 1973 oil crisis, Toyota saw its operating profit plummet 83 percent due to higher costs propelled by soaring oil prices and shrinking sales. In order to reduce its breakeven point for profitability to an operating rate of below 80 percent, Toyota picked its biggest seller, the Corolla, and established a Corolla Cost Kaizen Committee. The chairman of this committee (who was also a company director) was the superintendent of the Corolla plant. The Corolla Cost Kaizen Committee made the following proposals to the Cost Management Cross-Function Committee (a top-management decision-making group).

- Carry out a companywide cost-cutting campaign for the Corolla.
- Establish a Corolla Cost Reduction Committee, chaired by the Corolla plant superintendent.
- As substructures to the Corolla Cost Reduction Committee, establish three study groups, one each for:
  (a) Production and assembly
  (b) Design and engineering
  (c) Purchasing

- Set a cost reduction target of ¥10,000 (then about $40) per vehicle.
- Set a target achievement deadline of six months.

The Cost Management Cross-Function Committee accepted these proposals and, after six months of companywide efforts, Toyota realized a 128 percent attainment of the goal.

During this six-month effort, the Corolla Cost Reduction Committee thoroughly reviewed every part down to the last bolt and every production process, studying whether changes in dimensions, surface processing, or other factors would help cut costs. However, only so much cost reduction could be achieved through such incremental improvements. Therefore, they went beyond incremental changes—all the way back to the design stage to produce a new radiator grille design that uses less plastic, a new pressing process that eliminates a decorative part for the front hood air intake, and other cost-saving design changes.

30

Comparison of Japanese Kaizen Costing and Activity-Based Costing

Do Japanese Automobile Companies Need ABC?

This chapter compares activity-based costing (abbreviated as ABC), a method recently promoted in the United States, with Japan's kaizen costing and asks whether Japanese automobile companies need to adopt ABC. After briefly introducing ABC, we will examine the need for ABC from the perspective of Japanese automobile companies' cost configuration ratios. Next, we will further describe the kaizen costing approach that Japanese automobile companies use instead of ABC, and will compare and contrast the two approaches. Finally, we will explore the suitability (effectiveness) of ABC for Japanese industry in general.

Outline of ABC

The description here of the ABC approach is limited in scope, in line with the objectives stated above.

ABC is a type of accounting system that focuses on activities. The fundamental concept behind ABC is that activities consume resources (costs) and products consume activities.

The ABC approach says that cost elements (referred to as business resources) can be traced by the various activities that consume them. These costs, which are traced through such activities, are absorbed by various product models. At the second stage, the criteria for such cost absorption is the cost drivers that cause cost elements to be consumed by activities.

From the perspective of a conventional cost accounting system, we could say that these activities resemble what are called cost centers. The cost drivers are equivalent to the cost drivers that determine absorption of costs in conventional cost accounting systems.

ABC differs from conventional cost accounting in that its cost centers are subdivided in more detail; consequently they can be used for a wider range of cost absorption criteria, going beyond the conventional application of cost drivers as mainly operating rate-related criteria (direct operating time, machine operation time, direct materials costs, etc.).

Another difference is that the ABC approach subdivides what are conventionally called auxiliary department costs into activities, after which the absorption of costs goes directly to products. Therefore, we do not examine how auxiliary department costs are absorbed by the manufacturing division but instead jump directly to a product-specific accounting of costs. Therefore, the ABC approach tends to recognize as many types of costs as possible as direct manufacturing costs.

Cost Drivers That Explain the Behavior of Fixed Costs

It is well known, in conventional cost accounting, that variable costs are defined by their propensity to change with fluctuations in the short-term operating rate (basically, production volume). Costs that do not change with the short-term operating rate are defined as fixed costs.

Many important cost elements do change, however, due to causes other than fluctuations in production volume. These costs are conventionally regarded as fixed costs, since they are not affected by changes in production volume. They must be recognized, however, not as fixed-value costs but instead as variable costs that are influenced by different cost drivers.

While thus recognizing cost drivers not related to production volume, the ABC approach stratifies activities that are consumed by products into four levels. These are the (1) unit amount level, (2) batch level, (3) product type level, and (4) factory level.

Activities at the unit amount level are carried out for each product unit manufactured. Thus, activities at this level are very repetitive. Two examples are direct operation time and machine operation time. The costs for these activities vary according to the production volume.

Batch level activities are carried out each time a batch of goods is produced. Such things as machine retooling, order processing, and materials handling are more closely related to batch units than to product units. The costs for these activities are regarded as either common costs or fixed costs for all of the products in the batch, and these costs change according to the number of batches.

Activities at the product type level are carried out to support production of various kinds of products. Examples of activities at this level include making parts lists (bills of materials), updating work schedules, and some kinds of materials handling.

Activities at the factory level support production processes for the factory as a whole. Such costs are common to various products, and it is very difficult to trace any particular factory-level activity to any particular product.

Hitherto, the practice has been to divide the factory's indirect costs into variable costs and fixed costs. In relation to production volume, the costs for unit amount level activities are chiefly variable costs while those for activities at the other three levels are chiefly fixed costs. Incidentally, distinguishing among individual activities at the batch level and product type level is helpful when

selecting appropriate cost drivers for activities that create costs
that are seen as fixed costs in relation to production volume.
Various kinds of costs change. Many costs that are fixed costs in
relation to production volume are also variable costs in relation
to other cost drivers. This situation is especially true of activities
at the batch level and product type level. Costs incurred by activities at the factory level generally fall into the category of
fixed costs, and they can be allotted or traced to products by ar-
bitrary methods.

Figure 30-1 lists the various levels of activities, the costs used
for each level, and examples of cost drivers.

Applications of ABC

The ABC approach is useful for many types of business decision-making situations.

In decisions concerning business strategy, the ABC method can
be used to obtain reliable cost information. Such use enables top
managers to focus upon the most profitable products and product
types.

ABC also helps middle managers make marketing decisions, determine sales prices, plan promotional and advertising campaigns,
and correctly estimate product mixes and customer mixes. As for
production-related decisions, it helps managers make decisions
concerning product development and design and aids improvement activities (continuous operational improvements).

It is worth noting that both ABC and kaizen costing are intended to assist continuous operational improvements. Let us explore
this point a bit further.

The ABC approach is intended to continually provide evaluations that enable improvements to be identified (through cost
evaluations) and recommended for each activity. To achieve this
end, ABC measures, for example, the operating costs incurred by
changeover, by drafting manufacturing drawings and manuals, by
processing orders, and by clerical work associated with batch
transportation.

Activities at the unit amount level	Activities at the batch level
Activities: • Assembly activities • Press activities • Machining activities Resources consumed: • Operator wages and benefits • Cost of materials • Cost of consumables • Cost of energy consumption Cost drivers: • Operating time • Machine operating time • Direct manufacturing costs • Quantity of production units	Activities: • Batch changeover (retooling) • Materials handling • Order processing Resources consumed: • Operation costs for creating manufacturing manuals • Operation costs for order processing • Clerical costs for batch transport Cost drivers: • No. of batches • No. of changeovers • No. of orders to be processed
Activities at the product type level	**Factory-level activities**

Activities:
• Production scheduling
• Product design
• Part and product inspection
• Special transportation and special
  storage
 	
Resources consumed:
• Special-purpose equipment costs
• Design operation costs
• Cost of maintaining and updating
  files and records
 	
Cost drivers:
• Number of product types
• Number of part types
	Activities:
	• Factory supervision
	• Exclusive use of floor space
	• Personnel management
	
	Resources consumed:
	• Factory depreciation costs, taxes,
	  insurance fees
	• Factory superintendent's salary
	• General research-related costs
	
	Cost drivers:
	• Number of employees at manufacturing
	  activity centers
	• Distribution rate
	• Direct manufacturing costs
	• Volume of production units

Source: Adapted from Anderson and Sollenberger 1992, p. 82.

Figure 30-1. Cost Items and Cost Drivers for ABC's Four Levels of Activities

Japan's Kaizen Costing

As explained earlier, Japan's kaizen costing approach falls into two categories: (1) factory- or department-specific kaizen costing activities scheduled for each business term and (2) vehicle model-specific kaizen costing activities carried out as special projects.

Some department-specific cost reduction activities are implemented as a deployment of the short-term profit plan established for the following business term. Such activities are regarded as cost-reduction activities that seek to cut costs as part of budget management. The costs are broken down into variable costs and fixed costs, and term-specific target reduction amounts are set for the variable costs. The fixed costs are to be used as stated in the budget.

Cost Configuration at Japanese Automobile Companies and the Importance of Managing Variable Costs

In comparison to American automobile manufacturers, Japanese automakers have a much higher percentage of purchased parts costs in their overall configuration of costs, as American automakers manufacture more parts in-house whereas Japanese automakers tend to contract more to outside parts suppliers. The variable costs involved in these cases include the cost of purchased parts, the cost of materials used for parts manufactured in-house, and the direct labor cost (see Figure 30-2).

At Japanese automobile companies, variable costs account for more than 80 percent of overall costs. At Toyota, for example, direct materials costs are about 85 percent of the total, whereas direct labor costs are about 6 percent and operating costs are about 9 percent.

Accordingly, Japanese automobile companies can trace almost all cost behavior to operating rate-related cost drivers. And although they still need to trace the behavior of fixed costs using cost drivers that are not related to operating rate, which are the costs emphasized by the ABC approach, this part of total costs is not as important for Japanese automobile companies as it is for their American counterparts. Because the great majority of costs for Japanese automobile companies are variable costs, variable costs are clearly a more important issue for these companies.

Fixed costs are planned during the product planning and plant investment planning stages, and it is much more difficult

Manufacturing costs			
	Standard costs		
		Material costs	
			* Raw materials costs	Die-cast metals for engines and transmissions manufactured in-house, steel plates and plastics for vehicle bodies, etc.
			* Purchased parts costs	Interior equipment, tires, glass, seats, parts processed by outside contractors and assembled in-house, etc.
			* Paints, plastics, and adhesives	Exterior paints, thinner, gasoline, adhesives, etc.
		Processing costs	
			* Direct labor costs	Labor costs of technical staff (direct employees) of the Manufacturing Division who are directly involved in manufacturing automobiles.
			* Proportional indirect materials and operating costs	Cost of supplies for operators, tool and jig costs, off-spec losses, electricity and gas consumption, etc.
			Fixed processing costs	Labor costs of technical staff (indirect employees) of the Manufacturing Division (group leaders and improvement team leaders), operating costs other than those mentioned above, depreciation costs, and auxiliary department costs (maintenance and construction), etc.
	Other allocated costs		
		General departmental costs	Design, engineering costs (for testing, etc.), quality assurance costs, etc.
		Prototype development costs	Costs of prototype-related R&D and testing
		Die, jig, and tool costs	Depreciation costs for press dies, sheet metal jigs, etc.
		* Costs for transportation between factories	Costs for transporting parts and subassembly units between factories
General management and sales costs			
	* Direct sales costs (promotional costs)	Sales incentives, etc.	
	* Direct sales costs (other costs)	Costs for claims processing, cargo transportation, insurance, storage, etc.	
	Indirect management and sales costs	Management department costs, sales department costs, etc.	

Note: * indicates proportional (variable) costs

Figure 30-2. Cost Configuration for Automobiles

to reduce them when we come to budget management of overall costs during the production stage.

Measuring the Results of Workplace Improvement Activities as Part of Kaizen Costing

In kaizen costing, although many kinds of improvement activities take place at the workplace, the accounting division rarely keeps track of them. In factories, such improvement activities lead to cost reductions in various cost items for the factory, and the amount of such cost reductions resulting from these activities can be measured, but there is little effort to understand how specific improvement activities lead to specific cost reductions. In this respect, the accounting division does nothing more than encourage kaizen costing activities.

The factory's target reduction amounts for costs are established as kaizen costing targets for individual processes. Various methods and types of improvement activities are planned and implemented to reach these process-specific targets. For example, the planned improvement might be to reduce staffing requirements, increase the stroke per hour, shorten materials handling time, lower the defect rate, make minor line stoppages less frequent, shorten lead time, or reduce changeover time.

All these improvement activities are regarded as methods for achieving target cost reductions. The cost figures that result from these methods are seldom evaluated using an approach such as ABC. Naturally, costs that generally result from all improvements implemented at specific processes are measured, and the measured costs at each process are then compared with the target costs. However, even at companies that take the trouble to analyze the benefits gained from such improvements, bonuses or other rewards are rarely given for these accomplishments.

It is, though, a common practice among Japanese companies to provide bonuses and other rewards to shop-floor workers who devise and submit cost-effective improvement suggestions via the company's suggestion system.

Changeover Costs and Materials Handling Costs

Japanese automobile companies regard changeover costs and materials handling costs (conveyance, transportation, etc.) as variable costs under the category of labor-hour management. For accounting purposes, these costs are considered part of the direct labor costs. In such cases, standard operating time is defined as follows:

$$\begin{matrix} \text{Standard} \\ \text{operating} \\ \text{time} \end{matrix} = \begin{matrix} \text{direct} \\ \text{processing} \\ \text{time per unit} \end{matrix} + \frac{\text{total changeover time}}{\text{number of units in lot}}$$

The accounting division does not separate direct labor costs from changeover costs but instead regards changeover time and materials handling time as factory-based labor-hour management issues to be addressed when seeking to lower direct labor costs. Changeover costs and materials handling costs are included in direct labor costs because these two kinds of costs account for only a very small portion of overall costs.

This scale factor is also why Japanese automobile companies have not applied the ABC approach for these kinds of costs. Besides the fact that these costs are such a small portion of overall costs, they have also felt that companywide implementation of JIT techniques already works to minimize changeover time and other drivers for these costs.

Conclusion: Efforts to Reduce Fixed Costs

During the deep recession that hit Japan during the early 1990s, Japanese automobile companies began to strain under the burden of their fixed costs. Specifically, shrinking sales left an overabundance of labor—which meant excess labor costs, idle machinery (= excess equipment depreciation costs), and so on. As a result, the breakeven ratio for these companies was steadily worsening.

These conditions prompted Japanese automakers to place new emphasis on reducing not only variable costs but also fixed costs. As mentioned above earlier, however, the "continuous operational improvements" made at the production stage are relatively ineffective in reducing fixed costs when compared to target costing efforts at the product planning and development stages. Examples of such efforts include eliminating certain vehicle models, commonizing parts, or seeking greater economy of scale by dividing labor among several companies. There have also been efforts to restructure and/or reengineer to rationalize administrative departments. When applying the target costing approach for these purposes, companies use equipment-specific and process-specific cost tables that are more detailed than those used in conventional accounting systems.

In industries other than the automotive industry, it is not uncommon for companies to have fixed costs that account for as much as half of all costs (this is the case for process industries, such as the steel industry). In such industries, cost accounting and cost management must emphasize a variety of cost drivers that are not related to operating rate.

To reduce such cumbersome fixed costs, Japanese companies are employing not only target costing but also other methods that are substantially similar to the ABC approach.

Bibliography

Arranged by Company

Toyota

Ban, Shōji, and Kimura, Osamu. "Toyota jidōsha seisan bumon kihon no tettei to ju'nansei no torikomi" (Toyota Motor's production division: emphasizing the basics while working flexibly). *JMA Production Management.* October 1986: pp. 13-23.

Fukushima, Sachio. "Seihin kikaku dankai kara susumeru Toyota no buhin kyōtsūka" (Parts commonization starts from the product planning stage at Toyota). *IE rebyuu (IE Review).* March 1978 (special supplement issue): pp. 58-69.

Itō, Gorō, and, Yasuhiro Monden. *Toyota no genka kanri shisutemu (Toyota's cost management system).* 1993 (unpublished).

Monden, Yasuhiro. "Genka kikaku, genka kaizen, genka iji no kigen to hatten" (Sources and development of target costing, kaizen costing, and maintenance costing). *Kigyō kaikei (Corporate Accounting).* Vol. 45, No. 12, 1993: pp. 42-46.

Monden, Yasuhiro. *Shin Toyota shisutemu (The new Toyota system)*. Kodansha, 1991.

Monden, Yasuhiro. *Toyota shisutemu (The Toyota management system)*. Japan Management Association Management Center (JMAM), 1991.

Monden, Yasuhiro. *Toyota Management System: Linking the Seven Key Functional Areas*. Portland, Ore.: Productivity Press, 1993.

Monden, Yasuhiro. *Toyota Production System: An Integrated Approach to Just-in-Time, second ed*. Atlanta, Ga.: Industrial Engineering and Management Press, 1993

Monden, Yasuhiro. *Toyota Production System: Practical Approach to Production Management*. Atlanta, Ga.: IIE Press, 1983.

Morozumi, Takehiko. "Nyu moderu ga dekiru made: Serika keiretsu no baai" (The development story of the new line of Toyota Celica cars). *Mootaa fuan (Motor fan)*. January 1990: pp. 34-38.

Ozaki, Ryōsuke. "Jidōsha no hinshitsu hoshō shisutemu" (Quality assurance systems for automobiles). *Keiei shisutemu (Management Systems)*. Vol. 3, No. 3, 1993: pp. 159-166.

Tanaka, Takao. "Target Costing at Toyota." *Journal of Cost Management*. Summer 1993: pp. 4-11.

Tanaka, Takao. "Toyota no genka kikaku to kaizen yosan" (Toyota's target costing and kaizen budgeting). In Takao Tanaka, ed., *Fuiirudo sutadeii: gendai no kanri kaikei shisutemu (Field study: today's management accounting systems)*, ch. 1. Chūō Keizai-sha, 1993: pp. 29-58.

Tanaka, Takao. "Jidōsha meekaa ni okeru shin seihin kaihatsu to mokuhyō genka—Toyota no genka kikaku—" (Automakers' new product development and targets—Target costing at Toyota). *Kigyō kaikei (Corporate Accounting)*. Vol. 42, No. 10, October 1990: pp. 14-23.

Toyoda, Eiji. "Baburu e no hansei—aratanaru genka to no tatakai" (Looking back at the bubble economy—a new battle over costs). *Nikkan Kōgyō Shinbun (Japan Industrial News)*. December 24, 1993: p. 17.

Toyota Motor Company. *Yūka shōken hōkokusho sōran (Annual securities report)*. 1990, published by the Ministry of Finance printing office.

Watanabe, Yoshihiro. *Toyota ga Nihon o kaeru (Toyota can change Japan)*. Nikkan Shobō, 1992.

Daihatsu

Daihatsu Motors, Accounting Division. *Daihatsu kōgyō ni okeru genka kanri seido no gaiyō ni tsuite (Introduction to Daihatsu Motor's cost management system)*. February 1991 (unpublished).

Monden, Yasuhiro. "Genka kaizen no igi to mekanizumu— hyōjun genka keisan to no taihi" (The meaning and mechanics of kaizen costing—comparison with standard cost accounting). *Keisan (Accounting)*. Vol. 143, No. 2, February 1993 issue: pp. 63-75.

Monden, Yasuhiro. "Nihon no genka kaizen shisutemu to katsudō kijun genka keisan no hikaku—Nihon no jidōsha kaisha ni ABC wa hitsuyō ka" (Comparison of Japanese kaizen costing systems and standard cost accouting: is ABC needed at Japan's automobile companies?). *Kaikei-jin koosu (Course for Accountants)*. Vol. 28, No. 12, October 1993.

Monden, Yasuhiro. *Jidōsha kigyō no genka kaizen shisutemu— Daihatsu Kōgyō no jirei (Kaizen costing at automobile companies—case study of Daihatsu)*. 1991, (unpublished).

Monden, Y., and J. Y. Lee. "How a Japanese Automaker Reduces Costs: Kaizen Costing at Daihatsu." *Management Accounting*. August 1993: pp. 22-26.

Noboru, Yoshiteru and Yasuhiro Monden. "Jidōsha kigyō no genka kanri" (Cost management at automotive companies). In Kiyoshi Okamoto, Tada'aki Miyamoto, and Michiharu Sakurai, eds., *Haiteku kaikei (High-tech accounting)*, Case 4. Dōbunkan, 1988: pp. 272-289.

Noboru, Yoshiteru and Yasuhiro Monden. "Jidōsha kōgyō ni okeru sōgōteki genka kanri shisutemu" (Comprehensive cost management systems in the automotive industry). *Kigyō kaikei (Corporate Accounting)*. Vol. 35, No. 2, 1983: pp. 104-112.

Noboru, Yoshiteru. *Daihatsu kōgyō ni okeru genka keisan, genka kanri ni tsuite (Cost accounting and cost management at Daihatsu Motors)*. February 1982 (unpublished).

Nissan

Ebizaka, Sotoyuki, "Shinsha kaihatsu dankai ni okeru genka kanri" (Cost management at the new model development stage). *Keiei jitsumu (Managerial Practice)*. No. 438, October 1990: pp. 32-39.

Katō, Minoru. "Tokushū: kanri kaikei shisutemu no kaizen kadai, daini bu: waga sha no kanri kaikei shisutemu Nissan Jidōsha" (Special feature: kaizen in management accounting systems, part 2: our management accounting system at Nissan). *Kigyō kaikei (Corporate Accounting)*. Vol. 42, No. 10, October 1990: pp. 61-65.

Kato, Yutaka. *Soshiki henkaku kigyō rinen shintō katsudō to shōhin kaihatsu—Nissan Jidōsha no jirei—(Organizational restructuring, activities to implement corporate ideals, and product development—Case study of Nissan)*. March, 1992. (Unpublished).

Kato, Yutaka. "Genka kikaku kenkyū no imi—Nissan Jidōsha no jirei—" (The meaning of target costing research—Case study of Nissan). *Kokumin Keizai Zasshi (Japanese Economics Magazine)*. Vol. 166, No. 1, July 1992: pp. 101-132.

Kato, Yutaka. *Soshiki henkaku kigyō rinen shintō katsudō to shōhin kaihatsu—Nissan Jidōsha no jirei—(Organizational restructuring, activities to implement corporate ideals, and product development—Case study of Nissan)*. Kobe Daigaku Keiei Gakubu kenkyū nenpō (Annual research report of the Kobe University School of Business Administration). 1993.

Kimura, Katsutoshi. "Shinsha kaihatsu ni okeru genka kikaku katsudō" (Target costing activities at the new model development stage). *IE rebyuu (IE Review)*. Vol. 32, No. 2, May 1991: pp. 37-41.

Kimura, Katsutoshi. "Shōhin o jiku toshita genka kikaku katsudō" (Product-centered target costing activities). *JICPA jaanaru (JICPA Journal)*. No. 440, March 1992: pp. 61-65.

Sakai, Naoki. "Shin biggu kaa o tsuikyū shita Shiima" (The Nissan Cima: in pursuit of the new full-size car). In Takao Itai, ed., *Konseputo meekingu watakushi no hōhō (My concept making methods)*. Sannō University Press, 1991: pp. 148-158.

Shibata, Shōji. Naniga, *Nissan Jidōsha o kaeta noka (What has changed Nissan?)*. PHP Kenkyūkai (PHP Research Association), 1988.

Motohashi, Masami. "Nissan Jidōsha no rieki kanri to genka kikaku" (Profit management and target costing at Nissan). In Takao Tanaka, ed., *Fuiirudo sutadeii: gendai no kanri kaikei shisutemu (Field study: today's management accounting systems)*, ch. 2. Chūō Keizai-sha, 1993: pp. 59-83.

Honda

Fujimoto, T., and K. B. Clark. "The Power of Product Integrity." *Harvard Business Review*. Nov.-Dec., 1990.

Isuzu

Satō, Yoshihiko. "Manejimento no henkaku ni yoru buhin sakugen kyōtsūka—fukyō jidai o kokufuku suru—" (Reduction and commonization of parts through changes in management—overcoming the recession). *Baryuu enjiniiringu (Value Engineering)*. No. 154, February 1993: pp. 36-45.

Satō, Yoshihiko. "Gaiseihin izon-kei sangyō no kōbai katsudō" (Purchasing activities of industries dependent upon imported goods). *Keiei jitsumu (Managerial Practice)*. No. 442, February 1992: pp. 48-57.

Mazda

Takeda, Ryūji. "Kigyō paradaimu to jōhō shisutemu no sōgoteki eikyō—Matsuda no jirei kenkyū—" (Influences between corporate paradigms and information systems—A case study at Mazda). *Kigyō kaikei (Corporate Accounting)*. Vol. 42, No. 11, 1990: pp. 13-18.

Kanto Auto Works

Hakozaki, Masao. "Kōbai bumon ni okeru mokuhyō genka settei to genka kikaku katsudō ni tsuite" (Setting target prices in the purchasing division and other target costing activities). *Shizai kanri (Materials Management)*. Vol. 26, No 6., June 1983: pp. 1-7.

Nippondensō

Nishiguchi, Fumio. "Tōsha ni okeru genka kikaku katsudō no tenkai" (Development of target costing activities at our company). *Keiei jitsumu (Managerial Practice)*. No. 426, October 1988: pp. 279-293.

Watanabe, Oshie. "Nippon Densō no genka kanri katsudō to sono sapooto shisutemu" (Nippondenso's target costing activities and its support system). In Kigyō Keiei Kyōkai (Enterprise Management Association), ed., *Kanri Kaikei no Jissai—Riron to Jitsumu (The facts of management accounting—theory and practice)*. Zeimu Kenkyūkai Shuppan-kyoku (Tax Studies Publishing Office), 1988: pp. 279-293.

Xecel

Hakoda, Takashi. "Jiizeru kiki no genka kanri, teigen katsudōno jissai" (Facts about target costing and cost-reduction activiteis for diesel equipment). In Kigyō Keiei Kyōkai (Enterprise Management Association), ed., *Kanri Kaikei no Jissai—Riron to Jitsumu (The facts of management accounting—theory and practice)*. Zeimu Kenkyūkai Shuppan-kyoku (Tax Studies Publishing Office), 1988: pp. 295-317.

Yoshikawa, Yutaka. "Tōsha no genka kaizen katsudō to kōbai senryaku" (Kaizen costing and purchasing strategy at our company). *Keiei jitsumu (Managerial Practice)*. No. 442, February 1991: pp. 37-47.

Kubota

Iwahashi, Akio. "Kaihatsu sekkei dankai ni okeru genka kikaku katsudō to kosuto teeburu" (Target costing activities and cost tables at the design and development stages). *Keiei jitsumu (Managerial Practice)*. No. 426, October 1989: pp. 10-19.

Iwahashi, Akio. "Kakō, kumitate sangyō no genka kikaku katsudō—(kabu) Kubota ni okeru jirei to sono kaisetsu—" (Target costing activities in the machining and assembly industries—Analysis and case studies of Kubota). *IE rebyuu (IE Review)*. Vol. 32, No. 2, May 1991: pp. 21-28.

ASUMO

Nishiguchi, Fumio. *Kigyō keiei no genjō to genka kikaku kaizen katsudō (The current state of corporate management, target costing, and kaizen activities)*. 1993 (unpublished).

Matsushita Electric Industrial

Kato, Yutaka. "Genka kikaku to kanri kaikei—Matushita Denkō (kabu) A Kōjō no torikumi" (Target costing and management accounting—the struggle at Matsushita's Factory A). *Kokumin keizai zasshi (Japanese Economics Magazine)*. Vol. 162, No. 2, September 1990: pp. 15-35.

Hitachi

Tejima, Naoaki. "Seihin kaihatsu dankai no kosuto kanri—Kaihatsu danki e no VE no tekiyō—" (Cost management at the product development stage—Application of VE at the development stage). *IE rebyuu (IE Review)*. Vol. 32, No. 2, May 1991: pp. 42-51.

Tejima, Naoaki. "Genka kikaku ni kansuru itteigen—Seihin kai-hatsu dankai e no VE shuhō no tekiyō" (A proposal concerning target costing—Application of VE techniques at the product development stage). *Kigyō kaikei (Corporate Accounting)*. Vol. 44, No. 8, 1992: pp. 55-62.

NEC

Abe, Shōichi. *Atarashii kigyō kankyōka ni okeru genka kanri shistemu no arikata (How cost management systems work under new business environments)*. September 1991 (unpublished).

Abe, Shōichi. *NEC ni okeru genka kanri no dōkō (kaihatsu sekkei dankai ni okeru VE katsudō) (Cost management trends at NEC {VE activities at the design and development stages})*. March 1993 (unpublished).

Arai, Hideo. "Tōsha no seisan keitai-betsu genka kanri to VE kat-sudō" (Cost management and VE activities organized by types of production at our company). *Keiei jitsumu (Managerial Practice)*. No. 426, October 1989: pp. 1-9.

Fuji Electric

Yagi, Kimitoshi. "Tōsha ni okeru shizai gōrika katsudō no tenkai" (Development of materials rationalization activities at our company). *Keiei jitsumu (Managerial Practice)*. No. 442, February 1991: pp. 1-9.

TDK

Masujima, Suguru. *TDK-shiki "risō mokuhyō kanri" shisutemu (TDK's "ideal target management" system)*. Diamond-sha: 1991.

Masujima, Suguru. *Hinshitsu o agereba kosuto wa sagaru (When quality goes up, costs come down)*. Diamond-sha: 1992.

Victor Co. of Japan (JVC)

Suzuki, Naganari. "Kachi aru seihin-zukuri o mezasu VE kat-sudō" (VE activities that add value to products). *Keiei jitsumu (Managerial Practice)*. No. 426, October 1989: pp. 34-46.

Takubo, Takayuki. "Kaden seihin kaihatsu ni okeru kosuto enjiniaringu katsudō" (Cost engineering activities in the development of consumer electronics products). *IE rebyuu (IE Review)*. Vol. 32, No. 2, May 1991: pp. 13-18.

Ricoh

Aota, Eisuke. "Fukushaki jigyō de no genka kikaku katsudō" (Target costing activities in the photocopier industry). *JICPA Jaanaru (JICPA Journal)*. No. 440, March 1992: pp. 66-71.

Canon

Kan, Yasuhito. "Jimuki jigyō ni okeru genka kikaku katsudō" (Target costing activities in the business machine industry). *IE rebyuu (IE Review)*. Vol. 32, No. 2, May 1991: pp. 29-34.

Brother Industries

Mutō, Katsuhiko. *Burazaa kōgyō no genka kanri shisutemu (Brother Industries' cost management system)*. May 1993 (unpublished).

Sumitomo Heavy Industries

Shigeno, Katsumi. "Tōsha no shizai senryaku to sono tenkai" (Our materials strategy and its development). *Keiei jitsumu (Managerial Practice)*. No. 442, February 1991: pp. 10-19.

Daikin Industries

Tsukasa, Shirō. "Kūchō sangyō honbu no kōbai senryaku ni tsuite" (Purchasing strategy in the air conditioner industry). *Keiei jitsumu (Managerial Practice)*. No. 442, February 1991: pp. 20-36.

Arranged by Author

Abe, Shōichi. *Atarashii kigyō kankyōka ni okeru genka kanri shistemu no arikata (NEC) (How cost management systems work under new business environments) (NEC)*. September 1991 (unpublished).

Abe, Shōichi. *NEC ni okeru genka kanri no dōkō (kaihatsu sekkei dankai ni okeru VE katsudō). (Cost management trends at NEC [VE activities at the design and development stages])*. March 1993 (unpublished).

Akiba, Masao, Akiyuki Sakuma, Hiroyuki Takahashi, and Hiro'o Yoshida. *Seisan Kanri (Kaitei-ban) (Production Management [revised ed.])*, Daisan-shō: seisan kōtei no sekkei (Chapter 3: "Design of Production Processes"). JMA, 1987: pp. 59-118.

Anderson, L. K., and H. M. Sollenberger. *Managerial Accounting*, eighth ed. South-Western Pub. Co., 1992.

Aota, Eisuke. "Fukushaki jigyō de no genka kikaku katsudō" (Rikō) (Target costing activities in the photocopier industry) (Ricoh). *JICPA Jaanaru (JICPA journal)*. No. 440, March 1992: pp. 66-71.

Arai, Hideo. "Tōsha no seisan keitai-betsu genka kanri to VE kat-sudō" (NEC) (Cost management and VE activities organized by types of production at our company) (NEC). *Keiei jitsumu (Managerial Practice)*. No. 426, October 1989: pp. 1-9.

Arthur Andersen. *Cost Management*. Arthur Andersen & Co., 1993 (unpublished).

Arthur Andersen. *QCT Product Development*. Arthur Andersen & Co., 1993 (unpublished).

Arthur Andersen. *QCT Product Development Survey: Automotive Industry*. Arthur Andersen & Co., 1993 (unpublished).

Asanuma, Mari. "Sekkei tōshi kettei no purosesu to kijun— Nihon no jidōsha meeka no baai o chūshin toshite" (Process and standards for determining equipment design—a study centered on Japan's automobile makers). *Kokumin keizai zasshi (Japanese economics magazine)*. Vol. 152, No. 4, October 1985: pp. 37-59.

Ban, Shōji, and Kimura, Osamu. "Toyota jidōsha seisan bumon kihon no tettei to ju`nansei no torikomi" (Toyota Motor's production division: emphasizing the basics while working flexibly). *JMA Production Management*. October 1986: pp. 13-23.

Blanchard, B. S. *Design and Manage to Life Cycle Cost*. M/A Press, 1978.

Chow, W.C., Y. Kato, and D. M. Shields. "National Culture and the Preference for Management Control: An Exploratory Study of the Firm-Labor Market Interface.: Kobe University School of Business Administration, Working Paper 9313.

Cooper, R., and R. S. Kaplan. "Measure Costs Right: Make the Right Decisions." *Harvard Business Review*. Sept.-Oct., 1988: pp. 96-103.

Daihatsu Motors, Accounting Division. *Daihatsu kōgyō ni okeru genka kanri seido no gaiyō ni tsuite (Introduction to Daihatsu Motor's Cost Management System)*. February 1991 (unpublished).

Ebizaka, Sotoyuki, "Shinsha kaihatsu dankai ni okeru genka kanri" (Nissan) (Cost management at the new model development stage) (Nissan). *Keiei jitsumu (Managerial Practice)*. No. 438, October 1990: pp. 32-39.

Fujimoto, Takaharu. "Jidōsha no seihin kaihatsu soshiki to sekkei hinshitsu" (Automotive product development organizations and design quality). *Soshiki kagaku (Organizational Science)*. Vol. 22, No. 1, 1988: pp. 2-20.

Fujimoto, T., and K. B. Clark. "The Power of Product Integrity." *Harvard Business Review*. Nov.-Dec., 1990.

Fujita, Akihisa. *Shinpan IE no kiso (Foundation of the New IE)*, Kenpaku-sha, 1978.

Fukuda, Shuichi. *Konkarento enjiniaringu (Concurrent Engineering)*. Baifu-kan, 1993.

Fukuda, Yoshiaki. "Kōtei sekkei no dōkō to kadai" (Process design trends and themes). *Nihon keiei kōgaku-shi (Japanese Management Engineering Journal)*. Vol. 41, No. 4B, 1990: pp. B164-B168.

Fukushima, Sachio. "Seihin kikaku dankai kara susumeru Toyota no buhin kyōtsūka" (Parts commonization starts from the product planning stage at Toyota). *IE rebiyuu (IE Review)*. March 1978 (special supplement issue): pp. 58-69.

Hakoda, Takashi. "Jiizeru kiki no genka kanri, teigen katsudō no jissai" (Facts about target costing and cost-reduction activiteis for diesel equipment). In Kigyō Keiei Kyōkai (Enterprise Management Association), ed., *Kanri Kaikei no Jissai—Riron to Jitsumu (The Facts of Management Accounting—Theory and Practice)*. Zeimu Kenkyūkai Shuppan-kyoku (Tax Studies Publishing Office), 1988: pp. 295-317.

Hakozaki, Masao. "Kōbai bumon ni okeru mokuhyō genka settei to genka kikaku katsudō ni tsuite" (Kanto Auto Works) (Setting target prices in the purchasing division and other target costing activities) (Kanto Auto Works). *Shizai kanri (Materials Management)*. Vol. 26, No 6., June 1983: pp. 1-7.

Hashimoto, Ken'ichi, and Miyata, Takeshi. *Gijutsusha no tame no mitsumori genka keisan (Estimated Cost Accounting for Engineers)*. JMA, 1988.

Horiuchi, Ei'ichi. "Genka taishitsu o tsuyoku suru seisan seizō no kaikaku" (Manufacturing reforms that strengthen the cost structure). *IE rebiyuu (IE Review)*. March 1978 (special supplement issue): pp. 44-51.

Inoue, Shōgo, and Hatakeyama, Shigeo. *Keiei no tame no KJ hō nyūmon (Introduction to the KJ Approach to Management)*. JMA, 1978.

Ishimatsu, Yasuo. *Sekkei Seizō Bumon no tame no Genka Kanri to Genka Kaizen (Cost Management and Kaizen Costing for Design and Production)*. Nikkan Kōgyō Shinbun-sha: 1987.

Itō, Gorō, and Yasuhiro Monden. *Toyota no genka kanri shisutemu (Toyota's cost management system)*. 1993 (unpublished).

Itō, Hiroshi. "Nihon-teki genka kanri no kiseki to tenbō" (Japanese cost accounting today and tomorrow). *Kigyō kaikei (Corporate Accounting)*. Vol. 44, No. 8, 1992: pp. 17-47.

Itō, Yoshihiro. "Henkaku o semarareru genka kikaku—Seizō butsu sekinin, chikyū kankyō hozen rongi no takamari no nakade" (Target costing on the brink of change—amidst rising concerns over product liability and global environmental protection). *Sangyō keiri (Industrial Accounting)*. Vol. 52, No. 1, 1992: pp. 73-82.

Iwabuchi, Yoshihide. "Genka kikaku no kinō—Jōhō kyōtsūka to chishiki sōzō no kanten kara" (Target costing functions—from the perspective of information sharing and the creation of knowledge). *Kigyō kaikei (Corporate Accounting)*. Vol. 44, No. 8, 1992: pp. 41-47.

Iwahashi, Akio. "Kaihatsu sekkei dankai ni okeru genka kikaku katsudō to kosuto teeburu (Kubota)" (Target costing activities and cost tables at the design and development stages {Kubota}). *Keiei jitsumu (Managerial Practice)*. No. 426, October 1989: pp. 10-19.

Iwahashi, Akio. "Kakō, kumitate sangyō no genka kikaku katsudō—(kabu) Kubota ni okeru jirei to sono kaisetsu—" (Target costing activities in the machining and assembly industries—Analysis and case studies of Kubota). *IE rebyuu (IE Review)*. Vol. 32, No. 2, May 1991: pp. 21-28.

Iwamoto, Yukio. *Sekkei no hōhō—sōzō-teki sekkei e no apruoochi—(Design methods—an approach to creative design)*. JUSE Press, 1987.

JIPM Life Cycle Cost Council, ed. *Raifu saikuru kosutingu: shuhō to jitsurei (Life Cycle Costing: Techniques and Examples)*. JMA, 1981.

Kan, Yasuhito. "Jimuki jigyō ni okeru genka kikaku katsudō" (Target costing activities in the business machine industry). *IE rebyuu (IE Review)*. Vol. 32, No. 2, May 1991: pp. 29-34.

Kanazawa, Yūichirō, and Monden, Yasuhiro. *Genka kikaku ni okeru mokuhyō hanbai kakau no kettei hōhō (Setting Target Sales Prices as Part of Target Costing)*. 1994 (unpublished).

Kasanen, E., K. Lukka, and A. Siitonen. "The Constructive Approach in Management Accounting Research." *Journal of Management Accounting Research.* Vol. 5, Fall 1993: pp. 243-264.

Katō, Minoru. "Tokushū: kanri kaikei shisutemu no kaizen kadai, daini bu: waga sha no kanri kaikei shisutemu Nissan Jidōsha" (Special feature: kaizen in management accounting systems, part 2: our management accounting system at Nissan). *Kigyō kaikei (Corporate Accounting).* Vol. 42, No. 10, October 1990: pp. 61-65.

Kato, Yutaka. "Genka kikaku—senryaku-teki kosuto manejimento—" (Target costing—strategic cost management). *Nihon Keizai Shinbun-sha (Japan Economic News),* 1993.

Kato, Yutaka. "Genka kikaku katsudō no shintenkai: Daihatsu Kōgyō no jirei" (New development of target costing activities: Case study of Daihatsu). *Kaikei (Accounting).* Vol. 138, No. 1, Janurary 1990: pp. 46-63.

Kato, Yutaka. "Genka kikaku kenkyū no imi—Nissan Jidōsha no jirei—" (The meaning of target costing research—Case study of Nissan). *Kokumin keizai zasshi (Japanese Economics Magazine).* Vol. 166, No. 1, July 1992: pp. 101-132.

Kato, Yutaka. "Genka kikaku to kanri kaikei—Matushita Denkō (kabu) A Kōjō no torikumi" (Target costing and management accounting—the struggle at Matsushita's Factory A). *Kokumin keizai zasshi (Japanese Economics Magazine).* Vol. 162, No. 2, September 1990: pp. 15-35.

Kato, Yutaka. "Genka kikaku to SIS" (Target costing and SIS). *Kigyō kaikei (Corporate Accounting).* Vol. 42, No. 12, December 1990: pp. 103-108.

Kato, Yutaka. "Nihon kigyō no kaigai shinshutsu to genchika sareru ishi kettei kengen" (Overseas expansion by Japanese companies and local decision-making issues). *Sangyō keiri (Industrial Accounting).* Vol. 53, No. 1, 1993.

Kato, Yutaka. "Soshiki henkaku kigyō rinen shintō katsudō to shōhin kaihatsu—Nissan Jidōsha no jirei—(Organizational restructuring, activities to implement corporate ideals, and product development—Case study of Nissan)." Kobe Daigaku Keiei Gakubu kenkyū nenpō (Annual research report of the Kobe University School of Business Administration). 1993.

Kato, Y., G. Boer, and W. C. Chow. "Target Costing: An Integrative Management Process." Kobe University School of Business Administration, Working Paper 9321.

Kimura, Katsutoshi. "Shinsha kaihatsu ni okeru genka kikaku katsudō" (Nissan) (Target costing activities at the new model development stage) (Nissan). *IE rebyuu (IE Review)*. Vol. 32, No. 2, May 1991: pp. 37-41.

Kimura, Katsutoshi. "Shōhin o jiku toshita genka kikaku katsudō" (Product-centered target costing activities). *JICPA jaanaru (JICPA Journal)*. No. 440, March 1992: pp. 61-65.

Kobayashi, Hirotaka. "Genka kanri to VE" (Cost management and VE). *Kaikei (Accounting)*. Vol. 137, No. 3, 1990: pp. 62-74.

Kobayashi, Tetsuo. *Gendai genka keisan-ron—Senryaku-teki kosuto manejimento e no apuroochi (Today's Cost Accounting Theories: An Approach to Strategic Management)*. Chūō Keizai-sha, 1993.

Kobe University Management Accounting Research Association. "Genka kikau no jittai chōsa (1) - (3)" (Target Costing Surveys {1} - {3}). *Kigyō kaikei (Corporate Accounting)*. Vol. 44, Nos. 5-7, May-July 1992: pp. 86-91, 74-79, and 84-89.

Kondō, Tadamasa. "Shin shōhin kaihatsu dankai ni okeru shisaku zumen sekkei purocesu to sono tokuchōten—jidōsha meekaa no mokuhyō kosuto tassei katsudō ni kanren shite" (The process and key points of designing prototype drawings at the new product development stage—related to the target cost achievement activities of an automobile maker). *Dōshisa shōgaku (Dōshisa Commercial Studies)*. Vol. 41, Nos. 3 and 4, December 1989: pp. 320-335.

Kondō, Tadamasa. "Taagetto kosuto no sakutei purosesu ni kansuru ikkōsatsu—jidōsha meeka no jirei ni kanren shite— (Observations on the process for determining target costs: case study of an automobile maker). *Dōshisa shōgaku (Dōshisa Commercial Studies)*. Vol. 41, No. 1, June 1989: pp. 94-110.

Kondō, Tadamasa. "Waga kuni seizō kigyō no kanri kaikei jit-sumu—Bō jidōsha meeka no jirei (Oboegaki)—" (Management accounting practice at Japanese manufacturing companies— Case study of an automobile maker {Notes}). *Dōshisa shōgaku (Dōshisa Commercial Studies)*. Vol. 40, No. 2, August 1988: pp. 96-106.

Kondō, Tadamasa. "Genka kikaku ni kansuru ikkōsatsu—Kanri kaikei no kenkyū taishō to shite no ichi-zuke ni tsuite" (Thoughts about target costing—its role as a subject of man-agement accounting research). *Dōshisa shōgaku (Dōshisa Commercial Studies)*. Vol. 42, Nos. 4 and 5, February 1991: pp. 201-218.

Kondō, Tadamasa. "Genka kikaku ni okeru kanri kaikei no yakuwari—Sekushon-shikō kara chiimu-shikō e —" (The role of management accounting in target costing—from section-oriented to team-oriented management). *Genka keisan (Cost Accounting)*. Vol. 32, 1991: pp. 1-10.

Kondō, Tadamasa. "Genka kanri no henbō—Gijutsu shikō para-daimu kara shijō shikō paradaimu e —" (Sea-change in cost management—from a technology-oriented paradigm to a mar-ket-oriented paradigm). *Kaikei (Accounting)*. Vol. 137, No. 4, 1990: pp. 506-520.

Kura, Yoshimi, and Koyamada, Kenji. *Kyodai kigyō Toyota no genkai (Limits of Mega-Company Toyota)*. Nisshin hōdō, 1993.

Kurabayashi, Yoshio, Yoshio Sugasawa, and Kōichi Murata. *Chūshokigyō no tame no VE ni yoru sehin gijutsu kaihatsu" (Product and Technology Development via VE for Medium and Small Companies)*. Nikkan Kōgyō Shinbun-sha, 1987.

Lee, J. Y. *Managerial Accounting Changes for the 1990s*. Read-ing, Mass.: Addison-Wesley, 1987.

Masa, Shirō. "Kūchō sangyō honbu no kōbai senryaku ni tsuite" (Daikin Kōgyō) (Purchasing strategy in the air conditioner industry—Daikin Industries). *Keiei jitsumu (Managerial Prac-tice)*. No. 442, February 1991: pp. 20-36.

Masujima, Suguru. *Hinshitsu o agereba kosuto wa sagaru (When Quality Goes Up, Costs Come Down)*. Diamond-sha, 1992.

Masujima, Suguru. *TDK-shiki "risō mokuhyō kanri" shisutemu (TDK's "Ideal Target Management" System)*. Diamond-sha, 1991.

Miles, L. D. *Techniques of Value Analysis and Engineering*, second ed. New York: McGraw-Hill, 1972.

Monden, Yasuhiro. *Applying Just in Time: The American/ Japanese Experience*. Atlanta, Ga.: IEE Press, 1986.

Monden, Yasuhiro. *Cost Management in the New Manufacturing Age: Innovations in the Japanese Automotive Industry*. Portland, Ore.: Productivity Press, 1992.

Monden, Yasuhiro. "Genka kaizen no igi to mekanizumu— hyōjun genka keisan to no taihi" (The meaning and mechanics of target costing: comparison with standard cost accounting). *Kaikei (Accounting)*. Vol. 143, No. 2, February 1993: pp. 63-75.

Monden, Yasuhiro. "Genka kikaku ni okeru kōtei sekkei no yakuwari" (The role of process design in target costing). *Kigyō kaikei (Corporate Accounting)*. Vol. 45, No. 10, October 1993.

Monden, Yasuhiro. "Genka kikaku, genka kaizen, genka iji no kigen to hatten" (Sources and development of target costing, kaizen costing, and maintenance costing). *Kigyō kaikei (Corporate Accounting)*. Vol. 45, No. 12, 1993: pp. 42-46.

Monden, Yasuhiro. "Japanese Target-Costing System of Parts Supplier Committed to the Development Phase of the Automaker." IMVP Research Briefing Meeting, June, 1993.

Monden, Yasuhiro. "Nihon no genka kaizen shisutemu to katsudō kijun genka keisan no hikaku—Nihon no jidōsha kaisha ni ABC wa hitsuyō ka" (Comparison of Japanese kaizen costing systems and standard cost accouting: is ABC needed at Japan's automobile companies?). *Kaikei-jin koosu (Course for Accountants)*. Vol. 28, No. 12, October 1993.

Monden, Yasuhiro. *Jidōsha kigyō no genka kaizen shisutemu—Daihatsu Kōgyō no jirei (Kaizen Costing at Automobile Companies—Case Study of Daihatsu).* 1991 (unpublished).

Monden, Yasuhiro. *Jidōsha kigyō no kosuto manejimento—genka kikaku, genka kaizen, genka keisan—(Cost Management at Automobile Companies: Target Costing, Kaizen Costing, and Cost Accounting).* Dōbunkan, 1991.

Monden, Yasuhiro. *Shin Toyota shisutemu (The New Toyota System).* Kodansha, 1991.

Monden, Yasuhiro. *Toyota keiei shisutemu (The Toyota Management System).* Japan Management Association Management Center (JMAM), 1991.

Monden, Yasuhiro. *Toyota Management System: Linking the Seven Key Functional Areas.* Portland, Ore.: Productivity Press, 1993.

Monden, Yasuhiro. *Toyota Production System: An Integrated Approach to Just-in-Time, second ed.* Atlanta, Ga.: Industrial Engineering and Management Press, 1993

Monden, Yasuhiro. *Toyota Production System: Practical Approach to Production Management.* Atlanta, Ga.: IIE Press, 1983.

Monden, Y., and K. Hamada. "Target Costing and Kaizen Costing in Japanese Automobile Companies." *Journal of Management Accounting Research.* Vol. 3, Fall 1991: pp. 16-34.

Monden, Y., and J. Y. Lee. "How a Japanese Automaker Reduces Costs: Kaizen Costing at Daihatsu." *Management Accounting.* August 1993: pp. 22-26.

Monden, Y., and M. Sakurai. *Japanese Management Accounting: A World Class Approach to Profit Management.* Portland, Ore.: Productivity Press, 1989.

Monden, Y., R. Shibakawa, S. Takayanagi, and T. Nagao. *Innovations in Management: The Japanese Corporation.* Atlanta, Ga.: IIE Press, 1985.

Morozumi, Takehiko. "Nyu moderu ga dekiru made: Serika keiretsu no baai" (The development story of the new line of Toyota Celica cars). *Mootaa fuan (Motor Fan).* January 1990: pp. 34-38.

Motohashi, Masami. "Nissan Jidōsha no rieki kanri to genka kikaku" (Profit management and target costing at Nissan). In Takao Tanaka, ed., *Fuiirudo sutadeii: gendai no kanri kaikei shisutemu (Field Study: Today's Management Accounting Systems)*, ch. 2. Chūō Keizai-sha, 1993: pp. 59-83.

Motono, Shōzō. "Hōshin kanri" (Policy management). *Kōjō kanri (Plant Management)*. Vol. 36, No. 4, 1990: pp. 50-54.

Nihon Marketing Systems, ed., and Naotaka Torii, chief ed. *Jissen shin seihin kaihatsu handobukku (A Practical Handbook for New Product Development)*. JMA, pp. 170-181.

Nishiguchi, Fumio. "Tōsha ni okeru genka kikaku katsudō no tenkai" (Nippondenso) (Development of target costing activities at our company) (Nippondenso). *Keiei jitsumu (Managerial Practice)*. No. 426, October 1988: pp. 279-293.

Nishiguchi, Fumio. *Kigyō keiei no genjō to genka kikaku kaizen katsudō (ASUMO) (The Current State of Corporate Management, Target Costing, and Kaizen Activities) (ASUMO)*. 1993 (unpublished).

Nobeoka, K., and A. M. Cusumano. "Multi-project Management: Strategy and Organization in Automobile Product Development." IMVP Research Briefing Meeting, June 1993: pp. 1-53.

Noboru, Yoshiteru and Monden, Yasuhiro. "Jidōsha kigyō no genka kanri" (Cost management at automotive companies). In Kiyoshi Okamoto, Tada'aki Miyamoto, and Michiharu Sakurai, eds., *Haiteku kaikei (High-Tech Accounting)*, Case 4. Dōbunkan, 1988: pp. 272-289.

Noboru, Yoshiteru and Yasuhiro Monden. "Jidōsha kōgyō ni okeru sōgōteki genka kanri shisutemu" (Comprehensive cost management systems in the automotive industry). *Kigyō kaikei (Corporate Accounting)*. Vol. 35, No. 2, 1983: pp. 104-112.

Noboru, Yoshiteru. Daihatsu kōgyō ni okeru genka keisan, genka kanri ni tsuite (Cost accounting and cost management at Daihatsu Motors), February 1982 (unpublished).

Okada, Mikio. "Baraeti ridakushon ni yoru seihin seisan kōzō no kansoka" (Simplification of product and production structuring through variety reduction). *IE rebyuu (IE Review)*. Special issue, March 1978: pp. 29-36.

Otis, I. "Design for Manufacturing and Assembly." *Appliance Manufacturer*. Vol. 35, November 1990: pp.. 1-13.

Otis, I., "Seizō kumitate no tame no seisan sekkei hō—DFMA—" (DFMA: a design method for production and assembly). *IE rebyuu (IE Review)*. Vol. 34, No. 2, 1993: pp. 27-32.

Ozaki, Ryōsuke. "Jidōsha no hinshitsu hoshō shisutemu" (Toyota) (Quality assurance systems for automobiles) (Toyota). *Keiei shisutemu (Management Systems)*. Vol. 3, No. 3, 1993: pp. 159-166.

Sakai, Naoki, ed. *Konseputo meekingu watakushi no hōhō (My concept making methods)*, Sannō University Press, 1991.

Sakai, Naoki. "Shin biggu kaa o tsuikyū shita Shiima" (The Nissan Cima: in pursuit of the new full-size car). In Naoki Itai, ed., *Konseputo meekingu watakushi no hōhō (My Concept Making Methods)*. Sannō University Press, 1991: pp. 148-158.

Sakurai, Michiharu (moderator). "Entaku tōron kigyō kankyō no henka to kanri kaikei riron no gendai-teki kadai—Shigen no yūko riyō o mezashite —" (Round-table discussion on the changing corporate environment and current topics in management accounting theory—toward more effective uses of resources). *Kaikei (Accounting)*. February 1993: pp. 77-111.

Sakurai, Michiharu. *CIM kōchiku—Kigyō kankyō no henka to kanri kaikei—(CIM architecture—changes in the corporate environment and management accounting)*. Dōbunkan, 1991.

Sakurai, Michiharu. "Jidōka ga umu shinkei kanri kaikei" (A new kind of management accounting resulting from automation). *Nihon keizai shinbum (Japan Economic News)*. November 30, 1988, morning edition.

Sakurai, Michiharu. "Target Costing and How to Use It." *Journal of Cost Management*. Summer 1989: pp. 39-50.

Satō, Yasuo, ed. *Keesu sutadii—Nihon kigyō no kanri kaikei shisutemu—(Case Studies: Management Accounting Systems at Japanese Companies)*. Hakutō Shobō, 1993.

Satō, Yoshihiko. "Gaiseihin izon-kei sangyō no kōbai katsudō" (Isuzu) (Purchasing activities of industries dependent upon imported goods) (Isuzu). *Keiei jitsumu (Managerial Practice)*. No. 442, February 1992: pp. 48-57.

Satō, Yoshihiko. "Manejimento no henkaku ni yoru buhin sakugen kyōtsūka—fukyō jidai o kokufuku suru—" (Isuzu) (Reduction and commonization of parts through changes in management—overcoming the recession) (Isuzu). *Baryuu enjiniiringu (Value Engineering)*. No. 154, February 1993: pp. 36-45.

Shapiro, B. P., and B. B. Jackson. "Industrial Pricing to Meet Customer Needs." *Harvard Business Review*. Nov.-Dec. 1978: pp. 119-127.

Shibata, Shōji. *Naniga, Nissan Jidōsha o kaeta noka (What Has Changed Nissan?)*. PHP Kenkyūkai (PHP Research Association), 1988.

Shigeno, Katsumi. "Tōsha no shizai senryaku to sono tenkai" (Sumitomo Jūkikai Kōgyō) (Our materials strategy and its development) (Sumitomo Heavy Industries). *Keiei jitsumu (Managerial Practice)*. No. 442, February 1991: pp. 10-19.

Shimizu, Nobutada. "Genka kikaku katsudō ni okeru mokuhyō genka jōhō to chishiki sōzō katsudō no kankei" (The relation between target cost data and knowledge-building acititvies as part of target costing activities). *Sangyō keiri (Industrial Accounting)*. Vol. 51, No. 4, 1992: pp. 132-141.

Sugasawa, Yoshio. *Pasokon ni yoru seihin kinō bunseki to hyōka—kinō deetabeesu no katsuyō—(PC-Based Functional Analysis: An Evaluation of Products—Use of a functional database)*. Nikkan Kogyō Shinbun-sha, 1991.

Suzuki, Naganari. "Kachi aru seihin-zukuri o mezasu VE katsudō" (JVC) (VE activities that add value to products) (JVC), *Keiei jitsumu (Managerial Practice)*. No. 426, October 1989: pp. 34-46.

Suzuki, Toshio. *Konkarento enjiniarningu no susume (Concurrent Engineering)*. JMAM, 1992.

Takatate, Akiyoshi. "Tayōka to tei sōgyōdo taishitsu ni taiō suru baraeti ridakushon" (Variety reduction in response to diversification and low operating rates). *IE rebyuu (IE Review)*. Special issue, March 1978: pp. 21-28.

Takeda, Ryūji. "Jōhō shisutemu ni kakawaru paradaimu-kei model" (A paradigm model concerning information systems). *Kigyō kaikei (Corporate Accounting)*. Vol. 42, No. 4, 1990: pp. 4-11.

Takeda, Ryūji. "Kigyō paradaimu to jōhō shisutemu no sō goteki eikyō—Matsuda no jirei kenkyū—" (Influences between corporate paradigms and information systems—A case study at Mazda). *Kigyō kaikei (Corporate Accounting)*. Vol. 42, No. 11, 1990: pp. 13-18.

Takefuji, Katsuhiko. *Burazaa Kōgyō no genka kanri shisutemu (Brother Industries' Cost Management System)*. May 1993, (unpublished).

Takeuchi, Hirotaka, Nonaka, Ikujirō. "Seihin kaihatsu purosesu no manejimento" (Management of the product development process). *Bijinesu rebyuu (Business Review)*. Vol. 32, No. 4, 1985: pp. 24-44.

Takubo, Takayuki. "Kaden seihin kaihatsu ni okeru kosuto en-jiniaringu katsudō" (JVC) (Cost engineering activities in the development of consumer electronics products) (JVC). *IE re-byuu (IE Review)*. Vol. 32, No. 2, May 1991: pp. 13-18.

Tanaka, Masayasu, Michio Amagasa, and Tatsurō Aman. "Sekkei tokusei-chi ni yoru seijuku seihin no yosoku baika no settei hōhō" (Methods for setting predicted sales prices of mature products by using design characteristics). *Nihon Kanri Kaikei Gakkai-shi (Journal of the Japanese Management Accounting Society)*. Vol. 39, No. 4, 1988: pp. 211-217.

Tanaka, Masayasu. "Genka kikaku ni okeru genka kaizen hōhō" (Kaizen costing methods used in target costing). *Genka keisan kenkyū (Cost Accounting Studies)*. Vol. 17, No. 2, 1992: pp. 1-19.

Tanaka, Masayasu. "Genka kikaku ni okeru genka mokuhyō no settei to saibunka" (Setting and defining target costs as part of target costing). *Nihon Kanri Kaikei Gakkai-shi: Kanri kaikei gaku (Management Accounting: Journal of the Japanese Management Accounting Society)*. Vol. 1, No. 1, Autumn 1992 issue.

Tanaka, Masayasu. "Genka kikaku no kangaekata to susumeka-ta" (The philosophy and implementation of target costing). In

Kiyoshi Okamoto, Tada'aki Miyamoto, and Michiharu Sakurai, eds., *Haiteku kaikei (High-Tech Accounting)*, ch. 4.
Dōbunkan, 1988: pp. 53-63.

Tanaka, Masayasu. "Genka kikaku no susumekata I: Hitsuyōsei
to kangaekata" (Implementing target costing I: The need for
target costing and its philosophy). *IE rebyuu (IE Review)*. Vol.
33, No. 2, June 1992: pp. 61-67.

Tanaka, Masayasu. "Genka kikaku no susumekata II: Genka
mokuhyō no settei to saibunka" (Implementing target costing
II: Setting and defining target costs). *IE rebyuu (IE Review)*.
Vol. 33, No. 3, August 1992: pp. 59-67.

Tanaka, Masayasu. "Genka kikaku no susumekata III: Genka
mitsumori no kangaekata to hōhō" (Implementing target costing III: Cost estimating approach and methods). *IE rebyuu (IE
Review)*. Vol. 33, No. 4, October 1992: pp. 57-67.

Tanaka, Masayasu. "Genka kikaku no susumekata V: Genka
mokuhyō no tassei hōsaku" (Implementing target costing V:
Policies for achieving target costs). *IE rebyuu (IE Review)*. Vol.
34, No. 1, March 1993: pp. 55-62.

Tanaka, Masayasu. "Genka kikaku no susumekata VI: Seihin
konseputo zukuri" (Implementing target costing VI: Creating
product concepts). *IE rebyuu (IE Review)*. Vol. 34, No. 2, May
1993: pp. 54-64.

Tanaka, Masayasu. "Kosuto enjiniaruingu no honshitsu to Nihon
no genjō ni tsuite" (Fundamentals of cost engineering and the
current situation in Japan). *Genka keisan (Cost Accounting)*.
No. 274, 1984: pp. 42-44.

Tanaka, Masayasu. "Kosuto teeburu no honshitsu to katsuyō"
(Fundamentals and application of cost tables). *Genka keisan
(Cost Accounting)*. Vol. 20, No. 281, 1986: pp. 35-53.

Tanaka, Masayasu. "Mono no genka mitsumori to kinō leberu
no genka mitsumori—sekkei shiyō o hyōka suru genka mitsumori no taipu ni tsuite —" (Cost estimations of things and of
functional levels: types of cost estimations used to evaluate design specifications). *Genka keisan (Cost Accounting)*. Vol. 24,
No. 288, 1988: pp. 41-72.

Tanaka, Masayasu. "Nihon kigyō no shinseihin kaihatsu ni okeru genka kanri" (Cost management in the new product development of Japanese companies). *Kigyō kaikei (Corporate Accounting)*. Vol. 41, No. 2, 1989: pp. 19-25.

Tanaka, Masayasu. "Seihin no kaihatsu sekkei dankai ni okeru genka mitsumori no hōhō" (Cost estimation methods used at the product design and development stages). *Genka keisan (Cost Accounting)*. Vol. 22, No. 285, 1987: pp. 58-88.

Tanaka, Masayasu. *VE (Kachi bunseki) (VE [Value Engineering])*. Management-sha, 1985.

Tanaka, Takao. "Target Costing at Toyota." *Journal of Cost Management*. Summer 1993: pp. 4-11.

Tanaka, Takao. "Toyota no genka kikaku to kaizen yosan" (Toyota's target costing and kaizen budgeting). In Takao Tanaka, ed., *Fuiirudo sutadeii: gendai no kanri kaikei shisutemu (Field Study: Today's Management Accounting Systems)*, ch. 1. Chūō Keizai-sha, 1993: pp. 29-58.

Tanaka, Takao. "Genka kikaku" (Target costing). In Takao Tanaka and Hirotaka Kobayashi, eds., *Kanri kaikei-ron gaidansu (Guidance in Management Accounting Theory)*, ch. 4. Chūō Keizai-sha, 1993. pp. 50-61.

Tanaka, Takao. "Jidōsha meekaa ni okeru shin seihin kaihatsu to mokuhyō genka—Toyota no genka kikaku" (Automakers' new product development and targets—Target costing at Toyota). *Kigyō kaikei (Corporate Accounting)*. Vol. 42, No. 10, October 1990: pp. 14-23.

Tani, T., and Y. Kato. "Target Costing: A Contingency Approach." Kobe University School of Business Administration, Working Paper 9325, July 1993.

Tejima, Naoaki. "Genka kikaku ni kansuru itteigen—Seihin kaihatsu dankai e no VE shuhō no tekiyō" (Hitachi) (A proposal concerning target costing—Application of VE techniques at the product development stage) (Hitachi). *Kigyō kaikei (Corporate Accounting)*. Vol. 44, No. 8, 1992: pp. 55-62.

Tejima, Naoaki. "Seihin kaihatsu dankai no kosuto kanri—Kaihatsu danki e no VE no tekiyō (Hitachi)" (Cost management at the product development stage—Application of VE at the development stage) (Hitachi). *IE rebyuu (IE Review)*. Vol. 32, No. 2, May 1991: pp. 42-51.

Toyoda, Eiji. "Baburu e no hansei—aratanaru genka to no tatakai" (Toyota) (Looking back at the bubble economy—a new battle over costs) (Toyota), *Nikkan Kōgyō Shinbun (Japan Industrial News)*. December 24, 1993: p. 17.

Watanabe, Oshie. "Nippon Densō no genka kanri katsudō to sono sapooto shisutemu" (Nippondenso's target costing activities and its support system). In Kigyō Keiei Kyōkai (Enterprise Management Association), ed., *Kanri Kaikei no Jissai—Riron to Jitsumu (The Facts of Management Accounting—Theory and Practice)*. Zeimu Kenkyūkai Shuppan-kyoku (Tax Studies Publishing Office), 1988: pp. 279-293.

Watanabe, Yoshihiro. *Toyota ga Nihon o kaeru (Toyota Can Change Japan)*. Nikkan Shobō, 1992.

Womack, J. T., D. T. Jones, and D. Roos. *The Machine That Changed the World*. New York: Macmillan, 1991.

Yagi, Kimitoshi. "Tōsha ni okeru shizai gōrika katsudō no tenkai" (Fuji Denki) (Development of materials rationalization activities at our company) (Fuji Electric). *Keiei jitsumu (Managerial Practice)*. No. 442, February 1991: pp. 1-9.

Yokomoto, Toshirō. *Beikoku kanri kaikei-ron hattatsu-shi (The Development of Management Accounting Theory in the United States)*. Aoyama Shoten, 1993.

Yokomoto, Toshirō. "Waga kuni seizō kigyō no kanri kaikei—hitotsu no oboegaki" (Memorandum on management accounting in Japanese manufacturing companies). *Bijinesu rebyuu (Business Review)*. Vol. 33, No. 4: pp. 64-77./

Yoshikawa, Yutaka. "Tōsha no genka kaizen katsudō to kōbai senryaku" (Xecel) (Kaizen costing and purchasing strategy at our company) (Xecel). *Keiei jitsumu (Managerial Practice)*. No. 442, February 1991: pp. 37-47.

About the Author

Yasuhiro Monden is professor of managerial accounting and production management at the University of Tsukuba's Institute of Socio-Economic Planning, where he is currently serving as chairperson. He received his doctorate from the University of Tsukuba, where he also served as dean of the Graduate Program of Management Sciences and Public Policy Studies.

Dr. Monden has gained valuable practical knowledge and experience from his research and related activities in the Japanese automobile industry. He was instrumental in introducing the just-in-time (JIT) production system to the United States. His English-language book *Toyota Production System* is recognized as a JIT classic and was awarded the 1984 Nikkei Prize by the Nikkei Economic Journal. Recent books include *Japanese Management Accounting: A World Class Approach to Profit Management* (1989, cowritten with Michiharu Sakurai), *Cost Management in the New Manufacturing Age: Innovations in the*

Japanese Automobile Industry (1992), and *Toyota Management System* (1993), published by Productivity Press.

Dr. Monden taught at California State University at Los Angeles in 1991 and 1992. Previously he was a visiting professor at the State University of New York at Buffalo in 1980 and 1981. He is an adviser for the Production and Operations Management Society (POMS) and has been an international director of the management accounting section of the American Accounting Association. He serves on the editorial board of the AAA's *Journal of Management Accounting Research*.

Professor Yasuhiro Monden, Institute of Socio-Economic Planning, University of Tsukuba, Tsukuba-shi, Ibaraki 305, Japan.

Index

Books from Productivity Press

Productivity Press provides individuals and companies with materials they need to achieve excellence in quality, productivity and the creative involvement of all employees. Through sets of learning tools and techniques, Productivity supports continuous improvement as a vision, and as a strategy. Many of our leading-edge products are direct source materials translated into English for the first time from industrial leaders around the world. Call toll-free 1-800-394-6868 for our free catalog.

20 Keys to Workplace Improvement
Iwao Kobayashi

This easy-to-read introduction to the "20 keys" system presents an integrated approach to assessing and improving your company's competitive level. The book focuses on systematic improvement through five levels of achievement in such primary areas as industrial housekeeping, small group activities, quick changeover techniques, equipment maintenance, and computerization. A scoring guide is included, along with information to help plan a strategy for your company's world class improvement effort.

ISBN 0-915299-61-5 / 252 pages / $45.00 / Order 20KEYS-B252

Productivity Press, Inc., Dept. BK, P.O. Box 13390, Portland, OR 97213-0390
Telephone: 1-800-394-6868   Fax: 1-800-394-6286

Continuous Improvement in Operations
A Systematic Approach to Waste Reduction
Alan Robinson (ed.)

Here in one place is the world's most advanced thinking on Just-in-Time, Kaizen, Total Employee Involvement and Total Productive Maintenance. This handy book brings you a compendium of materials from our best-selling classics by world-famous manufacturing experts. The excerpts you'll read offer wisdom and experience that is unique to the developer of each approach. The authoritative introduction integrates the developments of these manufacturing gurus within a twofold theme—the elimination of invisible waste and the creation of a work environment that welcomes and implements employees' ideas.

ISBN 0-915299-51-8 / 406 pages / $35.00 / Order ROB2C-B252

Cost Management in the New Manufacturing Age
Innovations in the Japanese Automotive Industry
Yasuhiro Monden

Up to now, no single book has explained the new cost management techniques being implemented in one of the most advanced manufacturing industries in the world. Yasuhiro Monden has taught the principles of JIT in the U.S. and now brings us firsthand insights into the future of cost management based on direct surveys, interviews, and in-depth case studies available nowhere else.

ISBN 0-915299-90-9 / 198 pages / $45.00 / Order COSTMG-B252

Productivity Press, Inc., Dept. BK, P.O. Box 13390, Portland, OR 97213-0390
Telephone: 1-800-394-6868   Fax: 1-800-394-6286

Handbook for Productivity Measurement and Improvement
William F. Christopher and Carl G. Thor, eds.

An unparalleled resource! In over 100 chapters, nearly 80 front-runners in the quality movement reveal the evolving theory and specific practices of world-class organizations. Spanning a wide variety of industries and business sectors, they discuss quality and productivity in manufacturing, service industries, profit centers, administration, nonprofit and government institutions, health care and education. Contributors include Robert C. Camp, Peter F. Drucker, Jay W. Forrester, Joseph M. Juran, Robert S. Kaplan, John W. Kendrick, Yasuhiro Monden, and Lester C. Thurow. Comprehensive in scope and organized for easy reference, this compendium belongs in every company and academic institution concerned with business and industrial viability.

ISBN 1-56327-007-2 / 1344 pages / $90.00 / Order HPM-B252

The Hunters and the Hunted
A Non-Linear Solution for Reengineering the Workplace
James B. Swartz

Our competitive environment changes rapidly. If you want to survive, you have to stay on top of those changes. Otherwise, you become prey to your competitors. Hunters continuously change and learn; anyone who doesn't becomes the hunted and sooner or later will be devoured. This unusual non-fiction novel provides a veritable crash course in continuous transformation. It offers lessons from real-life companies and introduces many industrial gurus as characters. The Hunters and the Hunted doesn't simply tell you how to change; it puts you inside the change process itself.

ISBN 1-56327-043-9 / 582 pages / $45.00 / Order HUNT-B252

Productivity Press, Inc., Dept. BK, P.O. Box 13390, Portland, OR 97213-0390
Telephone: 1-800-394-6868   Fax: 1-800-394-6286

Japanese Management Accounting
A World Class Approach to Profit Management
Yasuhiro Monden and Michiharu Sakurai (eds.)

In response to innovations in manufacturing, Japanese companies have developed new management accounting techniques. Here, in 33 articles, dozens of experts reveal proven accounting practices with case studies, surveys, and the latest research. The book shows how to transform existing accounting structures into companywide cost management programs.

ISBN 0-915299-50-X / 568 pages / $65.00 / Order JMACT-B252

A New American TQM
Four Practical Revolutions in Management
Shoji Shiba, Alan Graham, and David Walden

For TQM to succeed in America, you need to create an American-style "learning organization" with the full commitment and understanding of senior managers and executives. Written expressly for this audience, *A New American TQM* offers a comprehensive and detailed explanation of TQM and how to implement it, based on courses taught at MIT's Sloan School of Management and the Center for Quality Management, a consortium of American companies. Full of case studies and amply illustrated, the book examines major quality tools and how they are being used by the most progressive American companies today.

ISBN 1-56327-032-3 / 606 pages / $50.00 / Order NATQM-B252

Productivity Press, Inc., Dept. BK, P.O. Box 13390, Portland, OR 97213-0390
Telephone: 1-800-394-6868   Fax: 1-800-394-6286

Performance Measurement for World Class Manufacturing
A Model for American Companies
Brian H. Maskell

If your company is adopting world class manufacturing techniques, you'll need new methods of performance measurement to control production variables. In practical terms, this book describes the new methods of performance measurement and how they are used in a changing environment. For manufacturing managers as well as cost accountants, it provides a theoretical foundation of these innovative methods supported by extensive practical examples. The book specifically addresses performance measures for delivery, process time, production flexibility, quality, and finance.

ISBN 0-915299-99-2 / 448 pages / $55.00 / Order PERFM-B252

Toyota Management System
Linking the Seven Key Functional Areas
Yasuhiro Monden

Here's the first comprehensive and systematic explanation of the management system that drives the world's leading auto maker. The development of JIT production at Toyota and the company's achievement of unprecedented levels of productivity were made possible by its supportive, integrated management system. This new book reveals for the first time exactly how that management system works. It looks carefully at each of Toyota's seven management subsystems and how they work as an integrated whole.

ISBN 1-563267-014-5 / 245 pages / $45.00 / Order TMS7-B252

Productivity Press, Inc., Dept. BK, P.O. Box 13390, Portland, OR 97213-0390
Telephone: 1-800-394-6868   Fax: 1-800-394-6286

The Unshackled Organization
Facing the Challenge of Unpredictability Through Spontaneous Reorganization
Jeffrey Goldstein

Managers should not necessarily try to solve all the internal problems within their organizations; intervention may help in the short term, but in the long run may inhibit true problem-solving change from taking place. And change is the real goal. Through change comes real hope for improvement. Using leading-edge scientific and social theories about change, Goldstein explores how change happens within an organization and reveals that only through "self organization" can natural, lasting change occur. This book is a pragmatic guide for managers, executives, consultants, and other change agents.

ISBN 1-56327-048-X / 208 pages / $25.00 / Order UO-B252

Vision Management
Translating Strategy into Action
SANNO Management Development Research Center (ed.)

For over ten years, managers of Japan's top companies have gathered at SANNO University to brainstorm about innovative corporate management methods. This book is based on the proven methodology that evolved from their ideas. It describes how the intangible aspects of vision-based strategy can be integrated into a concrete implementation model and clarifies the relationship among vision, strategy, objectives, goals, and day-to-day activities.

ISBN 0-915299-80-1 / 272 pages / $30.00 / Order VISM-B252

Productivity Press, Inc., Dept. BK, P.O. Box 13390, Portland, OR 97213-0390
Telephone: 1-800-394-6868   Fax: 1-800-394-6286

The Visual Factory
Bulding Participation Through Shared Information
Michel Greif

If you're aware of the tremendous improvements achieved in productivity and quality as a result of employee involvement, then you'll appreciate the great value of creating a visual factory. This book shows how visual management can make the factory a place where workers and supervisors freely communicate and take improvement action. It details how to develop meeting and communication areas, communicate work standards and instructions, use visual production controls such as kanban, and make goals and progress visible. Includes more than 200 diagrams and photos.

ISBN 0-915299-67-4 / 305 pages / $55.00 / Order VFAC-B252

TO ORDER: Write, phone, or fax Productivity Press, Dept. BK, P.O. Box 13390, Portland, OR 97213-0390, phone 1-800-394-6868, fax 1-800-394-6286. Send check or charge to your credit card (American Express, Visa, MasterCard accepted).

U.S. ORDERS: Add $5 shipping for first book, $2 each additional for UPS surface delivery. Add $5 for each AV program containing 1 or 2 tapes; add $12 for each AV program containing 3 or more tapes. We offer attractive quantity discounts for bulk purchases of individual titles; call for more information.

INTERNATIONAL ORDERS: Write, phone, or fax for quote and indicate shipping method desired. For international callers, telephone number is 503-235-0600 and fax number is 503-235-0909. Prepayment in U.S. dollars must accompany your order (checks must be drawn on U.S. banks). When quote is returned with payment, your order will be shipped promptly by the method requested.

NOTE: Prices are in U.S. dollars and are subject to change without notice.

Productivity Press, Inc., Dept. BK, P.O. Box 13390, Portland, OR 97213-0390
Telephone: 1-800-394-6868   Fax: 1-800-394-6286